Until Justice and Peace Embrace

by
NICHOLAS WOLTERSTORFF

The Kuyper Lectures for 1981
delivered at
The Free University of Amsterdam

WILLIAM B. EERDMANS PUBLISHING COMPANY
GRAND RAPIDS, MICHIGAN

Copyright © 1983 by Wm. B. Eerdmans Publishing Co.
255 Jefferson Ave. S.E., Grand Rapids, Mich. 49503
Printed in the United States of America

Reprinted, July 1987

Library of Congress Cataloging in Publication Data
Wolterstorff, Nicholas.
    Until justice and peace embrace.
    Includes bibliographical references.
    1. Sociology, Christian—Addresses, essays, lectures.
    2. Christian ethics—Addresses, essays, lectures.
    3. Social ethics—Addresses, essays, lectures.
    I. Title.
BT738.W56   1983   306.6   83-8976
ISBN 0-8028-1980-X

The author and publisher gratefully acknowledge permission to quote material
from the following publications:

Excerpts from *The Capitalist World-Economy* by Immanuel Wallerstein. Copy-
    right © 1979 by Maison des Sciences de l'Homme and Cambridge University
    Press. Reprinted with permission.

Excerpts from *The Challenge of World Poverty* by Gunnar Myrdal. Copyright
    © 1970 by Gunnar Myrdal. Reprinted with permission of Pantheon Books,
    a Division of Random House, Inc., and Penguin Books, Ltd.

Excerpt from *The City in History: Its Origins, Its Transformations, and Its Prospects*
    by Lewis Mumford. Copyright © 1961 by Lewis Mumford. Reprinted with
    permission of Harcourt Brace Jovanovich, Inc.

Excerpts from "The Demand from the Supply Side" by Robert L. Heilbroner,
    in *The New York Review of Books* 11 June 1981. Copyright © 1981 by NYREV,
    Inc. Reprinted with permission.

Excerpts from *For the Life of the World: Sacraments and Orthodoxy* by Alexander
    Schmemann. Copyright © 1973 by Alexander Schmemann. Reprinted with
    permission of St. Vladimir's Press.

Excerpt from *Global Reach: The Power of the Multinational Corporations* by
    Richard J. Barnet and Ronald E. Müller. Copyright © 1974 by Richard J.
    Barnet and Ronald E. Müller. Reprinted with permission of Simon & Schuster.

Excerpts from *Israel and the World: Essays in a Time of Crisis* by Martin Buber.
    Copyright © 1948, 1963 by Schocken Books Inc. Reprinted with permission
    of Schocken Books Inc.

Excerpts from *The Revolution of the Saints: A Study in the Origins of Radical
    Politics* by Michael Walzer. Copyright © 1965 by the President and Fellows
    of Harvard College. Reprinted with permission.

Excerpts from *A Theology of Liberation: History, Politics, and Salvation* by
    Gustavo Gutiérrez. Copyright © 1973 by Orbis Books. Reprinted with
    permission.

Excerpts from *Venice and the Defense of Republican Liberty: Renaissance Values in
    the Age of the Counter Reformation* by William J. Bouwsma. Copyright © 1968
    by The Regents of the University of California. Reprinted with permission.

Contents

11480 2

for my dear friend Allan Boesak,
black Reformed pastor and theologian from South Africa,
in whose speech
I have heard
both
the cries of the oppressed
and the Word of the Lord

Preface

What should be the Christian's overarching goals with respect to our present social order? Or, to put the question more pointedly, How should the Christian insert himself or herself into the present social order? A concern for an answer to this perennial question constitutes the basis for the lectures contained in this book.

The answer to this question is, I believe, largely the same as the answer to the question of what, from the Christian point of view, *a person's* overarching goals should be with respect to our present social order, since what the Christian should do is essentially, from the Christian point of view, what everyone should do. Accordingly, in the course of this discussion I will often be addressing the question in these terms.

It might be asked why, if this is true, I do not drop the reference to *Christian* and speak simply as one human being to another? The heart of the answer to that question is contained in a passage from Lucien Goldmann's profound book *The Hidden God:*

> The question How ought I to live? in no way admits a specifically moral reply, since it is meaningful only in a perspective which sees life as a relative temporal whole which fits into a larger whole that goes beyond and transcends it. As soon as one has asked the question How ought I to live? seriously and with all its implications, the reply is already implicit: by situating one's life inside an eschatological or historical whole in which it inserts itself by faith.
>
> . . . The essential truth of Augustinianism and of dialectical materialism is that we must believe in order to understand reality and to act in a humanly efficacious manner, and it is for this reason that there is no autonomous and independent Augustinian and Marxist ethic. [1]

The Enlightenment vision was that morality could be grounded in reason. A system of morality could be erected on the foundation of moral principles that every rational person accepts immediately. That is an illusion. It never goes that way and never could. When we converse with one another in our pluralistic world, we discover that we live with different moral visions, each vision intertwined with different understandings of reality and none grounded in what all rational persons accept immediately. In our conversations with one another we can sometimes offer our partners good reasons for giving up some part of their moral vision. Sometimes these good reasons are also effective reasons: our partners accept the reasons and change their views. And sometimes our partners have good reasons to alter their views apart from the reasons that anybody gives them; it doesn't all depend on conversation. The rationality of a moral vision lies mainly in whether one has responded adequately to these good arguments, not in whether that vision has been grounded on consensus foundations.[2]

Of course, in conversation with one another on moral issues we do not usually say everything we believe on the matter, showing how all the components of our view are hooked together. Often we probe for what we agree on and let the peculiar contours of our own vision go undescribed. But there come times when, to be fully open with each other, we try to show how our moral convictions are intertwined with our sense of the meaning of life. That is what I do here.

The substance of this book was first presented as the eight Kuyper Lectures at the Free University of Amsterdam in the fall of 1981. At its centennial the year before, the Free University had established this lecture series in honor of its founder, the great Dutch Christian statesman Abraham Kuyper. I am pleased to express in print the honor I feel in having been chosen by the Association of the University as its first lecturer in this new series. The experience of delivering these lectures was delightful and instructive in many ways. Many people helped to make it so. From a long list of persons that I could cite let me single out just one, Professor Henk Verheul, Rector of the University, for a word of special thanks. The establishment of the lectureship was in large measure due to his initiative. I hope that my accomplishment is not too much below the grandeur of his vision.

The rubric that the Association chose for the first several years of the Kuyper Lectures was "The Political Consequences of the Reformation." As is typical of lecturers participating in a series, I stretched the intent of those who set this topic, though not, I can safely say, to the point of ignoring it. My understanding of how Christians should insert themselves into society is substantially consonant with that of the original Calvinist reform. Accordingly, I open the discussion by considering what the social vision and practice of that reform was and subsequently bring the contributions of thinkers in the Reformed/Presbyterian tradition of Christianity into a discussion of more specific issues. Though my topic as such is thoroughly ecumenical, for the reasons indicated I here engage that tradition of Christianity more thoroughly than I do the others.

There is another reason as well for this emphasis in the discussion. The Reformed/Presbyterian tradition of Christianity is my own, and these lectures represent for me an attempt to appropriate its social vision. I say: *appro-*

priate. Appropriation of one's tradition implies neither uncritical acceptance nor total rejection; it entails a discriminating adaptation of its features to one's own situation. As I was growing up in the Reformed tradition, I saw very little of that world-formative impulse so prominent in its origins. For me the tradition represented a certain theology and a certain piety. The piety came through most clearly in the prayers. As I remember them, they were of the structure "We thank you, Lord, for the many blessings you have granted us, and we ask you to remember those less fortunate than we are." The attitude communicated was that it was God's business to take care of the oppressed and deprived of the world; our role was simply to pray that he not neglect to do so. If presented to me then, the thesis of Michael Walzer in his book *The Revolution of the Saints*, that "the Calvinist saint [is] the first of those self-disciplined agents of social and political reconstruction who have appeared so frequently in modern history,"[3] would have seemed comically perverse as a description of my own tradition.

Since then I have learned of the radical origins of the tradition in which I was reared. Learning of those origins has given me a deepened appreciation of my own identity. It has also produced in me a profound discontent over my tradition's loss of its radicalism. Why has it become so quiescently— sometimes even oppressively—conservative? I hope the words that follow will help to change matters. But in any case, all any of us can do with the traditions in which we locate ourselves is *appropriate* from those traditions what remains of worth as we struggle shoulder to shoulder with other human beings toward a society of justice and peace.

I must add that this is not a how-to-do-it book. I do not give a list of "things to do" to alleviate world poverty, to cure the virulent disease of self-righteous nationalism, to reduce urban ugliness. My goal is to contribute to the formation of a new consciousness and a firmer resolution. It is true that there are some who are already at the point of asking what can be done. Their eager, sometimes desperate questions deserve answers. There are some answers I could give. I am persuaded, though, that the deepest reason for the perpetuation of our predicament is that too few people in our Western society are persuaded that things *ought* to be different and that they are called to work toward a new order. If this book contributes toward changing that, and if it gives those already persuaded some support in their conviction, then my goal will have been achieved.

On 10 October 1898 a Dutchman visiting America spoke these words:

> A traveler from the old European Continent, disembarking on the shore of the New World, feels as the Psalmist says, that "his thoughts crowd upon him like a multitude." Compared with the eddying waters of your new stream of life, the old stream in which he was

moving seems almost frostbound and dull; and here, on American ground, for the first time, he realizes how so many divine potencies, which were hidden away in the bosom of mankind from our very creation, but which our old world was incapable of developing, are now beginning to disclose their inward splendor, thus promising a still richer store of surprises for the future.[4]

The words were spoken by Abraham Kuyper at the beginning of the Stone Lectures he delivered at Princeton Seminary. To give the lectures on which this present book is based I reversed his pilgrimage, traveling from the rapidly aging New World to the Old, arriving not by disembarking on its shores but by descending through its air space. As with him, thoughts crowded upon me like a multitude, among them the thought that the stream which flows through the Old World today is not so "frostbound and dull." But amidst my multitude of thoughts, one was uppermost: that the New and Old World together are living in dark and dangerous times. Dark, because we in the First World are continuing to refuse to share the wealth of our rich, indulgent societies with those impoverished millions whom we dominate; and dangerous, because in those two great Enlightenment experiments, the United States and the Soviet Union, there is now a deep sense of failed ideals. No longer seriously believing in their founding ideals, these two countries have taken to terrorizing each other with the threat of nuclear bombs, arming the world, and supporting repression in their "client states." Today a new order is desperately needed. What it must look like we do not yet know. In the meanwhile, I shall speak of darkness, but also of light; of danger, but also of hope.

N. P. W.
Amsterdam
December 1981

Love and Fidelity now meet,
  Justice and Peace now embrace;
Fidelity reaches up from earth
  and Justice leans down from heaven.
                    —from Psalm 85

O God, to those who have hunger give bread;
and to us who have bread
give the hunger for justice.
                    —a Latin American prayer

Chapter I

World-Formative Christianity

The entrance of the Christian gospel into history worked like a leaven through the Roman world, causing profound changes in the social order. But after some three or four centuries the leaven was no longer the source of much ferment except on the periphery. From then on through the high Middle Ages, the Christian church, with few exceptions, taught its members to acquiesce in the social world in which they found themselves, instructing them in how to regard the delights it yielded and how to endure the sufferings it caused as they worked within the roles offered them. Then in the sixteenth century a profoundly different vision and practice came forth from the "reformed" church in Switzerland and the upper Rhine valley. The structure of the social world was held up to judgment, was pronounced guilty, and was sentenced to be reformed. *World-formative Christianity,* as I propose to call it, came out from the wings of history onto center stage.

It has been there ever since—sometimes prominent, sometimes inconspicuous; sometimes acting with repressive triumphalism, sometimes with liberating modesty; sometimes breathing fire and fomenting revolution, sometimes only smoldering. Of that new way of inserting oneself into the social order that came into the lights there in central Europe three and a half centuries ago all of us in the modern world are inheritors.

In his book *The Revolution of the Saints,* political theorist Michael Walzer says of the late sixteenth- and early seventeenth-century English Puritans that "the saints were responsible for their world—as medieval men were not—and responsible above all for its continual reformation. Their enthusiastic and purposive activity were part of their religious life, not something distinct and separate."[1] Walzer does not use the phrase "world-formative Christianity," but I know of no more succinct characterization of this form of religion than his words here. The saints are responsible for the structure of the social world in which they find themselves. That structure is not simply part of the order of nature; to the contrary, it is the result of human decision, and by concerted effort it can be altered. Indeed, it *should* be altered, for it is a fallen structure, in need of reform. The responsibility of the saints to struggle for the reform of the social order in which they find themselves is one facet of the discipleship to which their Lord Jesus Christ has called them. It is not an addition to their religion; it is there among the very motions of Christian spirituality.

My project in this book is to ask how Christians should insert themselves into the modern social order. The pattern of thought and action that I have described as world-formative Christianity is the over-arching perspective of what I shall urge, and I propose to begin our discussion by looking at this pattern in its first appearance. I do not suggest that the program of those early Calvinists was in all respects admirable, and certainly I do not contend that we should try to implement it in our own century: not only is much of it simply irrelevant to our present-day world; much of it was misguided even in its own day. Neither do I hold that the ideology behind the early Calvinist version of world-formative Christianity ought to be recaptured: that too was not without fault. In short, I shall not be conducting an apology for the early Calvinist *version* of world-formative Christianity. Yet this form of life as such, apart from the peculiarities of the early Calvinist version thereof, constitutes one of the enduring patterns for the Christian's insertion into the social world. It is a pattern which is both biblically faithful and relevant to our modern world. And I think that there is no better way to grasp the essence of this enduring pattern— the issues it poses and the choices it makes—than to place it in the historical context within which it arose.

In his magisterial book *The Social Teaching of the Christian Churches,* Ernst Troeltsch remarks that original Calvinism was led

> everywhere to . . . a systematic endeavor to mould the life of Society as a whole, to a kind of "Christian Socialism". . . . it lays down the principle that the Church ought to be interested in all sides of life, and it neither isolates the religious element over against the other elements, like Lutheranism, nor does it permit this sense of collective responsibility to express itself merely in particular institutions and occasional interventions in affairs, as in Catholicism.[2]

To understand the full significance of the words in which Troeltsch here characterizes (accurately I think) the social practice of early Calvinism, we must remind ourselves of the characteristic medieval pattern of thought and action to which this practice was an alternative.

It is a truism that the medieval vision of human life was profoundly otherworldly. To the medieval, this physical world in which we find ourselves and of which we ourselves are part is not our home. We are aliens here, just traveling through. It is a reality ultimately unworthy of us, the inferior of another reality to which we have access—the world of the eternal, the immutable, the incorruptible, the imperishable. Our true happiness lies in becoming united with that supreme reality, God. Intellectual contemplation is the means for doing so. Some there are who are privileged already in this present existence seriously to begin the life of contemplation, doing their best to remove, by ascetic discipline, all hindrances. The rest of us must await our entrance into heaven for the serious beginning of that life. In the meanwhile we perform our religious duties so that we can be assured of eventual beatitude, and we perform the tasks of ordinary society—growing cabbages, building roads, running the affairs of government—not because such tasks have any religious significance, but because they are necessary to the maintenance of our earthly existence. We also enjoy such sensory delights as come our way, for this present material existence of ours, though inferior, is not evil; yet all the while we long for the day when our eyes will feast solely on God. Earthly life, though for some it already provides incidents and episodes of true beatitude, consists of waiting in the anteroom of our ultimate destiny. The true Christian, said the enormously influential Augustine in *The City of God,* should keep his gaze fixed on "the everlasting blessings that are promised for the future, using like one in a strange land any earthly and temporal things, not letting them entrap him or divert him from the path that leads to God."

"Otherworldly" I called this vision of human existence, using the conventional rubric. No doubt we all feel at once the propriety of this description. But in the course of this chapter I wish to lay out the vast structural difference between this vision of life and that which came to light in the Calvinist reform. For that, it will be important to go beyond this conventional description and sketch out some of the main elements in a typology of religion.

Fundamental in a vast array of religions is the conviction that in our ordinary existence there is something inferior, evil, or threatening, coupled with the conviction that for a life thus immersed in inferiority there is a cure, a cure which consists in turning one's concerns away from this realm of inferiority, averting oneself from it, so as to attain closer contact with a reality outside oneself which is higher, better, more real. That from which one is to turn and that with which one is to be united have both been conceived in a wide diversity of ways. But here I want simply to pick out that whole array of religions in which this turning away from a lower reality and this establishing of a closer relation with a higher reality is the fundamental goal. We may call these *avertive* religions, in contrast to *formative* religions, in which there is also the apprehension of something inferior in our ordinary existence, but in which, rather than acquiescing in this inferiority and then turning away, one seeks its reformation.[3]

In addition to avertive and formative religions, there are, of course, other forms. One such form apprehends our immersion in a realm of inferiority and responds with the conviction that there is nothing at all to be done about our human predicament.[4] Another form fails to find much of anything that is wrong or undesirable in our ordinary existence; if God is apprehended as active in a religion of this sort, his relation to us will typically be seen as that of *blessing* us, as distinct from *delivering* us.[5] In contrast to these additional forms, avertive and formative religion may together be called *salvation* religions: both look forward to salvation from what is defective in our present mode of existence.

I have presented these as if they were exclusive types. In fact that is not so. Adherents of a given religion may judge our ordinary existence to be undesirable in various distinct ways, and their response to these differences may be structurally different. They may believe that our ordinary existence is filled with sinful actions and that we must do battle to eliminate as many of these as possible. They may at the same time believe that this present embodied existence of ours is *inherently* inferior to disembodiment, when, released from all earthly cares, we can be united by contemplation to God.

In avertive religions, the action whereby one becomes more closely united to the higher reality, be that God or whatever, is customarily said to be contemplation. In principle it might be any one of a range of other actions. Indeed, it might be no action at all, but absorption into the divine. Furthermore, it may be that we by our own efforts cannot achieve this closer union, but that God must act within us. If this is true, it may nonetheless be the case that we must perform various "religious duties" to induce God to grant us this closer union. Then too, it may be that this closer union cannot be attained *now;* perhaps we must wait for it to be granted us upon death. Or perhaps we must wait to begin the contemplative life until the press of business diminishes or the flames of passion die down.

The practice of avertive religion may require a high degree of self-discipline, as may the practice of formative religion. But the regimentation of self required for the practice of the former will not have for its goal that of making oneself a better person—more pious, more virtuous, whatever—but that of removing the hindrances to closer union with the divine. It may be added that in avertive religions it will be customary to distinguish within reality a realm of the sacred from a realm of the secular.[6]

Medieval Christianity was not an unmixed example of any of the types I have distinguished, and neither was early Calvinism. Yet there can be no doubt that the dominant character of medieval Christianity was that of avertive religion, and, as we shall see, that the dominant character of original Calvinism was that of formative religion. The change from the one to the other of these represented a fundamental alteration of religious sensibility within Christendom.

At a later point in our discussion I shall return to some of these structural issues, but at this point I must once again take up the sketch I was drawing of the medieval vision. To the medievals' otherworldly vision of man's true end we must add their perception of all reality as having a hierarchical structure. The key idea here is that of the great chain of being, that out of the overflowing richness of his being God has brought forth a world of plenitude and continuity. Perhaps the best brief statement of this cosmic picture is the following, from the fifteenth-century jurist Sir John Fortescue:

In this order angel is set over angel, rank upon rank in the kingdom of heaven; man is set over man, beast over beast, bird over bird, and fish over fish, on the earth, in the air and in the sea: so that there is no worm that crawls upon the ground, no bird that flies on high, no fish that swims in the depths, which the chain of this order does not bind in most harmonious concord. . . . God created as many different kinds of things as he did creatures, so that there is no creature which does not differ in some respect from all other creatures and by which it is in some respect superior or inferior to all the rest. So that from the highest angel down to the lowest of his kind there is absolutely not found an angel that has not a superior and inferior; nor from man down to the meanest worm is there any creature which is not in some respect superior to one creature and inferior to another. So that there is nothing which the bond of order does not embrace.[7]

Human society was considered by the medieval to be both part and mirror of this cosmic hierarchical chain of plenitude and continuity. In the grave all persons are equal. In life they are not so. They are created unequal; more to the point, they are created for different and hierarchically unequal positions in the social order. Well on into the Renaissance, according to Walzer, this social inequality

was most often described in direct analogy to the cosmic hierarchy. Within the great chain there were discovered a whole series of lesser chains—the animal hierarchy, presided over by eagle and lion; and the nine angelic orders; the greater and lesser stars—and these were held to correspond closely to one another. The idea could hardly be avoided that such a lesser chain, corresponding to the order of animals and angels, existed also among men. Was not the society of men "even the diminutive and model of that wide-extending universe?" Indeed, the feudal hierarchy of status and degree seemed to imitate perfectly the great chain.[8]

God in his heaven, the bishop in his chair, the lord in his castle—to medieval man this was part of the very nature of things.[9]

You and I, shaped in our thought by the modern world, are prone to misinterpret this picture of society as a natural hierarchy. What comes before our minds is the picture of a complex, hierarchically ordered array of social *roles*. We then interpret the medievals as claiming that this hierarchical array was God-ordained. But that is not how they were thinking. They were not thinking—not first of all, anyway—of social *roles* and their inequalities; they were thinking of the inequality of the *persons* playing these roles. It was not the roles but the players in the social drama that they had their eyes on. They were first of all thinking of kings and serfs, not of king*ship* and serf*dom*. Some human beings are born to be kings, they thought, as lions are born to be king of the beasts. And some are born to be commoners.

From this perspective, society in all its hierarchical differentiation is seen as something natural, brought about by God, no more the free creation of human beings than is the society of animals a free creation of theirs! The medievals had not in general abstracted social structures from the persons filling those structures.[10] Even less had they seriously posed the issue of whether persons might be allowed to fill those structures other than those who actually did fill them. What they knew about was concrete particular human beings playing different roles and having different statuses into which with few exceptions they were born. This they regarded as part of the natural order of things. The metaphors they used to speak about it were metaphors of nature; they spoke, for example, of "the body politic."

Of course they knew of assassinations, intrigues, and seizures of power. They knew of usurpers who presumptuously stepped outside their assigned place in the social hierarchy. And they knew of struggles between these usurpers and those who had a rightful claim to the position usurped. They knew, in short, of human beings acting in violation of nature. Animals, too, sometimes acted unnaturally. But they knew nothing of bands of men who surveyed the whole structure of society, judged that structure to be fundamentally wrong, and then undertook for reasons of conscience to seize power in order to alter the structure. With rebels and usurpers they were well acquainted; of radicals and revolutionaries they knew nothing.

It is true that one hears of there having been programs for the reform of this and that in medieval times, but I think it safe to say that when medievals thought of society, they rarely thought of the whole as being in need of reform. So I think Ernst Troeltsch is fundamentally correct in his judgment that the Catholic social philosophy of the Middle Ages was "an all-embracing sociological system, but even at the height of its intellectual development it was not a programme of actual social reform. The Christian social doctrine of the Middle Ages was as far removed from being a programme of social reform as was the social teaching of the Early Church, although for different reasons."[11]

By way of contrast, consider these words from a sermon preached by the Puritan minister Thomas Case to the English House of Commons in 1641:

> Reformation must be universal . . . reform all places, all persons and callings; reform the benches of judgment, the inferior magistrates. . . . Reform the universities, reform the cities, reform the countries, reform inferior schools of learning, reform the Sabbath, reform the ordinances, the worship of God . . . you have more work to do

than I can speak. . . . Every plant which my heavenly father hath not planted shall be rooted up. [12]*

We have entered a different world. For all its vigor, the attack is not an attack on teachers, on sheriffs, on priests, on lords. Though Case surely knew well of licentious priests and corrupt judges, his attack here is not on persons, but on social structures. This Puritan preacher has in his mind's eye the general structure of his social world, and it is this that he subjects to his withering, somewhat hysterical attack. Clearly his assumption is that social structures are not something natural. They are not the reflection of true human nature. They are the result of human decision, and being made by us, they can be altered by us. Indeed, they *must* be altered, for they are fallen, corrupt. The structures *themselves* are corrupt and in need of reform, not only the persons who exist within these structures. And in those last lines we get a hint of why he judges England's social order to be in need of reformation: "Every plant which my heavenly father hath not planted shall be rooted up": England's laws and England's institutions are not the laws and institutions that God wills.

Equally extraordinary was the assumption of the Puritans that *the saints* are responsible for altering England's social structure. It is one thing to abstract the structure of the social order from the human beings filling that structure and then to realize that that structure is determined by our human actions, that it is capable of being altered, and that it is corrupt and in need of alteration; it is quite another thing to suppose that people other than those in authoritative positions have responsibility for such reform. In the medieval world no one at all was thought of as being responsible for determining the general structure of the body politic. The prince was of course responsible for the welfare of his subjects and for detailed laws and regulations; but the structure in its fundamentals was *given*. So too, no one was thought of as being responsible for determining the general structure of the church. The bishop was the overseer of the flock; but it was neither his nor anyone else's business to serve as an architect of church structure. That too was *given*. Now all is different. Not princes or bishops but commoners are assumed all together to bear responsibility for the general structure of England's laws and England's institutions. The passivity of its participants, so characteristic of the medieval social order, has been radically abolished. Subjects are becoming citizens. Walzer's comments are insightful:

> The idea that specially designated and organized bands of men might play a creative part in the political world, destroying the established

*Reading these words, one can well understand why the seventeenth-century English writer would say, "I had rather see coming toward me a whole regiment with drawn swords, than one lone Calvinist convinced that he is doing the will of God."

order and reconstructing society according to the Word of God or the plans of their fellows—this idea did not enter at all into the thought of Machiavelli, Luther, or Bodin. In establishing the state, these three writers relied exclusively upon the prince. . . . All other men remained subjects, condemned to political passivity.

     . . . it was the Calvinists who first switched the emphasis of political thought from the prince to the saint (or the band of saints) and then constructed a theoretical justification for independent political action. . . . This is surely the most significant outcome of the Calvinist theory of worldly activity, preceding in time any infusion of religious worldliness into the economic order. [13]

We shall want to investigate in more detail the religio-social vision of these early Calvinists. Already it is clear, though, that it is a species of what earlier I called *formative* religion. More precisely, it is *world*-formative religion. ("world" here meaning not the natural but the social world). I think it must be said that Lutheranism, when compared with medieval Christianity, also represents a form of religion in which the formative character has superseded the avertive component. But the focus of its formative efforts was mainly on ecclesiastical structures and on individual "inwardness." The stance of Lutherans toward the structures of the social world was as much acquiescence as was that of the medievals; that is why the distinction between religious and nonreligious components of life comes readily to them. Of course it's true that Calvinists were also insistent in calling for the reform of ecclesiastical structures and of inwardness. After a time they even absorbed the Baconian dictum that we have a religious duty to realize the potential of undeveloped nature. All together a quite extraordinary "totalism" began to characterize Calvinism, with its insistence that there is nothing at all in our experience that is not—so far as is necessary and possible—to be subjected to the will of God. But in speaking of Calvinism as *world*-formative Christianity, it is my intent to emphasize its impulse toward the re-formation of the *social* world.

     No doubt it is most customary for adherents of formative religion to understand that their formative activities are conducted in *obedience* to God. They may wish to say other things as well—for example, that they are to be done out of gratitude to God—but seldom will the notion of obedience be missing. Consequently, the fundamental impulse to reform will usually not be their desire to relieve the unhappiness they experience in present reality, but their desire to bring that reality closer to the will of God. And if the reality to be reformed is not just their own inwardness, but something outside themselves, they will tend to think of themselves as servants or agents of God. In avertive religion one desires to become a vessel of God; in world-formative religion one desires to become an instrument of God. Of course, those who adhere to a formative religion need not believe that their own human efforts will be successful in achieving the goal desired. Some direct intervention of God may well be necessary to bring reality fully into accord with his Will.*

I have suggested that the emergence of original Calvinism represented a fundamental alteration in Christian sensibility, from the vision and practice of turning away from the social world in order to seek closer union with God to the vision and practice of working to reform the social world in obedience to God. Before going on to investigate in detail the contours of this new vision, we would do well to consider the factors that account for the emergence of this new form of Christian life, for it did not arise without preparation and stimulus. Of course I cannot here offer a comprehensive account of the matter. All I can do is point to some factors which must find their place in such an account.

No doubt the drastic alteration in social relations taking place in Western Europe in the sixteenth century, along with the sense of crisis that pervaded all strata of society, played a significant role in the emergence of the new consciousness. Feudalism was in a state of collapse, being replaced by a market economy, by that fractionation and tightening of political authority that eventuated in the modern states, and by rapid urbanization. In this situation it was only natural that people would begin to reflect on alternative social structures and that the idea of social structure as part of the givenness of their surroundings would begin to seem entirely implausible. What may be added is that the rise of the cities within the context of decaying feudal imperialism forced issues of social structure onto people's attention simply because these cities, with respect both to their internal structure and their relation to their surroundings, did not fit at all into the hierarchical structure of feudal imperialism. As William Bouwsma puts it, "No longer viewing themselves as participants in a system of hierarchical gradations rooted in the nature of things, men . . . felt a heightened sense of personal responsibility. . . ."[14] Then too, participation in the reform of the church obviously served as schooling for the reform of society. Just as important as these factors, though, was the quality of social plausibility that this new vision took on in the fluid social situation of the sixteenth century. When the ordinary person is convinced that there is little he can do to alleviate the misery and injustice that surround him, then avertive religion in one or another of its forms or some inwardness version of formative religion will prove irresistibly attractive, and the social activism inherent in world-formative religion will seem profoundly irrelevant. But just the opposite

---

*For obvious reasons, the metaphor of *the Kingdom of God* will come naturally to the adherents of a world-formative religion when they wish to describe that ultimate state for which they work and hope. For reasons equally obvious, such a metaphor is quite out of place in avertive religions.

will be the case when the social situation appears fluid and open to influence in many different directions, as was the case in sixteenth-century Western Europe.

There were also developments in thought that served as transition from the vision of the medievals to that of the Puritans. The most important of these occurred in the humanist movement. Our understanding of the Renaissance humanists has undergone drastic revisions during the last quarter-century at the hands of such scholars as Paul Oskar Kristeller, Heiko Oberman, Charles Trinkaus, and William Bouwsma. The Burckhardtian picture of humanism as a secular, anti-Christian movement has lost its plausibility. Though no comprehensive alternative has yet gained consensus, some things do seem clear. Earlier I remarked that a commonplace in the thought-framework of those religions that are dominantly avertive is the distinction between the sacred and the secular. On exactly this point the Renaissance humanists represent a significant shift. In Oberman's words, there was in the Renaissance "the bridging of the distance between the sacred and the profane; one could say the elimination of the ontological opposition, contrast and gap between the sacred and the profane."[15] He adds that "if the closing of the gap between the sacred and the secular carries the marks of the time to come, we dare to see in the crisis of the later Middle Ages the birthpangs of the Modern Era."[16]

To this "closing of the gap between the sacred and the secular" there were many different dimensions. One of them was the emergence of the conviction among many humanists that the active life is to be preferred to the contemplative. As Bouwsma remarks, "salvation itself, on the basis of the Renaissance understanding of essential human nature, had to be conceived as the transformation of a total personality through love, not as intellectual union with eternal wisdom. Thus the Christian life, like civic life, was interpreted as basically active rather than contemplative."[17] In a more recent work, Bouwsma characterizes this strand of thought as Augustinian on the ground that it is derived from some of the later writings of Augustine,* and he argues that throughout the Renaissance period it was in conflict with Stoicism.[18]

Now humanist influences were of course strong in the training of the Swiss reformers, and evidence of both Augustinian and Stoic strands is to be found in their writings. But of these two, it was the Augustinian strand that was clearly dominant. Bouwsma says of Augustinian humanism that it "sought to meet the crisis of community in the age of the Renaissance not by protecting the individual from destructive involvement with the social world but by full engagement, if possible out of love, in meeting its deepest and most desperate needs."[19] Reading this, it is hard indeed not to see the Swiss reform as a sin-

---

*I am myself less confident than Bouwsma seems to be that this strand of thought that he identifies as *Augustinian* is in fact close to the thought of Augustine—who, it seems to me, never departs from his "otherworldliness."

gularly powerful intensification of the "Augustinian" strand present in Renaissance humanism. "From early boyhood," wrote Ulrich Zwingli, the reformer from Zurich, "the young man ought to exercise himself only in righteousness, fidelity and constancy: for with virtues such as these he may serve the Christian community, the common good, the state and individuals. Only the weak are concerned to find a quiet life: the most like to God are those who study to be of profit to all even to their own hurt."[20]

I have spoken of the breakdown of the old social relations and the emergence of new ones, along with the development among the humanists of an "Augustinian" climate of opinion, as both contributing to the development among the early Calvinists of the new vision of Christian social existence. One more factor must be mentioned: the new accessibility of the Bible, combined with a renewed emphasis on its importance for directing our lives and a new hermeneutic in which the prophetic literature of the Old Testament was brought forward into the light of attention. The reformers were "people of the Book."

We can do no better, as we now turn to investigate in more detail the contours of the Christian vision, than begin with Calvin himself. Once again, however, in doing so my intent will be to describe the general vision of the early Calvinists concerning our relation to the social order, rather than to outline their specific practices or ideas on social formation, or the influence of those practices and ideas on "modernization."[21]

Calvin opens his *Institutes* in the great medieval tradition of theological treatises with a discussion of the knowledge of God as the true end of man. But no one who reads what he says will miss the fact that beneath this commonality of language a profound alteration of perspective has taken place. Knowledge of God is no longer understood as contemplation of God's essence: it consists in the appropriate *response* to his *works*. Knowledge of God consists in *acknowledgment* of God. And *acknowledgment* of God occurs in life as a whole, comprising such things as trust, reverence, gratitude, service. This all comes out nicely in a small section of the *Geneva Catechism* (1541) on the end of man:

> MASTER: What is the chief end of human life?
> SCHOLAR: To know God by whom men were created.
>
> MASTER: What is the highest good of man?
> SCHOLAR: The very same thing.
>
> MASTER: What is the true and right knowledge of God?
> SCHOLAR: When he is so known that due honor is paid to him.
>
> MASTER: What is the method of honoring him truly?
> SCHOLAR: To place our whole confidence in him; to study to serve

him during our whole life by obeying his will; to call upon him in all our necessities, seeking salvation and every good thing that can be desired in him; lastly, to acknowledge him both with heart and lips, as the sole Author of all blessings.

The scholar here cites various things as belonging to that knowledge of God which is the true end of human life: placing one's whole confidence in God, serving him in one's whole life by obeying his will, calling upon him in need, seeking every good thing from him, acknowledging him with heart and lips as the sole author of all blessings. There can be no doubt that of all these it will often be obedience that becomes most prominent in later Calvinism. Correlatively, God will come to be apprehended predominantly as lawgiver. But we fail to grasp the structure of *original* Calvinist thought and piety if we think that obedience and law-giving are the most basic to it. Fundamental in the structure of Calvin's thought about God is the idea that he dispenses good gifts to us his children. To this our appropriate response is gratitude. What makes gratitude appropriate is not first of all that it is commanded (although, of course, it is), but simply that it is right and proper. Obedient action in society enters the picture as one of the manifestations of gratitude; as such, it is to God's glory. Thus, deeper in Calvin's thought than the image of God as lawgiver is the image of God as the "Author of all blessings," as the scholar in the *Catechism* puts it. God's law is itself one of his blessings. One has not caught the peculiar flavor of early Calvinist piety, nor indeed of much of later Calvinist piety, until one sees it as commitment to obedience out of gratitude for blessings received.*

At this very point Max Weber makes a fundamental mistake in his famous discussion of Calvinism in *The Protestant Ethic and the Spirit of Capitalism* when he argues that the peculiar activism of the Calvinist was energized by the desire to establish that one is among the elect. Certainly that is a caricature. The Calvinists' action was energized by their gratitude to God for his blessings, blessings that included the blessing of election, with its promise of eternal life.

It is obvious that Calvin's formulation of the true goal of human existence as the acknowledgment of God in one's life constitutes a profound turn toward this world and a repudiation of avertive religion. But we saw

---

*It has often been said that Calvinism was instrumental in the rise of our modern secularized society, and it is of course true that the Calvinists turned their religious endeavors toward this world, this *seculum,* and that they passionately resisted the worship of anything in this world as well as the granting of an authority to anyone who might compete with God's authority; but at the same time, they profoundly sacralized the world by recognizing within it the actions of God and by attempting to stamp it with the patterns of obedience. The Calvinist world is thoroughly secularized—and at the same time suffused with the sacral.

earlier that the preference for formative over avertive Christianity need not necessarily take the shape of *world*-formative Christianity; one's endeavors at reform may be confined, for example, to one's inwardness. Our next step will be to see why in this case it did take the world-formative path.

The terrain to be described here can be approached from many different directions. I shall approach it by speaking first of the Calvinist understanding of the relation between our actions of obedient gratitude and our social roles, and then speaking of the Calvinist notion of the holy commonwealth.

It is important to keep in mind that our social roles include more than what have customarily been labeled our "callings," that is, our occupations. On this Calvin himself was very clear. Although he speaks a good deal about how we ought to act in society, he speaks relatively little about callings. In the *Institutes* he devotes only two paragraphs to the subject (III, x, 6), and they are curiously unemphatic, as is clear from the opening: "Finally, this point is to be noted: the Lord bids each one of us in all life's actions to look to his calling." After a brief discussion he remarks, "But I will not delay to list examples. It is enough if we know that the Lord's calling is in everything the beginning and foundation of well-doing. And if there is anyone who will not direct himself to it, he will never hold to the straight path in his duties." The truth is that what the Calvinists wish to say about our callings is merely one aspect of what they wish to say about our social roles in general. Nonetheless, it has to be admitted that their teaching about callings is a paradigm of their teaching about social roles in general. I shall so treat it. Gratitude, obedience, and vocation— these are at the center of Calvinist social piety: obedience motivated by gratitude and expressed in vocation.

In the medieval church ordinary occupational roles would have been among the last things to be described as vocations, as callings. A vocation was some special religious occupation to which one was usually officially appointed by the church. Most Catholics today, at least in the United States, still talk the same way. They would find it strange to speak of the shopkeeper's occupation, for example, as a "vocation"; it is the person who is called by the church to do mission work in Venezuela who is said to have a vocation.

The change occurred in Lutheranism. There the ordinary occupations of the social world were spoken of as callings. The idea was that God calls us to them. However, though one is indeed called by God *to* some occupation, and though it would be disobedient to evade that call by going into some other occupation or trying to make do without an occupation, nonetheless what one does *in* one's occupation is thought of not so much as a matter of obedience as it is a matter of social necessity. Correspondingly, Luther still tended to think of the whole occupational structure of society as God-ordained rather than as something created by us to be rearranged if that seems desirable. Troeltsch sheds some valuable light on this distinction:

> Luther's view of vocation agreed with that of Paul, the Early Church, and the Middle Ages. To him the "calling" was simply the sphere of activity in which one was set, and in which it was a duty to remain. . . . Although at the same time Luther pointed out that it is precisely through the ordered work of one's calling, and the intricate network of mutual service that the preservation of the whole community is effected, and with that peace, order, and prosperity, he attributes it all to the wise ordering and the kindly guidance of Providence, and not to deliberate human initiative. The vocational system was not consciously designed and developed for the purposes of the holy community and of Christian Society, but it was accepted as a Divine arrangement. The individual, moreover, regarded his work, not as a suitable way of contributing to the uplift of Society as a whole, but as his appointed destiny, which he received from the hands of God. That is why it was possible for the Lutheran to regard the work of his vocation in an entirely traditional and reactionary way—as the duty of remaining within the traditional way of earning a living which belongs to one's position in Society. This point of view coincides with the traditional Catholic view. Christian morality was exercised *in vocatione* but not *per vocationem*. [22]

The core of what was different in the Calvinist concept of calling is alluded to in the concluding sentence of this passage: the Calvinist saw his occupation as something *through which* to exercise his obedience. *Remaining in that role* is not the thing which is to be done out of obedient gratitude; rather, *the actions performed in that role* are what is to be done out of obedient gratitude. However (and here I go beyond Troeltsch's point), each occupational role must either *be made* to serve the common good, or if in some case that cannot be done, then that role must be discarded. It's not true that if everyone works devotedly in the occupation to which God called him or her, the common good will automatically be served; one has to see to it that one's occupation serves the common good rather than simply assuming that it does, for—and here we come to perhaps the most profound of all breaches between the Calvinist and the medieval vision—we live in a fallen, corrupted society: the structures of our social world are structures which in good measure do not serve the common good.

What naturally follows among those who hold this perspective is the social activism that Weber found so striking. What also follows is that one will begin to think of the whole array of occupations as man-made. Once one is convinced that each occupational role ought to serve the common good, but that as a matter of fact many are corrupted so that they do not, then it will be impossible to think of the social order as given by God. One will inevitably think of it as made by human beings and capable of alteration. One will think of us as responsible for its structure.[23]

Yet another inference will follow naturally from the conviction that our obedience is to be rendered *per vocationem* and not merely *in vocatione* when it is coupled with the conviction that the structure of the social order is a fallen one: it will be increasingly difficult to tolerate the idea that a person is *born* into an occupation. If each of us is to reshape his or her occupation into a channel of obedience, then presumably each of us must also search for that occupation which will best serve as a channel of obedience. Thus in the Calvinist concept of the calling there is a powerful pressure toward the diminution of what sociologists call "ascriptivism," a phenomenon of which I shall speak in the next chapter. Calvin already remarked that "it would be asking for too much, if a tailor were not permitted to learn another trade, or a merchant to change to farming."[24]

One more thing must be added to have the full Calvinist concept of the calling before us—the fact that all those different modes of obedience rendered to God in the diversity of society-serving occupations are fundamentally equal in God's sight. Some may be more crucial than others for the welfare of society, but all are equal: "If the chambermaid and the manservant go about their domestic tasks offering themselves in their work as a sacrifice to God, then what they do is accepted by God as a holy and pure sacrifice pleasing in His sight."[25] What the Calvinists especially had their eye on with this radical levelling of occupations was of course the monasteries. For a thousand years, Christian Europe had said that the life of the monastery is the noblest form of life, inasmuch as it is dedicated to the contemplation of God. When the Calvinists levelled the occupations, they were saying that a career turned toward this world with God behind one's back is not inferior to a career turned toward God. It is no farther from the true end of man. Indeed, many Calvinists said it was closer—closer to that knowledge of God which is the true *ac*knowledgment of him in life.[26] A friend of mine told me how annoyed he was, upon visiting the St. Bavo Kerk in Haarlem, to see how the Calvinists had put representations of good solid Dutch burghers in the windows where the medievals would have had saints—until he realized that these *were* the Calvinist saints.

We have been considering what it was in the thought of the early Calvinists that made their turn toward the world take the shape of world-formative Christianity. I have argued for the importance of two convictions on their part: first, the conviction that the obedient gratitude that constitutes the basis of this turn ought to be exercised within our occupations; and second, the conviction that the occupational structures as presented to us are corrupted and would not serve that goal. Put these elements together and, with a few other assumptions that I shall mention shortly, one has a powerful argument for social reform and, in extreme cases, even for revolution.

But first, why were the Calvinists so persuaded that the social structures as presented to us are fallen? And where did they get their guidelines for reform? What was the root of their radical social critique? The answer is clear: it is the Word of God, presented to us in the Bible, that shows up for us the corruption of our social order. And it is that same Word of God that provides us with our fundamental pattern for reform. The reformation of society according to the Word of God: this was the Calvinist goal.

The Calvinists did not deny—indeed, they insisted—that the capacity for apprehending the will of God for our lives belongs to all human beings simply by virtue of our created nature. And no matter what the extent of a given person's perversity, that capacity is never entirely lost; indeed, the *workings* of that capacity are never fully *suppressed:* God's will is communicated in natural law. But our apprehension of that law is at best wavering and fallible. The Bible comes then to make clear to us the content of that law. Accordingly, it would be folly to try to extract the grounds for our critique of the social order from our faltering apprehension of God's natural law, and it would be worse than folly to try to extract it from the voice of reason within us, or from our inward desires for happiness or freedom, or from tradition. To that end, we have a word *from outside*—a word from God.*

To complete our attempt to grasp the contours of this original version of world-formative Christianity, I must now at one point broaden what has been said, and at another, deepen it. The broadening consists in recalling that though our discussion has been formulated in terms of the Calvinist doctrine of occupational callings, it in fact applies to the Calvinist teaching concerning social roles in general, and particularly to our roles in church and state, the great ordering institutions of human life. The deepening consists in bringing to light two assumptions in the line of thought as I have presented it.

For one thing, it is assumed that Christians, as they struggle to find or shape an occupation in which to exercise their obedience, will not stray far from those occupations characteristically found in our ordinary social world. We heard Calvin speaking of tailors, merchants, and farmers; such occupations

---

*If the Bible were to be a comprehensive guide for our social activities, it was essential that the Calvinist take the Old Testament seriously. Appeals to the Old Testament in Calvinism have a function similar to appeals to *nature* in Thomist Catholicism (and in Lutheranism). It is fascinating to observe, in his *Letters and Papers from Prison,* that as Bonhoeffer moves toward world-formative Christianity and away from a formative version of Christianity based on inwardness and religious practices, he also begins to emphasize the importance of the Old Testament. He saw, as did the Calvinists, that the New Testament in isolation gives insufficient guidance for the new praxis.

are of course thoroughly familiar to us. But why would Christians not exercise their obedience in a special set of occupations? Why in this range of relatively ordinary occupations? Why not all, say, become evangelists and medical workers?

The answer to this question lies in the Calvinist's understanding of the goal of God's redemptive activity. If we had lived as God meant us to live, we would all be members of an ordered community bound together by love for each other and gratitude to God, using the earth for our benefit and delight. In fact we do not live thus. A fall has occurred. God's response to this fall of mankind was to choose from all humanity a people destined for eternal life. They in obedient gratitude are now to work for the renewal of human life so that it may become what God meant it to be. They are to struggle to establish a holy commonwealth here on earth. Of course it is the mandate of all humanity to struggle toward such a community; what makes Christians different in their action is that they have in fact committed themselves to struggling toward this goal, that they recognize it as God's mandate, and that they struggle toward it not just in obedience to God the creator but in imitation of Christ. It is because Christians are committed in obedient gratitude to work for the renewal of the earthly community that they will render their obedience in such ordinary earthly occupations as tailor, merchant, and farmer.

The other assumption can be brought to light by asking this question: Suppose we grant that the holy commonwealth will be a truly earthly commonwealth with tailors and merchants and farmers; why, then, would it not be a *separated* community? Why would not the Christian pull out of general society and set up the holy commonwealth in a separated area? In short, why not follow the Anabaptist experiment?

Against the Anabaptists the Calvinists threw up a great flurry of arguments, far more than I can here review. But even if we had the time and space to review them, my guess is that in doing so we would not touch the real issues. The multiplicity of the Calvinist arguments against the Anabaptists, when viewed in conjunction with the violence of their rhetoric, leads one to surmise that their ideological defenses were not strong. The truth, I think, is that, on this issue especially, social realities shaped the thinking of the Calvinists. They assumed that the Constantinianism which Europe had known for more than a millennium was basically correct. They resisted questioning seriously the hoary assumption that the membership of the institutional church and the membership of civil society were identical. And though they never identified the elect with the membership of the institutional church, they resisted the idea of the "believers' church" on the ground that we had no way of making the separation between the elect believers and others. Accordingly, rather than calling for the church of believers to withdraw from mixed society and set up its own holy commonwealth, they went in the opposite direction and insisted that all the members of the institutional church—and thus all the members of civil society—were to be subjected to ecclesiastical admonition and discipline.[27] We all know of the repressiveness that this system entailed; on this point, social and psychic dynamics, if not theological arguments, made the system of original Calvinism intolerable almost everywhere within a century. One may well wonder whether the comparable social disciplines imposed by those secular saints of revolutionary regimes in our own century will ultimately fare any better!

As the Calvinists in their turn toward the world struggled to reshape society and institute the holy commonwealth on earth, they encountered resistance. It became their experience that humanity in general was not eagerly awaiting their program of social reform. They interpreted the Bible as telling them that this is what they should expect: the fallenness of the social order is not a result of mere blundering; behind it is a body of humanity committed to resisting the work of God. "You have great works to do," remarked the Puritan preacher Stephen Marshall in 1641, "the planting of a new heaven and a new earth among us, and great works have great enemies. . . ."[28] Beneath the social order the Calvinist discerned conflict, the Augustinian conflict between the City of God and the City of the World, the war of the Lamb with the Beast.[29] This conflict was not incidental to the social order. It was explanatory of its fundamental dynamics. Later this idea would be developed by Abraham Kuyper and his followers into the theory of *antithesis,* in which the concept of idolatry is used as a basic category of social analysis.* The Augustinian/Calvinist conviction that a fundamental conflict underlies the social order provides us with history's first version of conflictive social theory—a form of social theory of which we in our Marxist age have all become vividly aware.[30]

I have been speaking of the social thought of the early Calvinists, but of course what was remarkable about them was that this did not remain with them a pattern of thought, but became a component in their praxis. A new way of life came into being, its thought and practice interacting.** Along with it a typical psychological formation emerged—call it "the Calvinist social

---

*On this point one again finds a fundamental contrast between the vision characteristic of the Thomist Catholic and that of the Calvinists: the Catholic tends to see all humanity as reaching out for God, albeit often in misguided ways, whereas the Calvinist tends to see a fundamental division in humanity, between those who worship the true God and those who worship idols. This explains, of course, the tendency of Catholics to absorb a great many of the native religious practices into their liturgy, and the contrasting tendency of Calvinist Protestants to sweep away all such practices as "pagan."

**In later Calvinism the *world*-formative character of this new way of life will often diminish to the point of disappearance. All too typically what takes its place is a concern for the formation of *ideas*—especially theological ideas. Where the Lutheran becomes concerned with the formation of inwardness, the Calvinist becomes concerned with the formation of theology—or "philosophy."

piety"—at the heart of which was the awareness of a tension between demand and reality. The Calvinists knew that they ought to be exercising their obedient gratitude in their occupations and in their social roles in general, but the very Word of God which told them this also showed them that the social roles presented to them were corrupted and not fit instruments for obedience. In some people this double awareness produced a restless impulse toward reformism along with the self-discipline that Weber so strongly emphasized. In others it produced a feeling of guilt. These are the people who found themselves in the aching situation of being persuaded in their hearts that they ought to be working for reform but stymied by a will too weak to bring themselves to do so. One does not apprehend the contours of the characteristic Calvinist social piety until one discerns the pervasive presence of this form of guilt. Some will say that it is not guilt at all, but a peculiar form of hypocrisy: people saying that they ought to work at reform but not believing it and happily filling their social roles in the ordinary way. Perhaps in some cases this acquiesence is the result of hypocrisy, but my own experience suggests that it is more often otherwise.

There is nothing in the Calvinist system to assuage this form of guilt—nothing other than the general word of pardon for our human failings. By contrast there is a special word of consolation for the persons who have done their best to secure reform but failed: to them the Calvinist says that in this fallen world of conflicting demands there is nonetheless (often) a *best* thing to do, and that this best thing is the *right* thing to do. Those who do the best thing can live with an easy conscience. This stands in contrast to the typical Lutheran formulation that the best of one's options is often nothing more than the lesser of two evils, and that one must accordingly pray to be forgiven for doing the unavoidable evil. The Calvinist does not demand that a politics appropriate to heaven be practiced here already on this fallen earth.

Restless disciplined reformism, or guilt for not being restlessly reformist: these are the characteristic components of the Calvinist social piety. When these are missing, one can reliably surmise that one is confronted with a person who has some other understanding of his or her social role than that characteristic of early Calvinism—with one exception: sometimes one is instead confronted with that most insufferable of all human beings, the triumphalist Calvinist, the one who believes that the revolution instituting the holy commonwealth has already occurred and that his or her task is now simply to keep it in place. Of these triumphalist Calvinists the United States and Holland have both had their share. South Africa today provides them in their purest form.

Original Calvinism represented, then, a passionate desire to reshape the social world so that it would no longer be alienated from God. Thereby it would also no longer be alienated from mankind, for the will of God is that society be an ordered "brotherhood" serving the common good. Once this passion to reshape the social world entered Western civilization, it remained. Later it would be energized by the desire to make the world expressive of one's "self—to overcome the alienation between the desires of the self and the world. Originally it was energized by the passion to place on the world the stamp of holy obedience.

Is not that passion as relevant and imperative today as it was then? Admittedly, when we hear this word "obedience" we think immediately of the repressiveness of early Calvinism. Though the Calvinists spoke of justice, they failed to think through how they could live together in a just society with those with whom they disagreed. That was their great and tragic failing—though a failing scarcely unique to them. And a second failing, closely related, was their recurrent triumphalism. But is our need today for a society of justice and of peace not just as desperate as it was then? And when we struggle for such a society, do we not stand in continuity with the prophetic tradition of the Old Testament—and with Jesus Christ, who in the inaugural address of his ministry said that in him the words of the prophet Isaiah were fulfilled?

> The Spirit of the Lord is upon me,
> because he has anointed me to preach good news to the poor.
> He has sent me to proclaim release to the captives
> and recovering of sight to the blind,
> to set at liberty those who are oppressed,
> to proclaim the acceptable year of the Lord.

There are those in this world for whom the bonds of oppression are so tight that they cannot themselves work for a better society. Their lot falls on the shoulders of you and me. For I write mainly to those like myself who live in societies where the space of freedom is wide. To us I say: the Word of the Lord and the cries of the people join in calling us to do more than count our blessings, more than shape our inwardness, more than reform our thoughts. They call us to struggle for a new society in the hope and expectation that the goal of our struggle will ultimately be granted us.

Chapter II

The Modern World-System

The structures of our social world are fallen. They are alienated from the will of God. Instead of providing authentic fulfillment to us who live within them, they spread misery and injustice, squelching the realization of what human life was meant to be. In response to this we are not to avert ourselves from our social condition, seeking closer union with God by means of undisturbed contemplation, for God himself is disturbed by our human condition; rather, we are to struggle to alter those structures and the dynamics behind them, so that the alienation is diminished and the realization advanced. This is the core of that vision of human existence of which I spoke in the preceding chapter, calling it *world-formative Christianity*.

Indispensable to the implementation of this vision is an *architectonic* analysis and critique of our society, that is, an analysis and critique of its structure and dynamics. In this chapter I shall begin such an analysis; in subsequent chapters I shall expand upon this analysis in the context of a critique. First, though, a word as to what I have in mind when I speak of *structure*.

Every sizable group of human beings has an interrelated array of social institutions; those institutions *fundamental* to a given group, along with features *pervasive* throughout a group's institutions generally, will be regarded as belonging to the structure of that society. This dimension of our modern society will be part of what we here analyze. In addition, each member of every group of human beings performs actions that affect other members of the group and elicit a variety of responses from them. These we may call *socially significant actions*. In any group there will be complexes and sequences of such actions which, by virtue of their repetition, may be called *practices*. The *fundamental* social practices of a group, along with *pervasive* features of their practices generally, will also be regarded as belonging to the structure of that society of people, and this part of the structure of our modern society will also be the subject of our analysis.

On occasion I shall refer to the fundamental practices of a society as its *dynamics*. And sometimes I shall refer to the dual complex, consisting of a group's social institutions and its social practices, as *the social world* (or *order*) of that group. Using this terminology, we can say that our project in this chapter is to discern the structure that is characteristic of the modern social world. It should be noted that we are not at this point interested in investigating either the structure of *theories* concerning the modern social world or the issues of what one and another social institution *ought* to be like.

A fundamental thesis in our discussion is that not only are the individual members of society fallen and in need of reform, but that this is true as well of the structures of society. Our social world must be reformed. Medieval Christians assumed otherwise, and in this they have often been joined by twentieth-century American "evangelicals." But the truth is that our fundamental social institutions often do things they should not do—promote war when they should promote peace, for example, or promote unemployment when they should promote work—and the truth is that there are large-scale social practices and a whole system of social roles, often firmly approved by the members of society generally, that cause or perpetuate injustice and misery.

The conviction is widespread among social analysts that approximately five centuries ago a process was beginning in Western Europe that has led to a contemporary social world structurally different in profound ways from any that preceded it. Beyond this generality, however, one finds little consensus. Perhaps the most important discrepancy is between modernization theorists and world-system theorists. I call it a "discrepancy," rather than a dispute, because although there are indeed disputes between the two camps, the difference is more than can be captured by listing items of dispute. At issue are two different "ways of seeing" the situation—two different *paradigms,* to use the word made fashionable by Thomas Kuhn's *The Structure of Scientific Revolutions.* And we cannot avoid making a choice between these two ways of seeing.

Modernization theorists see our world as containing a large number of distinct societies, each at a certain point in the process of modernization. If one attends to the examples that they offer one sees that their maps of the distinct societies of the world come close to coinciding with the political map of the world. The United States constitutes a society, as does the Soviet Union, the Netherlands, and so on. Naturally modernization theorists realize that these distinct societies interact with each other. They typically conceive of the interactions of a given society with others by regarding the other societies as its social environment, parallel to the way in which a portion of the earth's surface constitutes the physical environment of that society. Any society will have a social environment and a physical environment, and perhaps other types of environment as well.[1]

By comparing societies that they consider to be at different stages in the process of modernization, the modernization theorists try to isolate the essential features of modernization and its crucial dynamics. The criteria cited by Talcott Parsons, dean of the modernization theorists, are these: a high degree of *differentiation,* a great increase in *adaptive upgrading,* an increase in the *inclusion* of differentiated structures into a finely articulated normative whole, and a trend toward *value generalization.*[2] (I shall have more to say about some of these later.) As to the driving force behind modernization, probably most Western theorists would say that it is the impulse toward expanding the scope of technology. What in turn accounts for this impulse is often not considered.

Apart from these claims concerning the defining features of the process of modernization, two theses lie at the very core of the modernization theorist's way of thinking: that it is in principle possible for all societies simultaneously to reach a high point of modernization without any fundamental structural alteration in the already established, highly modernized societies, and that the causes of a given society's low level of modernization are to be found in that society itself and not, to any significant degree anyway, in the impact of the highly modernized societies upon it. Something is amiss in the society that fails to become highly modernized: a lack of money for investment, the wrong kind of character formation, or whatever. Depending on what is thought to be amiss, perhaps the highly modernized societies can function as cure; perhaps they can supply the money needed for investment. But in any case they are not the *cause* of what is amiss.

Many intellectuals in the twentieth century have suggested that the process of modernization is an essentially destructive phenomenon that replaces concrete social formations with abstract formations in which individuals feel alienated from a social order not expressive of themselves.[3] There are signs that this mood of criticism is beginning to spread from intellectuals to the general public, but, at least until recently, the general public, both in the East and the West, regarded modernization as a *good* thing, typically giving it the honorific title "development." Development was touted as the cure to a multitude of human miseries and urged on the "undeveloped" and "underdeveloped" societies of the world.

In spite of the push since the Second World War toward developing the underdeveloped countries, things have mainly gotten worse. Not only has the income gap between the least- and the most-developed societies increased, but the standard of living of many people in underdeveloped societies has become *absolutely* and not just *relatively* worse. Furthermore, oppression, torture, and genocide have become commonplace. It is my judgment, along with that of a good many others, that in the face of these facts it is time for us to cease inventing excuses and start admitting that modernization theory is bankrupt. It simply provides no plausible, adequate account for these phenomena—nor, indeed, for similar phenomena going back five centuries. The lack of development among the underdeveloped cannot be explained without taking note of the impact of the highly developed areas on the underdeveloped; and the oppression characteristic of, say, South America can no more be explained without taking into account the influence of the United States on that area than can the oppression characteristic of Eastern Europe be explained without taking into account the influence of the Soviet Union. To understand our modern world, we shall have to look elsewhere than at the modernization theories so favored by both conservatives and liberals (progressives) in the West.

Where modernization theorists see the world as containing a number of distinct societies at various stages in the process of modernization, world-system theorists see the world today as containing just one society, or *social system* as they prefer to call it. This one social system displays the historically unique feature of having a single integrated economy combined with a multiplicity of distinct states and a multiplicity of distinct peoples (nations). Among the fundamental issues in dispute between these two ways of "seeing" is this then: What entities shall be taken as the fundamental units of our social analysis?

Both parties use similar terminology to denote their fundamental units of social analysis *(societies* and *social systems)*, and, curiously, both claim to be working with essentially the same concept of society (social system), namely, one in which the notion of *self-sufficiency* is central: both define a social system (society) as an almost entirely self-sufficient social group, or, alternatively, as that type of social group which is at the highest level of self-sufficiency.* Yet, the one theorist takes the United States and the Soviet Union and the Netherlands among his basic units of analysis, while the other insists that nothing less than all humanity is today the appropriate basic unit. Surely the world-system theorist is correct: there is no area in the world today that is not significantly influenced in its "development" by other areas. Indeed, so obvious is this fact that one is led to wonder whether perhaps the modernization theorist wishes not to notice the ways in which his or her own area of the world influences other areas. Perhaps modernization theory functions in part ideologically, concealing these influences from the attention of the theorist.

In filling out the world-system picture in more detail, I will for a while follow rather closely that particular development of the picture that is to be found in the writings of one of the foremost world-system theorists, Im-

---

*Parsons states that "in defining a society, we may use a criterion which goes back at least to Aristotle. A society is a type of social system, in any universe of social systems, which attains the highest level of self-sufficiency as a system in relation to its environments" (*Societies: Evolutionary and Comparative Perspectives* [Englewood Cliffs, N.J.: Prentice-Hall, 1966], p. 9). Later in his discussion, he explicitly speaks of "the self-sufficiency criterion we used in defining the concept of a society" (p. 17). Immanuel Wallerstein suggests that "what characterizes a social system in my view is the fact that life within it is largely self-contained, and that the dynamics of its development are largely internal. . . . If the system, for any reason, were to be cut off from all external forces (which virtually never happens), the definition implies that the system would continue to function substantially in the same manner" (*The Modern World-System: Capitalist Agriculture and the Origins of the European World-Economy in the Sixteenth Century* [New York: Academic Press, 1974], p. 347).

manuel Wallerstein. Suppose we use the following as our criterion for determining whether or not some group of people has a single integrated economy: Is there within the group "a division of labor, such that the various sectors or areas within are dependent upon economic exchange with others for the smooth and continuous provisioning of the needs of the area"?[4]* If we now distinguish among social groups on the basis of their (1) having a single integrated economy, (2) being distinct as a nation (people), and (3) being united under a single ultimate political authority, we can easily see that a variety of combinations are possible among such units. The traditional "primitive" social group, for example, comprises a single integrated economy and a single ultimate political authority, and all of its members belong to a single nation, or people. By contrast, a group that has a single entire economy may contain distinct peoples. Let us call such a group a *world-system:* its single entire economy ensures that it is indeed a *system,* and to call it a *world*-system is to stress that it ecumenically comprises distinct peoples. Within world-systems we may then in turn distinguish those which are world-*empires* from those which are merely world-*economies.* A world-empire will be a culturally diverse group which in addition to having a single entire economy also has a single ultimate political authority (an authority which may weaken almost to nonexistence in certain areas of the group). By contrast, a world-economy will be a culturally diverse group that has a single entire economy but more than one ultimate political authority. (It must be stressed that a social system is a *world*-economy not because it covers the whole globe, for it may be far short of doing that, but because it ecumenically contains diverse peoples.)**

So much for definitions and distinctions. "It turns out empirically that world-economies have historically been unstable structures leading either towards disintegration or conquest by one group and hence transformation into a world-empire," notes Wallerstein. "Examples of such world-empires emerging from world-economies are all the so-called great civilizations of premodern

*"We can regard a division of labor as a grid which is substantially interdependent. Economic actors operate on some assumption (obviously seldom clear to any individual actor) that the totality of their essential needs—of sustenance, protection, and pleasure—will be met over a reasonable time span by a combination of their own productive activities and exchange in some form. The smallest grid that would substantially meet the expectation of the overwhelming majority of actors within those boundaries constitutes a single division of labor" (Wallerstein, *The Capitalist World-Economy* [Cambridge: Cambridge Univerity Press, 1979], p. 14).

**If we were speaking with full accuracy here, we would not speak of certain groups as being world-empires and others not, but rather of groups as being world-empires to a greater or lesser degree. This is also true of world-economies, because whether or not a group has an integrated economy is a matter of degree, and whether or not a group is a nation is a matter of degree—even whether or not it has a single ultimate political authority is, strictly speaking, a matter of degree. This should be kept in mind throughout the discussion.

times, such as China, Egypt, Rome (each at appropriate periods of its history)."5 But, as he also notes, "It is the peculiarity of the modern world–system that a world–economy has survived for 500 years and yet has not come to be transformed into a world–empire—a peculiarity that is the secret of its strength."6 Although in principle there might have been several world–economies today, there is in fact just one. And although in principle there might have been sizable groups not incorporated into that world–economy, there is in fact none. Our one world–economy is global in scope. We are subjects of many distinct states and members of many distinct peoples, and yet we are all participants in one market–integrated division of labor.

By definition, a world–economy is a combination of distinct states and distinct nations with a shared economy, but the fact that our world–economy is a particular configuration of these three sorts of entities is not merely a formal, structural matter. Quite the contrary is true: to understand the shaping of our society, one must understand the internal dynamics of the component states, nations, and economy as well as the ways in which they influence and respond to one another. So too, if one is to understand the *origins* of our modern world–economy and the cause of its spread throughout the globe, one cannot treat separately the origin of the modern nations, of the modern states, and of the modern economy; one must construct an integrated account in which the influences of each on the other are brought to light. Such a treatment of the origins of our modern world–system lies well beyond my competence and is in any case outside the scope of this book (although I shall, in a later chapter, say something about the interplay of states and peoples in the world today). But because of its importance for almost all that follows, more must now be said about the nature and dynamics of the economy in our modern social system.

For one thing, this economy is overwhelmingly *capitalist*. Everyone would agree on that. But what does one say in saying that? What is it that makes one economy more capitalistic than another? There have been many attempts to pick out necessary and sufficient conditions for an economy's being capitalistic. One person says that wage labor is essential to capitalism; another disputes that claim. Another says that distribution of goods by means of the marketplace is essential to capitalism; another disputes that. So it goes. I think the lesson to be learned from these disputes is that it is best not to think of economies as simply capitalistic or non-capitalistic, but to think of them as being *more or less* capitalistic; the degree to which an economy is capitalistic can be gauged by the degree to which it exhibits certain typical traits. The list of those traits should include, I suggest, at least the following six, the totality being a blend of legal arrangements and social practices.

(1) An economy is more capitalistic (other things being equal) the

more it distributes articles, land, and services by means of a marketing system—instead of, say, by means of bartering or authoritative allocation. Of course, markets go back as far as history, but as Heilbroner remarks, "whether they be exchanges between primitive tribes where objects are casually dropped on the ground or the exciting traveling fairs of the Middle Ages, [markets] are not the same as the market system. For the market system is not just a means of exchanging goods; *it is a mechanism for sustaining and maintaining an entire society.*"[7]

I think we should resist adding that the market system must be free or even relatively free; if one looks at the five-hundred-year history of our capitalist world-economy, one sees that it has always, at many points, been far from free. That it should be so is no mystery: in any market it is to the interest of the buyer that he or she be allowed to choose freely from the products of competitors, whereas it is in the interest of the seller that the market not allow the buyer to choose freely. In spite of liberal ideology, sellers have always manipulated the market in their favor by conspiring with one another, by influencing the actions of the state, and so forth.[8]

(2) An economy is more capitalistic (other things being equal) the more the goal of economic enterprises within that economy is to make profit from sales in the market. In principle the making of profit might not enter into the goal of an enterprise at all: for example, the governing goal might be that of providing decent work for a group of people. In fact the pursuit of profit is pervasive in the modern economy—though surely even the most determined profit seekers are energized by other goals as well.

It is important to realize that whether the parties selling for profit are individuals or groups of individuals makes no essential difference. The owners selling may even be sovereign states. Indeed, there is strong evidence that the "socialist" states that sell in the international marketplace of our present world-economy do so with profit as a prominent goal, thereby exhibiting one of the primary traits of capitalism.[9] As Wallerstein remarks, "a state which collectively owns all the means of production is merely a collective capitalist firm as long as it remains—as all such states are, in fact, presently compelled to remain—a participant in the market of the capitalist world-economy."[10] To what extent the economies *within* such states are capitalist is of course quite another matter—though surely the truth is that the present "socialist" economies exhibit to a high degree at least three of the six traits we will be citing.

(3) An economy is more capitalistic (other things being equal) the more it secures labor by offering wages—which is to say, the more labor is itself an item on the market, the more there is a "labor market." Heilbroner makes the essential point forcefully: "Wage labor has the historically unique attribute of legally denying the worker the ownership of his labor-product, which belongs instead to the owner of the physical equipment with which he

works." By contrast, peasants "own what they produce, however much of it they must hand over to landlords. Even feudal serfs owned the output from their own strips of land, although not from the lord's strips that they were forced to cultivate. Only the slave could be said not to own his product. Hence the expression, 'wage slavery.' "[11]

(4) An economy is more capitalistic (other things being equal) the more *capital* enters into its production and distribution processes. *Capital* we may define as consisting of items to which persons (or corporate entities) have title, that are used in the production or marketing of goods or services, and whose use therein entitles the owner to income on account of the (purported) utility of those items in that process.[12] Normally the claim to income is enforced by the owner withdrawing or threatening to withdraw the use of his capital. Capital, suggests Alvin Gouldner, is "a product not employed for its consummatory satisfactions, but in order to produce *other* utilities and wealth. The object of capital is not consumption but instrumental mastery. It is thus 'goods producing goods.' "[13] There are many ways of acquiring income, among which are plunder, the exaction of tribute, and the contribution of one's capital to some process of production or distribution.

(5) An economy is more capitalistic (other things being equal) the more the participants in the economy use the income derived from capital to gain title to items that are in turn used as capital. All social systems other than the most primitive produce surpluses—that is to say, they all produce material wealth beyond what is needed to sustain the productive existence of the members of the system. But "what is distinctive about capitalism is the form that its surplus takes. Other social orders use surplus for war, public adornment, religious observances, and for the maintenance of privileged classes. Capitalism also uses its surplus in part for these purposes. . . . But its distinctive use is something else: *surplus is employed to create the means to gather additional surplus.* That is, 'wealth' under capitalism takes the form of machines, equipment, plants, factories. No such systematic use of surplus existed in any prior society."[14] No doubt it is especially this feature of capitalism that accounts for its uniquely expansive force, all the more so when the dominant mode of production is industrial.

(6) An economy is more capitalistic (other things being equal) the more capital is owned by private parties rather than by the public. Although it is less clear than might appear at first glance what constitutes a *private party* (presumably a corporation is a private party, but what about a cooperative or the socialist states of Russia and Eastern Europe?), it will not be necessary for our purposes to refine the concept.

We have been considering the structure of capitalism in order to explain the claim that the economy of our modern world-system is highly capitalistic. To perceive the full depth of the conflict between modernization theories and world-system theories, however, we must also note that this capitalist economy in our world-system has a horizontal structure of *core* and *periphery*, with a buffer zone between these two which may be called the *semiperiphery*.

Even a cursory glance at our world-system reveals the fact that wealth is not evenly distributed throughout the geographical areas of the system—and more importantly, that *capital* wealth is not evenly distributed; on the contrary, it is accumulated with extreme unevenness. Today its heaviest concentrations are to be found in North America, in northwest Europe, and in Japan. Those areas of heaviest capital accumulation constitute the core of our system; those of least capital accumulation, the periphery. Today the core of the system is heavily engaged in capital-intensive, high-technology, high-wage production, whereas the periphery is dominantly engaged in labor-intensive, low-technology, low-wage production. [15]

The idea behind calling certain areas *core* is not that they are the richest in capital but that they have the preponderance of economic voice and power in the system—this being both result and cause of their concentration of capital wealth. The core *dominates* the periphery and semiperiphery; or, to put it from the other side, the periphery is *subordinated* to the core and semiperiphery, and the semiperiphery, to the core. (To make the same point, other writers describe the periphery and semiperiphery as *dependent,* but that is misleading: the core is not *in*dependent; all areas are *inter*dependent.)

This domination of core over periphery and semiperiphery is in part a direct consequence of legal structures. Fundamental to capitalism is that curious legal arrangement whereby when one party contributes labor to some enterprise and another party contributes capital in the form of "means of production," the latter by virtue of contributing that capital is legally entitled to determine the policy of the enterprise and has legal title to all its proceeds, whereas the former does not by virtue of contributing his labor gain any entitlement to the determination of policy nor any title to proceeds. Wherever one finds labor and capital (in the form of "means of production") interacting, one finds legally sanctioned authority on the part of capital that is lacking on the part of labor. John Locke argued that a person acquires title to something by virtue of "mixing his labor" with it. Capitalism is as far from operating on that Lockean principle as an economic system could be.

The uneven distribution of capital in the modern world-system does not only reflect legal domination of core over periphery and semiperiphery; it also reflects *de facto* domination. Power, and not just authority, is concentrated in the core. This power has many facets, and its character has changed over the centuries. Today in good measure it consists in the fact that ownership of technologies much desired by enterprises outside the core is held exclusively by individuals and firms within the core. But there is another and more abiding form of domination of which we must take note. Insofar as laborers under capitalism have title to both income and a voice in the enterprise in which they work, those entitlements rest entirely on the contract they have with the capitalist, and not on the fact that they have mixed their labor with the product. Accordingly, insofar as the laborer's position in the bargaining situation is weak, he or she is at the mercy of the capitalist so far as the appropriation of the proceeds of the enterprise and the determination of its policies are concerned.

As one might well suspect, the gross unevenness of capital distribution in the modern world between core and periphery is in large part the result of the laborers in the periphery having long been in a weak bargaining position with respect to the capitalists in the core (though in principle there might, of course, have been other causes for the disparity). Often the laborers in the periphery are at a disadvantage simply because of the pressure of population in those areas and the consequent shortage of jobs. And often they are at a disadvantage because they lack certain skills, attitudes, and knowledge. But we in the West must be reminded of the fact that for five hundred years now, the laborers outside the core (and sometimes those inside) have in addition repeatedly been placed in a weak bargaining position by the armaments of the capitalists. It was guns that induced South American Indians to mine cheap gold for the Spaniards. It was guns that induced Indians to produce cheap textiles for the British. It is guns that induce Salvadorans to produce cheap coffee, and South African blacks to produce cheap gold, for the rest of the world. Behind the concentration of capital in Europe and the United States is the use of much gunpowder, elaborate torture, and many prisons.

It is characteristic of the world-system theorist to go yet one step farther and argue that the domination of core by periphery is indispensable to the expansion of a capitalist economy (the thought behind calling certain areas *core* also being that they are the center of the expansion of the system). Accordingly, it is assumed that development of all areas to an equally high level of capital (and consumer) wealth is impossible in our capitalist world-system. Modernization theory harbors a cruel illusion. Wallerstein puts the point thus:

> If we think of the exchange between the core and the periphery of a capitalist system being that between high-wage products and low-wage products, there then results an "unequal exchange" . . . in which a peripheral worker needs to work many hours, at a given level of productivity, to obtain a product produced by a worker in a core country in one hour. And vice versa. Such a system is *necessary* for the expansion of a world market if the primary consideration is *profit*. Without *unequal* exchange, it would not be *profitable* to expand the size of the division of labor. And without such expansion, it

would not be profitable to maintain a capitalist world-economy.
. . .[16]

The details of both the formulation and defense of the central contention here vary from writer to writer—Wallerstein himself seems to hold the highly controversial "labor theory of value"—but essentially the thought is this: to expand their market, sellers in an emerging core area find it necessary to pay their workers higher and higher wages—a practice which in turn reduces profits. To this, sellers in the core area make essentially three responses: they move their labor-intensive enterprises to other areas where wages are still cheap, they shift to capital-intensive enterprises in their own area, and they seek to expand and control the market for the capital-intensive goods beyond the core area. The conclusion then is that "it is not possible theoretically for all states to 'develop' simultaneously. The so-called 'widening gap' is not an anomaly but a continuing basic mechanism of the operation of the world-economy. Of course, *some* countries can 'develop'. But the some that rise are at the expense of others that decline."[17]*

I have made clear my conviction that we must see ourselves as living today in a global society that combines an integrated capitalist economy with a multiplicity of states and a diversity of peoples. I have argued that we must prefer the basic picture offered by the world-system theorist over that offered by the modernization theorist. In later chapters I shall fill in some more details of the picture. Yet if we are to understand the sorrows—and, yes, the triumphs—of modern man, we cannot simply ignore all those features of modernity to which modernization theorists have so regularly called our attention; instead, we must interpret their significance differently. They are indispensable accompaniments of our world-system in its expansion from its European origins to the encirclement of our globe. They are micro-structural features indispensable to the functioning of this capitalist economy which is combined with a pluralism of modern states—these being characterized by tightly defined geographical boundaries, precisely specified citizenries, and an impulse to wrap the tentacles of their authority snugly around the contours of our lives. I propose, then, that we look briefly at some of these micro-structural features. Once again we will be working with matters of degree. These micro-structural traits of modernity are not wholly unknown outside the pale of the modern world-system; indeed, here and there one sees them markedly present.[18] The situation is rather that our world-system requires and induces an intensification of these traits. Hence, insofar as our system overtakes areas where these traits are only dimly present,

---

*I am not able in this book to enter into the extremely complex question of why the core shifts around as it does; nor can I outline the specific advantages that enable a given region to become a core area.

it produces an alteration in the lives of those people down to the finest threads of their social fabric.

One of the most fundamental of these micro-structural features of modernity is the prominence of what Weber has taught us to call *rationalized* action, and, correspondingly, the relative insignificance of tradition as a guide and shaper of action. The background of all social existence is habit. No society can exist unless a vast array of the actions of its members is habitual. Choice is always performed against a background of habit.[19] It would be difficult to say whether our actions are on the whole any less habitual than those of the members of "primitive" societies, but it does seem clear that there has at least been a sizable shift in the grounds of our choices.[20] In choosing goals for their actions, the members of a traditional society characteristically do not mean to stray from the practices of their predecessors, and when they choose means for achieving their goals, they characteristically choose "the way it has always been done" without even raising the question of whether there might be some better way of achieving those goals. Nor do they, to any significant degree, raise the question of whether other goals would be more appropriate. In a traditional society the psychological mechanism of *modeling* is the great shaper of human action. What determines choice is that "this is how things are done, and not in any other way. This is how one marries (and whom); this is how one raises children, makes one's livelihood, exercises power, goes to war—and in no other way."[21]

In post-feudal Europe, tradition lost its grip. People increasingly began to set goals for themselves outside those characteristic of their predecessors, and to seek means for accomplishing their goals better than "the way it has always been done." This decline in the force of tradition as the great guide and shaper of human action was well under way by the beginning of the sixteenth century. Yet I think there can be no doubt that the Protestant Reformation, and particularly its Calvinist branch, contributed significantly to this decline. What is relevant here is partly the Reformers' insistence that the tradition of the church lacks the normative force of Scripture. What is much more relevant is their insistence that our personal lives and our social world must be reformed so as to accord with the Word of God. The Calvinist insisted on the "rational planning of the whole of one's life in accordance with God's will," as Weber puts it.[22] Tradition was bracketed by the Protestants; at best it was to be considered along with other options in one's attempt to determine how the Word of God is to be obeyed.

Rationalized action, in contrast to action modeled on tradition, emerges from more or less conscious reflection on how best to achieve one's goal, or on which goal to aim at. Such action is a hallmark of our modern social world, especially one species of rationalized action which we may call *technologically* rationalized action—action in which the agent makes use of the results of theorizing to determine the best means for achieving his goal. In arriving at an answer to the question of how best to achieve one's goals, one will, other things being equal, make use of whatever knowledge is available. We in the modern world have discovered, over and over, that *theoretical* knowledge is relevant to such determinations: we have discovered the value of technology. Initially, technologically rationalized actions mainly made use of the new physical sciences and were directed toward the alteration of physical nature; in our century, with the rise of the social sciences, they have also been directed toward altering social practices and institutions; and now, with the rise of psychology, they are directed as well toward altering the psychological dynamics of individual human beings.

So prominent among us is this technological use of the empirical and mathematical sciences that we have forgotten how extraordinary it is. The ancients and medievals did not consider the value of science to lie in its utility for altering the world; for them, theory was an aid to contemplation. By way of theory one became aware of the structure of the cosmos: it made possible a knowledgeable contemplation of the order of things, and in that lay its worth. For us its main worth resides in its utility for altering ourselves, our social world, and the natural world.[23]

A second fundamental feature of the micro-structure of our modern social world is a high degree of what sociologists call *differentiation.* Differentiation comes in two forms: differentiation of social roles and differentiation of institutions and organizations. In our modern world-system, one's role as parent is differentiated from one's role as operator of a small business, from one's role as member of a church, from one's role as chairman of the school board, from one's role as member of the local neighborhood association—thereby allowing the individual to fill a combination of roles different from those of other members of his or her society. (One facet of this differentiation of roles among us is the so-called division of labor,[24] although clearly differentiation of social roles extends well beyond the work place.) By contrast, in traditional societies the differentiation of roles tends to be minimal. Naturally, there too one can distinguish, in abstract fashion, an immense number of roles, but, to a far greater degree than among us, these roles cannot be put together in different combinations. To a far greater degree than among us they come clustered together.

Corresponding to this high differentiation of roles is a high differentiation—or perhaps one should say *pluralization*—of social institutions and organizations. In a traditional society, the number of distinct institutions and organizations is minimal. Among us it is vast. The philosophers start their own separate organization, then the philosophers of science theirs, then the philosophers of social science theirs, then the Catholic philosophers theirs, and so on. The result is a vast pluralism of institutions and organizations.*

*In connection with this point, we should also take note of a type of organization prominent in our modern world-system and prominent previously only

A third fundamental feature of the micro-structure of our modern world-system is a relatively low degree of *ascriptivism*. Ascriptivism pertains to the manner in which the participants in society are matched up to the whole array of roles and institutions. In traditional societies the social roles that individuals play are for the most part ascribed to them by virtue of features they possess over which they have no control: one's roles in society are determined by sex, by place of birth, by social status of parents, and so on. By contrast, in our modern world-system we see a radical diminution of ascriptivism—a trend that serves to render such surviving ascriptive phenomena as sexism and racism all the more noticeable and infuriating. One can think of the decrease of ascriptivism as introducing a considerable degree of looseness between the role structure of the social world and the way in which that structure is matched up to its participants—this looseness to be taken up by someone's choice. The more totalitarian a particular state within our relatively nonascriptive world-system, the more the matching up of persons to roles will be determined by the fiat of some administrator. The more free it is, the more that matching up of persons to roles will be accomplished by the persons themselves (there being, of course, limits to this sort of personal autonomy: as ascriptivism has diminished in significance, the functional consideration of whether the person can competently perform the role has risen).*

A fourth important feature of the micro-structure of our modern world-system pertains to the interrelation between the structure of our social world and its cultural and motivational context, which underlies several of the other features to which I have pointed. The feature I have in mind is the presence of a high degree of what sociologists have called *value generalization*. In traditional societies the rights and obligations of a person are almost entirely con-

---

in those societies that were world-empires—namely, the organization with a bureaucratically organized administration. A high degree of role differentiation belongs to the very essence of the bureaucratic organization: not only is there horizontal differentiation, which we experience when, as a client of such an organization, we are referred to the office down the hall for someone authorized to deal with our case, but also vertical differentiation, which we experience when our case is referred by the functionary with whom we are dealing to one of his superiors. It is well known that Weber regarded bureaucracies, with their articulated array of delineated areas of competence and generalized procedural rules, as being, after technology, the most decisive manifestation of rationalized action in the modern world.

*The more freedom a state gives to its members in matching up persons to roles, and the more highly differentiated the institutional structure in that area, the more will that area of the world-system display what sociologists call *associationism*—that phenomenon whereby membership in institutions and organizations is determined by the choice of the person. In traditional societies there is very little associationism: seldom is an individual a member of some social institution or organization by virtue of having decided to associate himself with it. By contrast, all of us in modern Western society are members of large numbers of institutions and organizations with which we have *chosen* to associate ourselves.

nected to his or her various social roles. By contrast, we to a great extent acknowledge the rights and responsibilities of the person *qua* human being, regardless of the roles he or she fills.

Ethical universalism has to a great extent replaced the ethical particularism of traditional societies. This comes to expression, for example, in those lists of human rights with which we are all familiar, from the preamble of the United States Declaration of Independence to the Universal Declaration of Human Rights of the United Nations. It comes to expression in the formulation of generalized codes of law and the insistence that everyone is equal before the law, and no one above it. It comes to expression in the proscription of discrimination among individuals on the basis of such things as race, color, creed, sex, age, social status, and wealth. Likewise, it comes to expression in the replacement of the ideal of honor by the ideal of dignity. "It is important to understand that it is [the] solitary self that modern consciousness has perceived as the bearer of human dignity and inalienable rights," suggest the authors of *The Homeless Mind* in an interesting discussion of this succession of ideals; they go on to say,

> Dignity, as against honor, always relates to the intrinsic humanity divested of all socially imposed roles or norms. It pertains to the self as such, to the individual regardless of his position in society. . . .
>
> *The concept of honor implies that identity is essentially, or at least importantly, linked to institutional roles. The modern concept of dignity, by contrast, implies that identity is essentially independent of institutional roles.* [25]

We must not exaggerate the extent to which value generalization has taken hold in our modern world-system: the ethics of loyalty, as it is sometimes called, has not been totally displaced, nor would any of us want it to be (we would, I think, all agree that one should treat one's own children differently from the way one should treat children generally, just *because* they are one's children). As we shall see in a later chapter, the prominence of nationalism in the modern world is a flamboyant exception to the trend toward value generalization.

In summary, then, the increase in rationalization over what was characteristic of most earlier societies, the increase in differentiation, the reduction of ascriptivism, and the increase in value generalization: these are fundamental features of the micro-structure of society wherever the dynamics of our modern world-system have done their work.* Though I cannot here argue the point,

---

*Of the four principal aspects of societal micro-structure, the increase in rationalization is the most fundamental, in the sense that no matter what impels the departure from tradition into genuine history, an increase in rationalization will mark the resultant actions.

I would suggest that they are necessary accompaniments of our modern world-system in all of its modifications of preexisting social structures. This is not to deny, of course, that factors other than those energizing the spread in scope and intensity of the system itself have contributed to the emergence of these micro-structures. The original Calvinists, for example, were clearly in favor of a society in which the role of tradition and of many forms of ascriptivism would be reduced, a society in which there would be an increase in social differentiation and value generalization. If Walzer is correct, their advocacy of such a society played a significant role in its emergence. (Whether they advocated anything like the modern state or many of the features central to capitalism is quite another matter. Naturally, they may have contributed to the rise of these things without advocating them.)[26]

The new world-system, as I have already suggested, was in good measure forced upon people. Dwellers on distant shores did not stand there eagerly beckoning the Europeans to introduce their social innovations. As late as 1793, the Emperor of China wrote the following to George III, King of England: "As your Ambassador can see for himself, we possess all things. I set no value on objects strange or ingenious, and have no use for your country's manufactures."[27] It has been said that the principal advantage of the Europeans in their initial contact with the Orient was that they had better ocean-going ships—and better artillery.[28]

Yet I do not think we can deny that there is something about this new system that has proved irresistibly alluring to masses of humanity, something that proves deeply satisfying to those who experience it. If that were not so, the system would have disappeared long ago.

Down through the ages, man has found himself with desires that his physical situation left unsatisfied: he was hungry, but there was no food; he longed to live to a ripe old age, but found himself on his deathbed at thirty; he loved his children and wanted them to live, but half died in childhood; he longed to fly like the birds, but found himself earthbound. Life was experienced as a vale of tears. In response to this experience, human beings learned to eliminate some of those desires that they had no hope of satisfying and to endure the unhappiness of life in the shadow of those they could not eliminate.

Our modern world-system holds out to all the allure—and, to many, the satisfaction—of a stunning alternative. To an astonishing degree we have learned how to alter our physical situation so that ancient desires are now satisfied. Where previously humanity, to gain freedom from unsatisfied desires, had to eliminate those desires, we now have gained freedom by *satisfying* them. A radical expansion of what may be called *freedom by mastery* is the great triumph of our modern world-system: that constitutes its most powerful allure and its deepest satisfaction. Of course, this system, in satisfying some desires, also suggests and stimulates others; some of these desires, in turn, are satisfied by yet further mastery of nature, but in the process yet others are aroused, and so forth. Happiness keeps receding.

There is yet another achievement to the credit of our modern world-system, another triumph, which also functions to allure many and satisfy some. We have seen that the incursion of our modern world-system has been accompanied by a radical diminution of ascriptivism and a radical increase in value generalization. Often the modern state, in totalitarian fashion, has moved in to forestall whatever freedom these alterations would otherwise have introduced. Where once one's occupation as farmer was sealed by having a farmer as father, now in much of the world it is sealed by the command of some bureaucrat. But not everywhere, and especially not in the West. Here such determinations are made in good measure by the choice of the person concerned. Thus there has been in the West a truly remarkable increase in what may be called *freedom of self-direction*—the freedom granted by social structures to determine the course of one's own life. In our relation to nature we have gained in freedom by mastery; in our relation to social structures we have gained in the freedom of self-direction. [29] One need only observe the rapid spread of the Solidarity union through Poland in the years 1980 and 1981 to see how powerful a lure is this increase in freedom of self-direction. (I write these words two months after the crushing of Solidarity by the military regime on 13 December 1981.)

Expansion of freedom by mastery and expansion of freedom of self-direction—these, I suggest, are what we find of fundamental worth in our modern world-system. Together they constitute an expansion in our range of choice. If there is compensation for the sorrows produced by our modern world-system, that compensation must lie in this truly remarkable expansion of range of choice. *For some.* And there lies perhaps the deepest challenge to this new system. The expansion of range of choice is distributed with appalling unevenness. Gross inequality of benefits pervades the system. But is it not true that the longing for a measure of equality is just as deep in mankind as the longing for expanded choice? Inequality always has to be justified. Equality speaks for itself.

Our deepest dilemma today, causing deep rifts within our world-order, is our inability or refusal to devise a social system that comes at all close to satisfying both of these deeply human motivations. The West grasps freedom at the cost of inequality, thereby consigning the economically impoverished to all the constraints of poverty. The East grasps equality at the cost of freedom, thereby consigning the politically powerless to all the inequities of tyranny.

ADDENDUM
Religious Pluralism and Secularization

One of the structural features of modern society of which I have said nothing is that particular manifestation of the rise of associationism and the diminution of ascriptivism that is *religious pluralism*. Neither have I said anything about the natural consequence of such pluralism, namely, *secularization*. I have not done so because, though there is indeed some connection between, on the one hand, the spread in scope and intensity of our modern world-system and, on the other hand, the rise of religious pluralism, the connection seems to me much weaker than in the case of the other micro-structural phenomena to which I have called attention.[30] Nevertheless, the phenomenon is of obvious relevance to our topic in this book, so let me here make a few remarks about it.

The original Calvinists were open advocates of many features of our modernized society, but they were most emphatically not in favor of religious pluralism, nor were any of the other mainline Protestants. Of course the early Protestants were fully aware of the fact that by their actions they had as a matter of fact introduced religious pluralism into European society as a whole, but that had not been their intention. They neither desired nor anticipated that *within a given civil polity* there would be a pluralism of religions. In fact they fought vigorously, oppressively, and sometimes bloodily against this possibility. *Cuius regio, eius religio.* They lost the battle. Religious pluralism was introduced *within* the Protestant countries of Europe and not only *amongst* them. As a result, religion has unavoidably become a matter of choice in many areas of the modern social system. By contrast, in a traditional society one's religion was above all what one *did not* choose: it above all was taken for granted, defining one's social identity.

In several of his books, Peter L. Berger seems to me especially perceptive regarding the social consequences of religious pluralism. Let me point to two of these consequences, which are especially significant for our subject in these lectures. For one thing, the emergence of religious pluralism goes a long way toward explaining the phenomenon of secularization, whereby religion has to a great extent lost its hold on the public consciousness and whereby religious institutions have to a great extent lost their voice in society. The connections are explained by Berger thus:

> A religious worldview, just like any other body of interpretations of reality, is dependent upon social support. The more unified and reliable this support is, the more these interpretations of reality will be firmly established in consciousness. The typical premodern society creates conditions under which religion has, for the individual, the quality of objective certainty; modern society, by contrast, un-

dermines this certainty, deobjectivates it by robbing it of its taken-for-granted status, *ipso facto* subjectivizes religion.[31]

Additionally, when a society becomes religiously pluralistic, then obviously religion no longer binds it together by giving it a shared legitimating structure and a shared interpretation of reality. Then religion no longer serves as the ultimate basis of public discourse; instead, it becomes part of the private domain:

> While the presence of religion within modern political institutions is, typically, a matter of ideological rhetorics, this cannot be said about the opposite "pole." In the sphere of the family and of social relationships closely linked to it, religion continues to have considerable "reality" potential, that is, continues to be relevant in terms of the motives and self-interpretations of people in this sphere of everyday social activity. . . . Such private religiosity, however "real" it may be to the individuals who adopt it, cannot any longer fulfill the classical task of religion, that of constructing a common world within which all of social life receives ultimate meaning binding on everybody. Instead, this religiosity is limited to specific enclaves of social life and may be effectively segregated from the secularized sectors of modern society. The values pertaining to private religiosity are, typically, irrelevant to institutional contexts other than the private sphere. For example, a businessman or politician may faithfully adhere to the religiously legitimated norms of family life, while at the same time conducting his activities in the public sphere without any reference to religious values of any kind. . . .
>
> The over-all effect of the afore-mentioned "polarization" is very curious. Religion manifests itself as public rhetoric and private virtue.[32]

The question that this brings to mind, of course, is whether something else in the modern polity plays the integrating interpretative and legitimating role that religion once played. It was the suggestion of the Enlightenment that Reason, and Science as its child, *could* play this role. By contrast, it was the thesis of Durkheim that if we look closely we will see that religion still does play this role, but that it has become a new, scarcely recognizable form of religion, a *civil* religion, which bears as uneasy relation to the plurality of official religions. It is my own view that Durkheim is correct, and that here we touch on the deep dynamics of loyalty to nation in the modern social order. This is a topic to which we will return in Chapter V.

Chapter III

Lima or Amsterdam: Liberation or Disclosure?

Our modern social world is a world of striking triumphs. Many in this world have experienced that unprecedented expansion in range of choice of which we spoke in the preceding chapter. But this world of ours is also a world of deep sorrows.

There are, for one thing, the *sorrows of injustice.* Those who enjoy a vast range of choice coexist in our world-system with nearly a billion others who live in a state of perpetual poverty, and with hundreds of millions for whom political terror, torture, and tyranny are the ever-present context of their lives—their oppression often being perpetrated or supported by those very governments whose own citizens enjoy great freedom.

There are also the *sorrows of misplaced values,* as one might call them. The desires we choose to satisfy by our conquest of nature and our alteration of society are often profoundly perverse. Hundreds of billions of dollars are spent each year on armaments to terrorize and kill our fellow human beings. Tens of billions more are stupidly spent each year by the well-to-do on outrageous luxuries.

In addition there are all those miseries that *result* from our social order—call them the *sorrows of undesired consequences:* the destruction of traditions, the loss of a sense of rootage and support and belongingness resulting from the destruction of concrete communities, the agonies of indecision resulting from constantly being confronted with the need to make choices concerning one's social roles and one's world-view, the boredom resulting from work utterly lacking in intrinsic satisfaction and performed merely as a means to acquire the money to support one's family, the loss of freedom resulting from the encroachment of bureaucracies, the elimination of environments expressive of our inner selves resulting from the pervasive rationalization of our lives.

This is not even to mention the threats, which we in the core area all acutely sense, to the maintenance and direction of this social system that we have created. The shared frameworks of belief whereby we interpret our experience and legitimate our actions, thus to undergird our life together, are slipping away, often being transformed into little else than chauvinistic nationalism. The limits of that natural world which provides the indispensable context for the social order are being severely pressed by pollution of the environment and exhaustion of resources. And through it all, our system acts in ways we either do not understand or cannot control.

This is the world we have made for ourselves. It is a world with which only the privileged, and the imperceptive at that, could be satisfied. What we must now begin to consider is how Christians should act in this world, and how, as they see it, others should act as well. In a world such as this, what should be our *project?* As background to these considerations we shall also want to reflect on how the picture drawn of our society fits into the larger Christian vision of life and reality. How does it all hang together?

I propose that, rather than conducting these reflections from the ground up by ourselves, we see what we can learn from two of the most penetrating contemporary articulations of world-formative Christianity: *liberation theology,* especially in its South American, mainly Catholic form; and the *neo-Calvinism* which has its sources in the Netherlands of the late nineteenth and early twentieth centuries. I pick these two because in both one finds a penetrating analysis of our contemporary social world combined with a comprehensive Christian vision of history and society. All too often one finds either or both of these missing in the approach of contemporary Christians to social issues; their analysis is typically superficial, or their vision pinched. We shall see that there are some fundamental affinities between these two patterns of thought, but we shall also uncover some substantial disagreements. At several points we shall find ourselves forced to choose, and the decision-making process will help greatly in illuminating some of the profound issues at stake.

Since it is not my aim to give a comprehensive description of the social thought of these two movements, but rather to elicit from them two patterns of Christian social thought, I propose that we concentrate our attention on representative spokesmen. For liberation theology I shall concentrate mainly on Gustavo Gutiérrez; for neo-Calvinism, on Herman Dooyeweerd and Bob Goudzwaard. In effect, we will be engaging in what Max Weber called "ideal-type" analysis; but rather than doing so in the abstract, we will look at the formulations of those who come as close as any to expressing the ideal type.

To grasp the thought of the liberation theologians, let us begin where they themselves begin: with the cries of suffering humanity for deliverance, or, more pointedly, with the cries of those whose misery is grounded in the social order. Liberation theologians are not indifferent to the suffering caused by disease, anxiety, or other pandemic maladies, but they are especially attuned to the poor, the hungry, the voiceless, the terrorized of the world. And since they live in the Third World, it is the cries of those in that part of our world-system that they hear most clearly.

Liberation theologians, who are urged to their reflections by the cries of the wretched of the earth, begin having already come to certain conclusions as to the cause of their misery. Why are those with whom they identify so wretched when others in the world—some in their own country, and very many in the core areas of our world-system—are so wealthy and powerful? Of course they know the traditional answer—something within the structure of Third World societies causes lack of development—but they no longer accept it as the full truth. Says Gutiérrez, "there will be a true development for Latin America only through liberation from the domination by capitalist countries. That implies, of course, a showdown with their natural allies: our national oligarchies."[1] In short, the liberation theologians have chosen decisively for the world-system interpretation of the underdevelopment of the Third World, an interpretation that considers underdevelopment to be in good measure rooted in the exploitative domination of the periphery of our world-system by the core.

They have seen the coming and going of development programs since the Second World War; none has alleviated the misery of their people. Their net result has always been greater development for the core areas along with luxury for the oligarchies of the Third World. The benefits of development do not trickle down to the masses. Hunger and poverty remain their daily ration. One of the most significant sources of the misery of their people is the fact that they belong to the periphery of the capitalist world-economy and in their exchange with the core areas find themselves constantly the losers. The oppressive political structures of the periphery are among the mechanisms that ensure this. Voicelessness and terror join hands with hunger and poverty.

In short, the liberation theologians' analysis of the misery of their people leads them to the conclusion that those people are *being wronged*—they are being exploitatively dominated by the core areas of the world-system and by the small but powerful oligarchies in the periphery. Their analysis leads the liberation theologians to take sides with those whose cries they hear, to stand against those who oppress them. They declare their solidarity with the people, and to implement that declaration they resolve to contribute as best they can to the relief of this oppression. Their theorizing is openly done on behalf of the miserable. They intend to give the wretched of the earth their voice. Their theorizing is a species of *praxis-oriented* theory. Their theology "does not stop with reflecting on the world, but rather tries to be part of the process through which the world is transformed."[2]

It is obvious now why such individuals are called *liberation* theologians (though we shall shortly see that the theme of liberation resonates yet more deeply in their theology than this). They have heard the cries of their people and perceived that a deep root of their misery is oppression: the people are being wronged. In response, liberation theologians declare that the people must be liberated from oppression if they are to be released from their misery—and that liberation is their project. Says Gutiérrez, "to speak of transformation of history from the perspective of dominated and exploited peoples, from the perspective of the poor of this world brings us to see it as a *liberating* praxis [which] acquires a *subversive* perspective. It is subversive of a social order in which the poor person, the 'other' of this society, scarcely begins to be heard."[3]

I have been describing the situation in which the liberation theologians do their theorizing: they intend their theorizing as *a reflection on* that situation and as *an instrument in* its alteration. But we are not yet done. The situation, as our theologians see it, includes more; it includes the spreading of a certain consciousness in the masses—namely, an awareness that a fundamental cause of their misery lies in their domination by the rich and powerful of the world. In other words, the liberation theologians' own analysis of the situation of their people is increasingly being shared by those very people.[4] "The poor countries," says Gutiérrez, "are becoming ever more clearly aware that their underdevelopment is only the by-product of the development of other countries, because of the kind of relationship which exists between the rich and poor countries. Moreover, they are realizing that their own development will come about only with a struggle to break the domination of the rich countries" (*TL*, p. 26).[5]

It is important for us in the West to let these words sink in. Most of us are still in the thrall of development (modernization) theory. We believe that a bit of economic aid scattered here and there around the globe will get things moving, and we expect those to whom these crumbs are tossed to applaud our largess. But those in the periphery of the world increasingly see us as predators rather than benefactors. The buildup of this discrepancy of perception is filled with explosive potential. From what I said in the preceding chapter, it will be evident that my own conviction is that the Third World is largely right on this issue and that we are wrong. (I shall have more to say on the matter in the next chapter.)

Of course the concepts of domination and exploitation are common tools of the trade for Marxists, and, as one might well expect, liberation theologians are regularly accused of being Marxists. Their answer is that they are simply trying to understand what it is that perpetuates the social misery of their people. They find Marxist analysis, in its general contours, to provide the most plausible explanation of their situation. They are not committed to Marxism as an ideology by which to live and die; if someone offers them an alternative analysis, they will consider it. Furthermore, some such social analysis is unavoidable. The Christian gospel cannot be applied *immediately* to the issues of society. A mediating analysis is imperative.*

---

*The liberationists' interaction with Marxism goes beyond the basic social analysis they share: they are committed, remember, to working substantively for the liberation of their people, and many Marxists are committed to working for the same goal. Thus the liberationist shares with the Marxist the *praxis* of liberation as well as

Gutiérrez and his colleagues argue that the spreading consciousness of domination, and the spreading determination to throw off the shackles of that domination, must be set in the yet larger context of an alteration taking place in the consciousness of mankind generally. "A historical vision in which mankind assumes control of it [sic] own destiny" is emerging today, suggests Gutiérrez; "the social praxis of contemporary man has begun to reach maturity. It is the behavior of man ever more conscious of being an active subject of history; he is ever more articulate in the face of social injustice and all repressive forces which stand in the way of his fulfillment; he is ever more determined to participate both in the transformation of social structures and in effective political action" (TL, pp. 25, 46).

This spreading consciousness of man as "an active subject of history" is taking the form, says Gutiérrez, of an increasing commitment to liberation from all that binds and enthralls: "A broad and deep aspiration for liberation inflames the history of mankind in our day, liberation from all that limits or keeps man from self-fulfillment, liberation from all impediments to the exercise of his freedom. Proof of this is the awareness of new and subtle forms of oppression in the heart of advanced industrial societies . . ." (TL, p. 27). The point here is so important that it is worth citing one of Gutiérrez's liberation colleagues as well; J. Severino Croatto puts it this way:

> The struggle of so many oppressed peoples who are seeking to "say their word," who desire to "be" what now they know they can be and must be, is perhaps the characteristic phenomenon of our time. There is new *value* placed on freedom. . . .
>
> The massive cry of humankind, which suddenly feels itself groaning under the human-made yoke of "being-of-another," now attains an unprecedented volume thanks to the new method of "conscientization" orchestrated by the social sciences and the mass media. The degree of maturity achieved by the people of our century does not permit them to attribute their ills to *fate.* . . .[6]

Thus Gutiérrez and his colleagues do not merely reflect on that longing for political and economic liberation which is now so pervasive among the miserable of the Third World; they reflect as well on this broader and deeper "liberation consciousness": "At a deeper level, *liberation* can be applied to an understanding of history. Man is seen as assuming conscious responsibility for his own destiny. . . . In this perspective the unfolding of all of man's dimensions

---

the analysis of social dynamics. One senses that it is here, at the level of praxis, that the relation of these two becomes most problematic: although their background ideologies are profoundly different, their short-term goals are similar. What then is the advisability of cooperation? The Argentinian theologian José Míguez-Bonino examines this issue with care in his book *Christians and Marxists* (London: Hodder and Stoughton, 1976).

is demanded—a man who makes himself throughout his life and throughout history. The gradual conquest of true freedom leads to the creation of a new man and a qualitatively different society. This vision provides, therefore, a better understanding of what in fact is at stake in our times" (*TL*, pp. 36-37). For the liberation theologian, history both is, and is increasingly seen to be, "a process of the liberation of man"; and the liberation in question is "a historical conquest": "the step from an abstract to a real freedom is not taken without a struggle against all the forces that oppress man. . . . The goal is not only better living conditions, a radical change of structures, a social revolution; it is much more: the continuous creation, never ending, of a new way to be a man, a *permanent cultural revolution*" (*TL*, p. 32).

It is here that I find one of the most unsatisfactory points in Gutiérrez's thought. What exactly is this liberation that he sees as taking place in history, by virtue (in good measure) of man's *determination* to be free? What, for him, is liberation in its comprehensive sense? That it *includes* liberation from exploitative domination is clear, but that it goes beyond this is also clear. Often Gutiérrez makes the point that comprehensive liberation includes liberation from sin—that is, from hostility among men and between man and God. And he insistently adds that sin must not be seen as something *in addition* to social oppression; to the contrary, structures of unjust domination and exploitation are *manifestations* of sin:

> In the liberation approach sin is not considered as an individual, private, or merely interior reality. . . . Sin is regarded as a social, historical fact, the absence of brotherhood and love in relationships among men, the breach of friendship with God and with other men, and therefore, an interior, personal fracture. When it is considered in this way, the collective dimensions of sin are rediscovered. . . . Sin is evident in oppressive structures, in the exploitation of man by man, in the domination and slavery of peoples, races, and social classes. Sin appears, therefore, as the fundamental alienation, the root of a situation of injustice and exploitation. It cannot be encountered in itself, but only in concrete instances, in particular alienations. It is impossible to understand the concrete manifestations without understanding the underlying basis and vice versa. (*TL*, pp. 175-76)[7]*

But does Gutiérrez wish to say that *all* liberation is liberation from sin? As we shall shortly see, it does seem that sin constitutes for him the key link between liberation and salvation; yet, is it at all plausible to read history

---

*I would add that it seems to me doubtful that all injustice has its roots in sin, if we are understanding sin as hostility; some injustices, for example, are committed through ignorance.

as an increasing liberation from sin? And does Gutiérrez not also have in mind, when he speaks of "liberation," certain processes not connected with sin, such as improvement in living conditions? My own guess is that when he describes our actual history as a growth in liberation, he is in fact describing the process I outlined earlier as the unprecedented expansion in the range of choice that has come to many in the modern world-system as a result of our expansion of mastery over nature and corresponding alterations of social structure. Yet when Gutiérrez gives his *theological* interpretation of history as the history of liberation, he tends to have something different in mind: liberation from *sin* and its effects—particularly its social-structural effects.

Apart from these last critical comments, I have thus far been describing what Gutiérrez sees as our present situation and what his commitments are within that situation. He considers his task as Christian theologian to be that of reflecting critically on this situation in the light of the Word of God; Christian theology in general, as he sees it, is "a critical reflection in and on historical praxis in confrontation with the word of the Lord lived and accepted in faith."[8] Mainly, says Gutiérrez, he will reflect on the relation "between salvation and the historical process of the liberation of man," or in other words, on the relation "between the Kingdom of God and the building up of the world" (*TL*, p. 45).[9]

Two principles are fundamental here, he says. First, "there are not two histories, one profane and one sacred, 'juxtaposed' or 'closely linked.' " There is not a history of the world and then in addition a history of the church, with only the latter being of abiding significance. Our history is the history of the world with the church in it: "there is only one human destiny, irreversibly assumed by Christ, the Lord of history" (*TL*, p. 153). Second, this history has a salvific significance; or, better, this history is the *scene* of salvation. It is not the case that salvation is to be found only at the end of history, with all that preceded it having been nothing more than a preparation; it is, as Gutiérrez states, "an intrahistorical reality." After all, the sin from which we are saved

> is not only an impediment to salvation in the afterlife. Insofar as it constitutes a break with God, sin is a historical reality. . . . One looks then to this world, and now sees in the world beyond not the "true life" but rather the transformation and fulfillment of the present life. The absolute value of salvation—far from devaluing this world—gives it its own autonomy, because salvation is already latent there. . . . The history of salvation is the very heart of human history. . . . The salvific action of God underlies all human existence. The historical destiny of humanity must be placed definitively in the salvific horizon. Only thus will its true dimensions emerge and its deepest meaning be apparent. (*TL*, pp. 152-53)

If we grant that history is in essence the history of liberation, then we must conclude that Gutiérrez is suggesting that the liberation of mankind and the salvation of mankind are not two separate things, but one and the same. Salvation is the total liberation of humanity in all dimensions of its existence, achieved by Christ: "the liberating action of Christ—made man in this history and not in a history marginal to the real life of man—is at the heart of the historical currency of humanity . . ." (*TL,* p. 168). But what exactly is the link here between liberation and salvation? Far and away the dominant thrust of Gutiérrez's discussion is that the link is sin: the salvation Christ secures is salvation from sin, and liberation at its deepest level is also liberation from sin. "Christ the Savior liberates man from sin, which is the ultimate root of all disruptions of friendship and of all injustice and oppression. Christ makes man truly free, that is to say, he enables man to live in communion with him; and this is the basis for all human brotherhood" (*TL,* p. 37).

But despite his insistence that salvation from sin constitutes the essence of liberation, one senses in Gutiérrez a hesitant awareness of the point I made earlier: that much of what he wants the word *liberation* to denote within the context of history as the history of liberation has been achieved not by the conquest of sin but by the mastery of nature. In an extended consideration of the relation between creation and salvation (*TL,* pp. 153-60), Gutiérrez takes note of the teaching of Genesis 1 that, as he puts it, "man is the crown and center of the work of creation and is called to continue it through his labor" (*TL,* p. 158). No doubt a development of this point could go a long way toward providing the missing link. Yet in this same passage he devotes most of his efforts to arguing that God's (and, correspondingly, man's) creative activity must itself be seen as salvific. The evidence that he presents for this conclusion is the fact that when Israel confessed God as creator, it spoke of the God whom it already knew as liberator, and furthermore that it never ceased to link its confession of God as creator with its confession of God as savior. In short, what we see in Gutiérrez is an example of that regular practice among contemporary theologians of treating creation as an act of salvation—without ever being able to say what creation saves us from—rather than setting salvation within the context of (a disrupted) creation. As a result, salvation and history, in spite of the deepest motivations on the part of Gutiérrez, remain unlinked. If we understand liberation in such a way as to make it plausible to read history as the history of liberation, then there is no plausible direct link between liberation on the one hand and salvation from sin on the other. But if we understand liberation in such a way that it is directly linked to salvation from sin, then it becomes implausible to read history as the history of liberation.

But let us return to Gutiérrez's argument. If salvation is ultimately liberation from sin, and if sin manifests itself in oppressive social structures, then it follows that the struggle to eliminate those structures has salvific significance. Although "the liberation of Christ cannot be equated with political liberation," still "it takes place in historical and political liberating acts. It is not possible to avoid those mediations," he asserts.[10] "All struggle against exploitation and alienation . . . is an attempt to vanquish selfishness, the negation of love. This is the reason why any effort to build a just society is liberation. . . . It is a salvific work, although it is not all of salvation" (*TL*, pp. 176-77).

On the other hand, "the process of liberation will not have conquered the very roots of oppression and the exploitation of man by man without the coming of the Kingdom, which is above all a gift." Although "the historical, political liberating event *is* the growth of the Kingdom and *is* a salvific event . . . it is not *the* coming of the Kingdom, not *all* of salvation" (*TL*, p. 177). "Radical liberation is the gift which Christ offers us. By his death and resurrection he redeems man from sin and all its consequences . . ." (*TL*, p. 176).

In short, the movement of history toward *freedom*, whereby man shapes his own destiny, is the movement toward God's *salvation* of mankind, and political and economic liberation is an indispensable component in this process; consequently,

> when we assert that man fulfills himself by continuing the work of creation by means of his labor, we are saying that he places himself, by this very fact, within an all-embracing salvific process. To work, to transform this world, is to become a man and to build the human community; it is also to save. Likewise, to struggle against misery and exploitation and to build a just society is already to be part of the saving action, which is moving toward its complete fulfillment. All this means that building the temporal city is not simply a stage of "humanization" or "pre-evangelization" as was held in theology up until a few years ago. Rather it is to become part of a saving process which embraces the whole of man and all human history. (*TL*, pp. 159-60)

To conclude our presentation of Gutiérrez's views, let us circle back and bring to light one last feature of the situation in which he sees himself as doing his theologizing. Not only is there a growing longing in mankind for comprehensive liberation, of which the growing awareness of oppression amongst the miserable of the Third World (along with their growing determination to throw off the bonds of that oppression) is a reflection; there is also a growing conviction amongst *Christians* of the Third World that it is their evangelical calling to participate in these revolutionary movements. Gutiérrez sees himself as giving expression to, and reflecting on, this new Christian consciousness. "From the viewpoint of faith," he writes, "the motive which in the last instance moves Christians to participate in the liberation of oppressed peoples and exploited social classes is the conviction of the radical incompatibility of evangelical demands with an unjust and alienating society" (*TL*, p. 145). More and more this conviction is spreading throughout the Christians of the Third World:

> The different sectors of the People of God are gradually committing themselves in different ways to the process of liberation. They are becoming aware that this liberation implies a break with the status quo, that it calls for a social revolution. In relation to the entire Latin American Christian community it must be acknowledged that the number of persons involved is small. But the numbers are growing and active and every day they are acquiring a larger hearing both inside and outside the Church. (*TL*, p. 102)[11]

It is here that I wish to pose my last question to Gutiérrez, a question intimately connected with the preceding ones: What exactly is the historical project in which he sees the Christian as called to work? Toward what goal do we devote our efforts and call others to devote theirs as well? Liberation is a process, a movement *from* something *toward* something. In choosing the word *liberation* our theologian wishes, among other things, to emphasize that often this process is a *conflictual struggle*. But what are we to move from and what are we to move toward? After liberation, what?

Often the answer to this question given by liberation theologians is "freedom." After liberation, freedom. Freedom is the end-state toward which we aim. Consider, for example, these words of Croatto: "we discover ourselves as 'called to freedom' "; at the same time, we "become conscious that we do not possess it—whether as individuals or as a people. In the face of both the danger of frustration and the attraction of that vocation, we initiate a *process* of liberation. Hence the important goal is not liberation, but freedom. The former is a process 'toward' the latter, which is the ontological 'locus' wherein human beings can be fulfilled."[12] But what are we to understand by *freedom* here? The answer to that question does not become clear; or rather, insofar as it becomes clear, it becomes equally clear that *freedom* is a poor word for the end-state envisaged. It sometimes appears that Croatto has in mind what he calls *creativity*.

Similar difficulties haunt Gutiérrez's discussion. In one important passage he cites Descartes, Kant, Hegel, Marx, Freud, and Marcuse as the great "freedom thinkers," though indeed he also makes it clear that he does not "endorse without question every aspect of this development of ideas" (*TL*, pp. 28-32). Now, for Hegel, Marx, Freud, and Marcuse, I think it is indeed accurate to say that the goal they envisage for liberation is simply *freedom*, for in their view the great evil from which we must be saved is that of being shaped by influences external to ourselves, whether those influences take the form of external formation or of internal inhibition; correspondingly, the goal is self-determination, autonomy, maturation.

It is my own view that this vision of our goal is deeply unsatisfactory. In the first place, it is psychologically untenable. We are all shaped in countless ways by the people who surround us, unavoidably so. Nobody is and nobody could be self-determining.[13] Everybody is "dominated." The relevant question is not how to eliminate influence on the self, but instead the normative question as to which forms of influence are desirable and which not—and, in particular, which forms of influence constitute oppression.

In the second place, we all know from experience that when each of us is given a voice in the direction of society, we say different things, and clearly we cannot all have our way. Some can, some cannot. I know of course that to solve this dilemma there have been attempts to distinguish the voice of the "real self" from the voice of the "unreal self," the assumption being that all true selves speak with one voice. I also know that the ideology which sometimes lies behind the so-called "dictatorship of the proletariat" is that the Party knows what the real self of the proletariat is saying, and that that voice is in turn the voice of the real self of all members of society.[14] This metaphysics of real and unreal selves is as implausible as the oppression is tangible among those in the contemporary world who find themselves saddled with these dictators who tell them what their true selves are saying.[15]

There is yet a third reason for finding it unacceptable to say that freedom, understood as self-determination, is the overarching goal of our social endeavors. We human beings are a mixture of good impulses and bad, amongst these latter being even, on occasion, the impulse to do what one knows one should not do. The Christian reads these impulses as having, at bottom, the character of sin: hostility toward God and one's fellows. But if this is true, then obviously the goal for each cannot be self-determination, maturation, removal of all external influence and all internal inhibition. Our sinful impulses ought not to be satisfied but to be conquered, inhibited—dominated, if you will. To acknowledge the presence of sin in our existence is to acknowledge that we have no choice but to engage in the difficult task of *normative reflection,* asking, among other questions, which impulses of the self are to be satisfied and which suppressed.

As I have already indicated, Gutiérrez also sees sin as a profound factor in the human self. Consequently, although the direction of Enlightenment thought clearly has some allure for him, his awareness of sin prevents that line of thought from being dominant in his thinking. Never does he link his understanding of salvation with his reading of history by proposing that Christ saves us for autonomy and self-determination. Christ saves us from sin. But once again, for what? "For love" is the answer most prominent in Gutiérrez: after liberation, love. "Liberation from sin and communion with God in solidarity with all men" is the end-state (*TL,* p. 238). He does indeed say such things as that "the utopia of liberation [is] the creation . . . definitively, of freedom," but immediately he makes it clear that by "freedom" he has in mind "the communion of all men with God. This communion implies liberation from sin, the ultimate root of all injustice, all exploitation, all dissidence among men" (*TL,* p. 237).

Surely this is better than positing that illusory state of self-determination as the goal of our human project. But now our old question returns to haunt us. Love pertains to the relation among human persons, and between them and God. How does our mastery of nature fit into this image of the goal of our human project? Once again the failure of linkage between salvation and history becomes manifest—though what never comes undone in Gutiérrez is the link between salvation from sin and liberation from oppression.

The paradigmatic biblical event for the liberation theologian is the Exodus. Yet the hexateuch does not use *freedom* to describe the end-state of this great liberation. Characteristically when it wants a single word to describe that rich and complex reality which Israel found in the promised land, that word is *rest.* Is there a clue in that? And contrary to Croatto's interpretation, Genesis does not say that mankind's uniqueness lies in our call to freedom; it lies in our being responsible, in our being created for responsible action: to be human is to be *called.* Is there also a clue in that?

Let us move on to see whether some of the questions we have posed are answered in the neo-Calvinist vision—hanging on, however, to the core of the liberation theologian's message: that the Gospel calls us to struggle for the liberation of the oppressed.

Turning from liberation theology to neo-Calvinism as expressed in Herman Dooyeweerd, one is struck first by the differences. Here the cries of the wretched of the earth are not given voice. Here there is little talk of oppression, and consequently little of liberation from oppression; the talk is more of "authority structures." And here there are no reflections on violence (which, incidentally, makes neo-Calvinism significantly different also from early Calvinism). There is indeed talk of conflict in society, but it is the religious conflict between believer and idolater and not the social conflict between oppressor and oppressed that is discussed.

It must frankly be said that in this respect the second generation of the neo-Calvinist movement, of which Dooyeweerd is representative, is different from the first generation. The movement began at the end of the nineteenth century by listening to the cries of certain oppressed people—the *kleine luyden* (little people) of nineteenth-century Holland.[16] Victimized economically by agricultural crises and industrialization, they felt themselves even more profoundly threatened in matters of both church and state by the liberalism of the regnant bourgeoisie. Their religious convictions were being trampled on, alien ideologies were being forced on them and their children, and all voice in the political-social and ecclesiastical shaping of Dutch society was being denied them. The neo-Calvinist movement arose out of commitment to the cause of these people. It was a struggle for their liberation—mainly successful, it may be added.

There can be no doubt that the social theory of the movement today continues to reflect its origins—as, for example, in its perception of the basic conflict in society as the Augustinian conflict between the City of God and the City of the world. And in general, the themes that Dooyeweerd develops were present in embryonic form in the movement at its beginning, but at that stage they were balanced by other themes as well—such as, importantly, those of oppression and liberation.

Basic to the neo-Calvinist analysis of society is the perception of history as fundamentally the interaction of two deep dynamics. One of these is the dynamic just mentioned—call it the dynamic of *faith/idolatry*. The other is the dynamic of *differentiation*. In the discussion that follows, our interest will not so much be in attaining a thoroughgoing understanding of these dynamics as such; rather, we will attempt an analysis of contemporary society in terms of these dynamics using the insights of Bob Goudzwaard contained in his book *Capitalism and Progress*. Nevertheless, if we are to understand Goudzwaard's thought, it will be essential first to say a bit about the dynamics of differentiation.

The foundation of human history, says Dooyeweerd, lies in a particular form of human activity which may be called *cultural* activity. Though cultural activity always does and always must occur in the context of tradition, yet in its essence it is in conflict with tradition, since it "always consists in giving form to material in free control over the material. It consists in giving form according to a free design."[17]* Cultural activity consists in breaking from tradition so as to attain mastery over the natural world—and presumably over the social world and oneself as well. And insofar as cultural activity occurs, we are in the presence of genuine human history.

Dooyeweerd observes that cultural activity, thus identified, is indissolubly linked with the exercise of power. "Free control," he says, "reveals itself in the historical formation of *power*" (*RWC*, p. 66). Thus, in his view power lies at the very foundation of history—the power of forming one's world. Cultural activity involves *mastering*. Likewise, he sees social conflict as

---

*It is clear that cultural activity, as Dooyeweerd understands it, is a version of what in Chapter II, following Weber's lead, I called *rationalized* activity. What makes it a version of this, rather than identical with it, is Dooyeweerd's stipulation of cultural activity as involving *control* over *material*. But perhaps we are to understand this stipulation rather freely.

a pervasive component in history. "All historical formation," he says, "requires power. Formation thus never takes place without a struggle. The progressive will of the moulder of history invariably clashes with the power of tradition, which, as the power of conservation, opposes every attempt to break with the past" (*RWC,* p. 70).

Already we are confronted with an important normative issue: are the mastery and conflict that lie at the very foundation of genuine human history to be seen as good or bad? Is history, as such, progress or decline? Dooyeweerd's answer is emphatic: mastery is good; only its misuse is bad. Power "is rooted in creation and contains nothing demonic. Jesus Christ explicitly called himself the ruler of the kings of the earth. . . . Only sin can place power in the service of the demonic. But this holds for every good gift of God. . . . Power is the great motor of cultural development. The decisive question concerns the *direction* in which power is applied" (*RWC,* p. 67) Similarly, the conflictive struggle against tradition is, as such, good. Granted, there could be no human society, and so there could be no cultural development, without tradition. Nonetheless, "truly historical development also demands that a culture not vegetate upon the past but unfold itself" (*RWC,* p. 71).

The ultimate ground of the neo-Calvinist's conviction that the cultural activity that underlies history is good is the conviction that such activity is God's will, and thereby, normative for humanity. God at creation gave to humanity a cultural mandate. The obligation to act culturally, and thereby to set loose the dynamics of history, belongs to the very essence of what it is to be human; it is indigenous to our creatureliness:

> The story of creation itself indicates that the cultural mode of formative activity is grounded in God's creation order. God immediately gave man the great cultural mandate: subdue the earth and have dominion over it. God placed this cultural command in the midst of the other creational ordinances. It touches only the historical aspect of creation. Through this aspect, creation itself is subject to cultural development. (*RWC,* pp. 64-65)

It is the calling of humanity to bring to realization the potentials stored in creation. I think we should see in this neo-Calvinist vision an advance over that of liberation theology, which indeed was struggling toward the same point, but was hindered from attaining it by its acceptance of the contemporary theological dictum that God's creation is of merely salvific significance.

As we have already seen, the pursuit of mastery and the social conflict which together constitute the essence of cultural activity, and which thus lie at the foundation of the emergence from the bonds of tradition into genuine history, can both be misused. So of course the question arises: What constitutes their proper use? In short, what constitutes genuine progress in history as opposed to nonprogressive alteration? The beginning of Dooyeweerd's answer is that *differentiation* is the norm for history. Cultural activity, and thereby history itself, ought to move in the direction of increasing differentiation. Insofar as cultural activity does not do so, it is regressive and thereby disobedient, for differentiation is at the heart of the realization of creation's potentials. Dooyeweerd himself saw Hitler's Germany as an example of historical regression inspired by romantic nationalism.

What does the neo-Calvinist mean when he speaks of "differentiation"? Well, after saying that the norm for history is *the opening or disclosure of culture,* Dooyeweerd states that "this norm requires the differentiation of culture into spheres that possess their own unique nature. Cultural differentiation is necessary so that the creational ordinance, which calls for the disclosure or unfolding of everything in accordance with its inner nature, may be realized also in historical development" (*RWC,* p. 74).* "This differentiation," he continues, "occurs . . . by means of a 'branching out' of culture into the intrinsically different power spheres of science, art, the state, the church, industry, trade, the school, voluntary organizations, etc." (*RWC,* p. 79). In traditional undifferentiated societies "there was as yet no room for the formation of life spheres characterized by their own inner nature" (*RWC,* p. 74). "Only in the differentiation of culture can the unique nature of each creational structure reveal itself fully. . . . Undifferentiated forms gradually differentiate into the various societal structures through a lengthy process of historical development" (*RWC,* p. 79).**

How is differentiation, thus understood, related to the differentiation

---

*It should perhaps be noted that Dooyeweerd views historical-cultural differentiation as part of a whole *cosmic* pattern of differentiation: "Historical development is nothing but the cultural aspect of the great process of becoming which must continue in all the aspects of temporal reality in order that the wealth of the creational structures be concretized in time. . . . In all its aspects, the process of becoming develops, in conformity to law, from an undifferentiated phase to a differentiated phase. The organic development of life begins from the still undifferentiated germ cell, out of which the separate organs gradually differentiate. The emotional life of a newborn child is completely undifferentiated, but gradually it unfolds into a differentiation of sensuous feeling, logical feeling, lingual feeling, artistic feeling, juridical feeling, and so forth. The course of human societal development is no different" (*RWC,* p. 79). In an important way, God too is caught up in this pattern of differentiation. In spite of his emphasis on God's difference from creation, Dooyeweerd speaks of the unity of God's being as expressed in the cohering diversity of creation. In this respect, there is a striking similarity between his thought and that of Plotinus, who saw the diversity of reality as emanating in stages from the simplicity and unity of God.

**It is clear that Dooyeweerd is using the term *differentiation* to denote a process of social structuration. It is striking, then, that in his answer to the question of what norm our progressive mastery of the natural and social worlds should follow, he says nothing at all about how *nature* should be treated, but only about how *society* should be structured.

of which I spoke in the preceding chapter when I discussed some of the characteristic micro-structural features of our modern world-order? It is the same phenomenon. There I explained differentiation as having two aspects: differentiation of social roles and differentiation of social formations (institutions and organizations). The neo-Calvinist's eye is mainly on the latter: in the course of history, political formations differentiate themselves from economic formations, from educational formations, from family formations, from ecclesiastical formations, and so on. Of course this sort of differentiation is inevitably accompanied by a differentiation of social roles as well.* The neo-Calvinists add an additional note, however. They do not merely observe and approve this process of social differentiation; they give it an ontological interpretation, albeit a highly controversial and problematic one: they hold that there are certain irreducibly different abiding *types* of social formations—the State, the Family, the School, the Production Enterprise, etc.—and that originally (most of) these types were not exemplified. In traditional societies, one could not pick out any distinct formations that were their schools, their governments, etc. But as differentiation gradually and fitfully takes place in the course of history, these types are exemplified in distinct institutions. And so neo-Calvinists interpret our fundamental cultural-historical obligation as the obligation toward God of working for the exemplification of these social types (structures) in order to "open up" creation's potentials.

I shall have more to say about this shortly, but first let me remark here that what I find seriously lacking in Dooyeweerd (as indeed in Parsons) at this point is any serious consideration of what has *caused* this increase in differentiation and its cognates in our modern world. Why has this radical increase in differentiation taken place in the modern Western world (and spread out from there into the whole world), when most of the world's societies remained statically traditional? In the preceding chapter I made clear that in my own judgment this question can only be answered by studying the rise of our capitalist world-economy. This is the energizer of differentiation and its cognates. Dooyeweerd's failure to see this—his failure, in fact, even to consider the question of causation seriously—implies that his thought is really a version of modernization theory. What may be added is that inasmuch as one cannot adopt

---

*Talcott Parsons, you will recall, also cited the importance of an increase in differentiation in his list of the four basic traits of the evolution of human society— the others being increases in inclusion, adaptive upgrading, and value generalization. Regarding these latter three traits, we would note that Dooyeweerd considered *integration* (a trait essentially equivalent to Parsons's *inclusion*) to be a necessary counterpart of differentiation; he considered adaptive upgrading to be the most fundamental of all of the processes, since it accounts for our breaking from tradition in order to increase our mastery over nature and society; and he failed to take any explicit note of value generalization as a significant feature in the process (ignoring the factor of a decrease in ascriptivism as well).

the world-system approach without recognizing the pervasive role of domination—and exploitative domination at that—in the "development" of our
world, a recognition of the role of this factor in historical formation has no
place in Dooyeweerd's thought.

We were speaking of the neo-Calvinists' ontological understanding
of differentiation as the gradual manifestation in history of abiding types: the
State, the Productive Enterprise, etc. What must now be added is that they see
each of these types as having a nature—specifically, a *normative* nature. Just as
we may consider what constitutes the well-formed lion, so in a similar way we
may consider what constitutes the well-formed state, the well-formed school,
the well-formed family, and so forth. In short, there are abiding norms for the
State, for the School, and all the other categorically distinct social structures.

With this in mind, Dooyeweerd suggests that the cultural-historical
project of humanity should focus on achieving the following three goals in a
differentiated society:*

(1) We should see to it that each social formation realizes the normative nature of its particular type, or structure. Political institutions must
follow the norm for the State, economic organizations, for the Productive Enterprise, etc. In that way, life within each sphere must unfold and flower in its
own unique but normed way.

(2) As a direct corollary to this, we should see to it that the institutions belonging to one sphere do not dominate those belonging to another,
because when one sphere is dominated by another, life in the former is distorted
and cannot flower in its own unique normed manner. We are to work for the
sovereignty of the spheres: "A process of over-extension in culture . . . conflicts
with the norms that God established for differentiation in his creation order.
Every extreme expansion of the historical power sphere of a specific life sphere
occurs at the expense of other life spheres, for it retards their unfolding in an
unhealthy way" (*RWC,* pp. 80-81).

---

*If these goals are indeed the whole of the matter, then the idea com-
municated is that our human social obligation amounts to no more than an obligation
to God to see to it that each sphere unfolds in accord with its proper nature. It would
also imply that human misery is a *symptom* of something having gone wrong in the
unfolding of the spheres rather than something that is itself wrong. Accordingly, the
implication would be that one ought not to set out to combat misery as such; instead,
one should try to bring about a proper unfolding of the spheres, in which case misery
would be relieved as an incidental (though no doubt desirable) by-product. And,
indeed, the modern Afrikaner, who has often made use of Dooyeweerd's thought,
insists that we must not really pay much attention to social misery, since in the long
run if we just see to it that structures are unfolded properly, misery will vanish. In my
judgment this is "cultural mandate" thinking gone to seed. I think Dooyeweerd himself
is not entirely without blame here. Too often he gives the impression that mankind
was created to unfold social structures, rather than that social structures *have no justification* unless they serve mankind. Fortunately, Goudzwaard is clear on this point,

(3) We must seek what may be called *disclosure*. Life within each sphere of activity, though it must find its own fulfillment free from domination by other spheres, must at the same time be *open to* the norms of the other spheres. Economic activity, for example, is never exclusively economic in its significance: it has moral significance, it involves the use of language, and so forth; accordingly, it must be faithful not only to economic, but to moral, linguistic, and all other norms.

All this is extraordinarily general and abstract. Nonetheless it is this pattern of thought that is contained in the critique of modern society found in Goudzwaard's *Capitalism and Progress,* to which I now turn. I choose Goudzwaard because of the imaginative and penetrating use he makes of this pattern of thought—a use, I may add, which points in a thoroughly progressive, even radical, direction.*

What is the root of what has gone wrong in Western society? That is Goudzwaard's guiding question. That something has gone wrong, *profoundly* wrong, he has no doubt. He presents as evidence for this judgment many of the same phenomena I cited at the beginning of this chapter.

Goudzwaard's suggestion, supported with great richness of example, is that the fundamental root of what has gone wrong is that we in the West have accepted economic growth and technological advance as the ultimate social good. In the private sphere we subordinate everything to the production of ever more surplus by making profit the sole decisive goal of our enterprises and then using this profit to obtain more capital goods—which are then used to produce yet more surplus, and so on. On the national level we subordinate everything

---

stating, among other things, that "the purpose of norms is to bring us to life in its fullness by pointing us to paths which safely lead us there. Norms are not straightjackets that squeeze the life out of us" (*Capitalism and Progress: A Diagnosis of Western Society* [Toronto: Wedge Publishing Foundation; Grand Rapids, Mich.: Eerdmans, 1979], pp. 242-43). It is the *fullness of human life* that is the decisive test, not the proper realization of each sphere's inner nature. On the whole, Goudzwaard does a good job of staying clear of that mankind-for-the-sake-of-structures way of thinking by emphasizing his third goal for humanity's cultural-historical project—*disclosure*—far more than Dooyeweerd himself does.

*It ought to be noted that Dooyeweerd's thought has regularly been used by social conservatives to undergird their position: they use his stress on the importance of resisting the expansion of government outside its sphere to justify their indifference to—and, indeed, their practice of—economic exploitation; they use his stress on the importance of recognizing governmental authority within its own sphere to justify their opposition to all who preach or practice resistance to government dictates; and so forth. Dooyeweerd's thought is one more example in that long line of "creation ordinance" theologies and philosophies that have been used to support conservative positions. We might well suspect that, as Karl Barth insisted, there is an affinity here to which we must be constantly alert. Some will argue that only by misinterpreting Dooyeweerd can the conservative find support among his ideas, but I am not persuaded of that. It seems to me that at the very least they contain certain ambiguities.

to growth in the Gross National Product. Economic growth, technological innovation, and scientific advance supersede all other values, and are in turn raised above all normative appraisal; they have, in fact,

> attached themselves to our society as forward-moving forces which are *their own justification,* as sources of progress which are good in themselves, and therefore in principle need not be subjected to any critical assessment. Technical innovations are by definition considered desirable, all scientific findings are positive contributions, and in economics it is self-evident that bigger is always better. . . . The forces of economic growth, technical innovation, and scientific aggrandizement have established themselves securely in our society as *ultimate standards.* They need not measure up to society, but society must measure up to them.[18]

The result is that we have created what Goudzwaard aptly calls a "tunnel society."

The structural manifestations of this overriding commitment to the production of ever more surplus are threefold. In the first place, the economic sphere has come to dominate all others: our society has become economized. Government, education—everything is bent to the demands of the economy. Our social order throughout has been overwhelmingly shaped by production for profit on the market. Like a cancerous growth, the economy has violated the "sovereignty of the spheres."

Secondly, economic life itself has not followed its own appropriate norms. Goudzwaard's conviction is that the concept of *stewardship* best captures the norm for life in the economic sphere. But we have not been guided by the norm of stewardship; we have instead been guided by the goal of increasing production. He makes the point interestingly and forcefully:

> In classical antiquity two distinct Greek words were used to describe human economic activity: *oikonomia* and *chrematistike. Oikonomia* (the origin of our word *economics*) designated the behavior of the steward whose task it was to manage the estate entrusted to him in such a way that it would continue to bear fruit and thus provide a living for everyone who lived and worked on it. Central to this concept, therefore, was the maintenance of productive possessions on behalf of everyone involved. *Chrematistike,* however, meant something quite different. This word expressed the pursuit of self-enrichment, for ever greater monetary possessions, if need be at the expense of others. It is remarkable to observe that in western civilization the meaning of the word *economics* has increasingly become synonymous with *chrematistike,* while progressively it lost the meaning of *oikonomia,* the careful maintenance as steward on behalf of others of all that is entrusted to man.

A business is not run economically if it is efficient merely in a monetary sense. *It is economically responsible only if it possesses the ability to render a net economic fruit.* In terms of a normative-economic cost-benefit analysis, many financially viable businesses may be called economic fiascos, whereas the opposite might be true of a number of businesses which are losing money. As an example of the first we might cite producers of goods which can actually be marketed only by means of intensive advertising campaigns, but which pollute the environment (either during production or consumption), are energy intensive, and use up the world's dwindling supply of nonrenewable resources. Another example would be those firms which damage the health of their laborers during the process of production (health, too, is an economic good!), fail to utilize their workers' mental capacities, or even brutalize them by over-doses of mechanical and deadening drudgery. Corporations can also fail economically—despite great apparent success from a financial point of view—in their operations in developing countries. . . .

Business enterprises, in other words, should be genuinely economic organizations, that is, institutions of stewardship. That is the key norm by which they should be judged, without neglect of market factors. (*CP,* pp. 211-12)

Thirdly—and it is especially this last point that Goudzwaard emphasizes—we have not allowed the economic sphere to be genuinely open to the norms of the other spheres. We have prevented "disclosure." We have not insisted that economic activity also be morally responsible, technologically responsible, and so on. We have not pursued "simultaneous realization" of norms:

A certain fixed sequence arises in which questions are asked and problems are solved. The first question concerns how we can ensure sufficient economic, scientific, and technological growth. Only thereafter is it asked to what extent we are able to counteract whatever harmful effects may result from such growth; for example, its effects on the environment, on the working conditions of laborers, on the economic status of the poor nations of the world, on the decreasing world reserves of energy and natural resources, on the freedom of consumers, and on interpersonal relationships in society. In a tunnel society such an order of priorities is self-evident. . . . A society with a measure of disclosure will be characterized by a conscious effort to reverse this sequence of posing questions. Its first concerns will be man's responsibility to protect and respect nature, the meaning of human labor, the human dignity of the consumer, and the opportunities for development of the poor nations; and to preserve for posterity sufficient energy and other natural resources. (*CP,* p. 194)

Earlier we saw that Dooyeweerd outlined three ways in which the development of the spheres can go wrong once they have been differentiated from each other. I think we all sense that Goudzwaard's analysis, which is clearly conducted in terms of these three types of misadventure, is a profoundly insightful one. But for most of us that sense of illumination is combined with the uneasy question: To what extent must one accept that background ontology of Dooyeweerd in order to go along with the essentials of Goudzwaard's analysis? Must we hold that there are such categorically distinct types as the State and the Business Enterprise, each with its distinct normative nature; that these gradually become exemplified as societal differentiation takes place; and that we owe it to God to see to it that the inner nature of each of these types is opened up? In a word, *no*. We do *not* have to adopt this ontology in order to preserve the core of Goudzwaard's contribution. Let me briefly sketch out an alternative picture.

Every society contains a certain array of institutions (or *formations* if you prefer a more neutral word). Our own society exhibits a dizzyingly complex array of them. We owe it to God and to our fellow human beings to see to it that our society's array of institutions adequately serves the life of its members—that they serve the cause of justice and shalom. (I shall speak of *shalom* shortly.) In our assessment of our society's institutions, it is our obligation to engage in normative reflection; we must not allow certain institutions and goals to be placed above all normative assessment. And as we conduct our normative reflections, we must be especially sensitive to the stultification of human life that occurs when one institution (or type of institution) dominates all others: it is our obligation to promote pluralism. Likewise, we must be especially sensitive to the stultification of human life that occurs when, in tunnel-vision fashion, the need for "simultaneous realization" of norms is forgotten.

The institutions in every society will perform certain functions. We must ask whether the functions that they perform in our society are being performed well, whether there are some that ought not to be performed at all, and whether there are others not presently being performed by any institution that ought to be performed. And we must ask how the functions performed are best parcelled out among the institutions of society: which should be assigned to different institutions, and which to the same. When we look at the various societies to be found in the course of history, we find certain basic functions regularly performed, but we find them parcelled out among institutions in all sorts of different ways. Functions that we assign to one institution may in other societies be assigned to different ones, and functions that we assign to different institutions may in other societies be assigned to the same one. In societies quite different from ours we can still pick out institutions that are recognizably schools, states, and so on (though we cannot do so in all). But the assignment of functions to these is often quite different from what it is in our society. Is our assignment a good one *for us*? That must be our question.

In considering which functions ought to be performed in our society, and which institutions should be assigned to perform them, we should keep in mind the guiding principle I mentioned earlier: what serves best the cause of justice and shalom. And our considerations must always be "situated," concrete. We must ask what *this* institution in *this* institutional array ought to be doing, or what redistributions of function ought to occur in *this* array. We must not ask what *the* State should be doing, as if what are recognizably states should in all times and all places have the same assignment of functions. We do not owe it to God to realize the inner nature of the State; rather, we owe it to God that our own institutional array, including our state, serves humanity.

Dooyeweerd argues that *the* task of *the* State is the administration of justice. My own government, and most others in the world as well, provides certain services that enhance our life together: it builds roads, runs a post office, offers fire protection, and so on. This is not the administration of justice, as Dooyeweerd understands it; nonetheless, it is important that these functions be performed, and perhaps it is best in our situation that these functions be performed by the same institution that administers justice. In another institutional array, it might not be wise, but that case would have to be argued not by reference to the inner nature of the State, but by reference to the lives of human beings.*

We can still classify the functions performed by our social institutions into types. So too we can classify obligations into types: ecological responsibilities, intellectual responsibilities, moral responsibilities, aesthetic responsibilities, etc. And of course we can classify institutions into types. But the matching up of functions (and their correlative responsibilities) to institutions is not to be done by asking what *the* State and *the* Business Enterprise ought to do, but by considering what *our* states and *our* business enterprises ought to do in *our* situation.

But let us return to Goudzwaard, for he has one more important point to make. How, he asks, are we to understand this pursuit of economic growth which has so profoundly shaped not only our economy but our entire social order? Perhaps it is best to see ourselves as dealing here with *religious* dynamics; perhaps we are dealing here with a "faith": "Insofar as western man attributes divine stature to the forces of progress, we might well be confronted with a situation parallel to that of idol worship in primitive cultures. These forces are given divine prerogatives as soon as man puts an unconditional *trust* in them; that is, as soon as economic and technological progress are depended

---

*It is true, of course, that an institution could scarcely be considered a state unless, among other things, it saw to the administration of justice in that society. But it does not by any means follow from this that the administration of justice is the *sole* appropriate function of the state. In some instances this may be the case, but it is not universally so.

upon as the guides to the good life and as mediators of our happiness" (*CP*, p. 152).

We have here touched on the second of the fundamental dynamics that the neo-Calvinist sees as operative in history—the dynamic of idolatry and of its struggle with authentic faith. Goudzwaard's suggestion is that our practice of giving decisive consideration to economic growth should be seen as an example of idolatry: something of *some* worth is being treated as if it were of *ultimate* worth. Like idols generally, this idol not only distorts life but eventually enslaves the very person who trusts it. We are enslaved by the very technology and bureaucracy which are among our principal agents of economic growth:

> As in primitive cultures, powers that are regarded as gods and saviors can gain a dominant influence over our lives from which we cannot readily extricate ourselves. . . . One cannot choose one's own masters in life without accepting the status of servant. It appears therefore that the sense of powerlessness present in western culture may well be closely connected with the *faith dimension* of the progress motive. Powerlessness results when one's own power is delegated; but it is precisely a *faith* (in progress) that can elicit such a delegation of power. (*CP*, p. 152)

But there is more involved here than simply the *practice* of treating economic growth as a social good of autonomous and ultimate worth. A whole ideology—a framework of justifying beliefs—has arisen within the society shaped by this practice, and this too must be seen as a component of our idolatry. The meaning of history lies for us in human progress, and we consider increase in the production of goods to be the decisive instrument of that progress: *we have faith in progress.* Our society has rewarded us with goods beyond comparison. Therein we see its justification. We assume that whatever problems arise along the way will be solved by technological advance and economic growth.

Goudzwaard realizes that we do not eliminate this idolatry from our lives simply by renouncing its constituent ideology and by intellectually repudiating growth as a good of ultimate value—for at the heart of this idolatry is a *practice,* the practice of taking growth as a good of unquestioned and ultimate worth. It is this *practice* that must be rooted out of our lives. We can do so only by adopting alternative practices in which growth is no longer treated thus. Furthermore, Goudzwaard is fully aware that this practice is at the very heart of what we know as capitalism. Once we no longer follow the practice, capitalism will be altered beyond recognition. It must be added, though, that this very same practice shapes life in the "socialist" countries. They, too, in their own way—indeed, often in the same way—are in the grip of the idol of growth.

To release ourselves from this idol (without succumbing to another) we must once again bring normative considerations to bear on economic life, no longer letting ourselves be tyrannized by something placed above all normative appraisal. We must retract our abdication from normative reflection and decision. And as we begin once again to engage in such reflection, we must be constantly alert to the dangers of "tunnel vision," constantly open to the rich diversity of norms for our lives, in that way working for "the disclosure of society."*

In the preceding chapter I suggested that capitalism was a blend of certain legal arrangements and practices. Goudzwaard's discussion leads us now to see these practices in a new light. All together they amount to a "faith," a "social idolatry." I myself think that what we find of fundamental worth in our modern world-system is less accurately described as *increased production* than as *increased mastery of nature and society so as to satisfy our desires* (since, for example, the prolongation of life, which surely we regard as one of the good things which our system has yielded, is not directly a matter of more goods available for use and consumption). I also think that the ideology accompanying the emergence of our world-order is somewhat less academic in its origins than Goudzwaard's discussion would suggest; as I see it, academics gave expression to an ideology which had already gained currency—though, indeed, by so doing they reinforced the grip of that ideology. But these are minor disagreements.

I have noted several points of difference between the neo-Calvinist analysis of our society and the liberationist analysis in the course of this discussion; there remains one more that I would like to address. It is also important, however, to take note of some of the deep affinities between these two patterns of thought, affinities that tend to be obscured by the obvious and substantial differences. Let me attend to that first, stressing affinities with which I am myself in agreement.

Liberation theology and neo-Calvinism have similarities that extend beyond the fact that they are both contemporary versions of world-formative Christianity. Both express, for example, a significant concern for the *victims* of modern society (though it is true that they differ in their specific definitions of which groups constitute the victims of a given society). In addition, both express concern for the victims in essentially the same manner: not by applying bandages, but by searching out what it was that inflicted the wounds and seeking to effect changes in that quarter. Both find the culprit in the structure of modern society and the dynamics underlying that structure rather than in acts of individual waywardness. Both offer architectonic analyses of the ills of modern society, and both locate the crucial dynamic in the economic sphere—and in the political sphere insofar as it supports the economic.

*"Taking norms seriously is the essence of every genuine process of disclosure"—Goudzwaard (*CP*, p. 248).

Furthermore, both the liberationist and the neo-Calvinist perceive the processes afoot in the modern world not as incidental to the ultimate fulfillment of human destiny, but as foundational to it. The neo-Calvinist interprets the grand sweep of history as the development of the potentials implicit in creation, with art eventually coming into its own, science coming into its own, and so on.[19] The liberationist sees the grand sweep of history as the attainment of freedom (while remaining somewhat ambiguous concerning what exactly constitutes this freedom). Thus, both perceive progress in history, though by no means a smooth, uninterrupted progress. Neither objects in principle to the growth of technology, nor indeed to bureaucratic organization, but both object to the *direction* in which these developments have been turned in the modern world. In neither is there any of the regressive romanticism of the late Frankfurt School (which, in despair over the invasion of modern society by what it called *instrumental reason,* eventually turned to art for salvation, because it came to believe that art was the one remaining area of life in which such reason did not yet hold sway, in which life was still characterized by wholeness and expressiveness and concreteness).

In addition, both consider the making of humanity in history to be intrinsic to the coming of the Kingdom of God—while at the same time both see the Kingdom in its fullness as a gift and not as an accomplishment; neither etherealizes human destiny. Life in history is incorporated into our destiny. Correlatively, both are so bold as to suggest that we human beings play a role in the coming of the Kingdom. Our relation to the Kingdom is not only obedient waiting, but active contribution. Whether one interprets history as a fitful movement toward differentiation or as a fitful movement of liberation, it remains something that we contribute to, not merely something inflicted upon us.

There are indeed more affinities than these, but let us in conclusion move on to the most important of the differences not yet considered. Liberationists focus on domination and exploitation, which they see as age-old manifestations of the age-old phenomenon of sin—resistance to love; neo-Calvinists, on the other hand, focus on the widespread faith in economic growth, which they see as a modern form of the age-old phenomenon of idolatry. For one the category of sin is prominent; for the other the category of idolatry is prominent.

It ought here to be recognized that although these interpretations are different, they are not mutually exclusive: it is possible, and advisable, to incorporate both into a larger perspective. We do in fact live in a world-system in which the core dominates the periphery, characteristically out of greed and a lust for power. What is that but sin? We do in fact live in a world-system shaped by the practice of treating economic growth as an autonomous and ultimate good. What is that but idolatry?

The liberation theologians typically conclude from their analysis of the predicament of their people that they must work for the formation of a socialist society in which there is no longer private appropriation of the surplus of production. Goudzwaard also decries the arrangement whereby only the owner of capital and not the worker has voice in the operation of, and title to the proceeds from, the enterprise to which they jointly contribute; but his analysis makes clear that the members of a socialist society—whether defined as a society in which private ownership of the means of production has been abolished or a society in which labor and capital have co-responsibility in the enterprise—can also treat growth as an autonomous and ultimate good, with results scarcely better than what we witness under capitalism. Our ills are deeper than such restructuring can cure.

On the other hand, the liberationist analysis corrects an important deficiency in the neo-Calvinist analysis: our situation is not merely that we are all dominated by the idol of growth; it is also that certain groups of *persons* are exploitatively dominated by other groups of *persons*. The neo-Calvinists scarcely take note of this *conflictual* aspect of our social order. Of course they are aware of *certain* conflicts—they recognize the differences of opinion people have as to the norms we ought to follow and the policies we ought to adopt, for example—but they pass by that conflict of wills between those who have power in the system and those who lack it. Accordingly, though they suggest strategies for freeing ourselves from the idol of growth, they say nothing about groups of people struggling to *liberate* themselves from oppression and exploitation. But the truth is surely that there is no disclosure without liberation.

It would be pleasant if we could stop with this *both/and:* each vision has insights that we should incorporate into a larger picture and each has limitations that the other helps to correct. But when it comes to practice, and to reflection that guides practice, we cannot stop with a *both/and.* The sorrows produced by our world-system are many. Among them is the domination of some by others which the system encourages. And, as one would expect, when one party dominates another, it customarily also takes advantage of the other and exploits it. In such a situation one cannot simply say that we all suffer from the idolatry of growth. One cannot just say that we are all in this boat together. One has to say that one human being is being wronged by another, and to say that is to take sides with the former. It is to declare solidarity with him or her in opposition to the oppressor. It is to take sides on a struggle occurring *within* the boat. And if one's declaration of solidarity is serious, the actions of liberation will flow forth. On all this the liberation theologian is right.

Moreover, not only will Christians thus *take sides* as they concern themselves with the miseries of contemporary mankind, but this taking sides will be a priority for them. The exploitative domination experienced by many

threatens their very livelihood, their very sustenance. The elimination of starvation, and the alleviation of the tyranny that supports it, has priority over,
say, relieving the boredom of the well-to-do in a society devoted to growth.

This taking of sides will of course produce conflict (of which there
was much already). The powerful will try to hang on to their positions. One
will not be able to avoid reflecting seriously on the place of violence in that
conflict. Sad to say, it is not a conflict in which the church is to be found
exclusively on the side of the exploited. *Christ* was there, and is there, but his
"body," the church, is not—not all of it in any case. So in taking the side of
the exploited, Christians will find themselves in opposition to some of those
who confess the same Lord. That, for them, is yet another of the great sorrows
of our world.

For Justice in Shalom

In Chapter II we saw that there are two fundamental dynamics shaping the modern world: freedom by mastery and freedom of self-determination. In the light of this, we may perhaps summarize the discussion contained in Chapter III in this way: liberation theology, with its emphasis on salvation, affirms the importance of freedom of self-determination, but never succeeds in incorporating into its vision, in any satisfactory way, freedom by mastery. The Amsterdam school, with its emphasis on creation, affirms the importance of freedom by mastery, but never succeeds in incorporating into its vision, in any satisfactory way, freedom of self-determination. To guide our thoughts, we need some vision yet more comprehensive than either of these. Of course there is no substitute for careful, informed, and specific reflection; but is there some comprehensive vision that can serve to orient those reflections and thereby keep us from losing our way? When architects design buildings, they begin with an image of forms and lights and shadows to which they gradually give increasing articulation. Is there any such image for us here?

I think there is. It is the vision of *shalom*—*peace*—first articulated in the Old Testament poetic and prophetic literature but then coming to expression in the New Testament as well. We shall see that shalom is intertwined with justice. In shalom, each person enjoys justice, enjoys his or her rights. There is no shalom without justice. But shalom goes beyond justice.

Shalom is the human being dwelling at peace in all his or her relationships: with God, with self, with fellows, with nature. It is shalom when

> The wolf shall dwell with the lamb,
>   and the leopard shall lie down with the kid,
> and the calf and the lion and the fatling together,
>   and a little child shall lead them.
> The cow and the bear shall feed;
>   their young shall lie down together;
>   and the lion shall eat straw like the ox.
> The sucking child shall play over the hole of the asp,
>   and the weaned child shall put his hand on the adder's den.
>   (Isa. 11:6–8)

But the peace which is shalom is not merely the absence of hostility, not merely being in right relationship. Shalom at its highest is *enjoyment* in one's relationships. A nation may be at peace with all its neighbors and yet be miserable in its poverty. To dwell in shalom is to *enjoy* living before God, to *enjoy* living in one's physical surroundings, to *enjoy* living with one's fellows, to *enjoy* life with oneself.

Shalom in the first place incorporates right, harmonious relationships to *God* and delight in his service. When the prophets speak of shalom, they speak of a day when human beings will no longer flee God down the corridors of time, a day when they will no longer turn in those corridors to defy their divine pursuer. Shalom is perfected when humanity acknowledges that in its service of God is true delight. "The mountain of the house of the Lord," says the prophet,

> shall be established as the highest of the mountains,
>   and shall be raised above the hills;
> and all the nations shall flow to it,
>   and many peoples shall come, and say:
> "Come, let us go up to the mountain of the Lord,
>   to the house of the God of Jacob;
> that he may teach us his ways
>   and that we may walk in his paths."
>
> (Isa. 2:2-3)

Secondly, shalom incorporates right harmonious relationships to other *human beings* and delight in human community. Shalom is absent when a society is a collection of individuals all out to make their own way in the world. And of course there can be delight in community only when justice reigns, only when human beings no longer oppress one another. When "justice shall make its home in the wilderness, / and righteousness dwell in the grass-land"—only then will it be true that "rightousness shall yield shalom, / and its fruit be quietness and confidence for ever" (Isa. 32:16-17). In shalom,

> Love and Fidelity now meet,
>   Justice and Peace now embrace;
> Fidelity reaches up from earth
>   and Justice leans down from heaven.
>
> (Psalm 85)

Thirdly, shalom incorporates right, harmonious relationships to *nature* and delight in our physical surroundings. Shalom comes when we, bodily creatures and not disembodied souls, shape the world with our labor and find fulfillment in so doing and delight in its results. In speaking of shalom the prophet spoke of a day when the Lord would prepare

> a banquet of rich fare for all the people,
> a banquet of wines well matured and richest fare,
> well matured wines strained clear.
>
> (Isa. 25:6)

He spoke of a day when the people "shall live in a tranquil country, / dwelling in shalom, in houses full of ease" (Isa. 32:18).

I said that justice, the enjoyment of one's rights, is indispensable to shalom. That is because shalom is an *ethical* community. If individuals are not granted what is due them, if their claim on others is not acknowledged by those others, if others do not carry out their obligations to them, then shalom is wounded. That is so even if there are no *feelings* of hostility between them and the others. Shalom cannot be secured in an unjust situation by managing to get all concerned to feel content with their lot in life. Shalom would not have been present *even if* all the blacks in the United States had been content in their state of slavery; it would not be present in South Africa *even if* all the blacks there felt happy. It is because shalom is an ethical community that it is wounded when justice is absent.

But the right relationships that lie at the basis of shalom involve more than right relationships to other human beings. They involve right relationships to God, to nature, and to oneself as well. Hence, shalom is more than an ethical community. Shalom is the *responsible* community in which God's laws for the multifaceted existence of his creatures are obeyed.

Shalom goes beyond even the responsible community. We may all have acted responsibly and yet shalom may be wounded, for delight may be missing. Always there are sorrows in our human existence that we are at a loss to heal. It is in this context that we must ultimately see the significance of technology. Technology does make possible advance toward shalom; progress in mastery of the world can bring shalom nearer. But the limits of technology must also be acknowledged: technology is entirely incapable of bringing about shalom between ourselves and God, and it is only scarcely capable of bringing about the love of self and neighbor.

I have already cited that best known of all shalom passages, the one in which Isaiah describes the anticipated shalom with a flourish of images of harmony—harmony among the animals, harmony between man and animal: "Then the wolf shall live with the sheep. . . ." That passage, though, is introduced with these words:

> Then a shoot shall grow from the stock of Jesse,
> and a branch shall spring from his roots.
> The spirit of the Lord shall rest upon him,
> a spirit of wisdom and understanding,
> a spirit of counsel and power,
> a spirit of knowledge and the fear of the Lord.
>
> (Isa. 11:1-2)

That shoot of which Isaiah spoke is he of whom the angels sang in celebration of his birth: "Glory to God in highest heaven, and on earth his *peace* for men on whom his favor rests" (Luke 2:24). He is the one of whom the priest Zechariah said that he "will guide our feet into the way of *peace*" (Luke 1:79). He is the one of whom Simeon said, "This day, Master, thou givest thy servant his discharge in *peace;* now thy promise is fulfilled" (Luke 2:29). He is the one of whom Peter said that it was by him that God preached "good news of *peace*" to Israel (Acts 10:36). He is the one of whom Paul, speaking as a Jew to the Gentiles, said that "he came and preached *peace* to you who were far off and *peace* to those who were near" (Eph. 2:17). He is in fact Jesus Christ, whom Isaiah called the "prince of peace" (Isa. 9:6).

It was this same Jesus who said to the apostles in his Farewell Discourse, "The words that I say to you I do not speak on my own authority; but the Father who dwells in me does his works. Believe me that I am in the Father and the Father in me; or else believe me for the sake of the works themselves" (John 14:10-11). And then he added, "I say to you, he who believes in me will also do the works that I do; and greater works than these will he do" (John 14:12).

Can the conclusion be avoided that not only is shalom God's cause in the world but that all who believe in Jesus will, along with him, engage in the works of shalom? Shalom is both God's cause in the world and our human calling. Even though the full incursion of shalom into our history will be divine gift and not merely human achievement, even though its episodic incursion into our lives now also has a dimension of divine gift, nonetheless it is shalom that we are to work and struggle for. We are not to stand around, hands folded, waiting for shalom to arrive. We are workers in God's cause, his peace-workers. The *missio Dei* is *our* mission.[1]

An implication of this is that our work will always have the two dimensions of a struggle for justice and the pursuit of increased mastery of the world so as to enrich human life. Both together are necessary if shalom is to be brought nearer. Development and liberation must go hand in hand. Ours is both a cultural mandate and a liberation mandate—the mandate to master the world for the benefit of mankind, but also the mandate

> to loose the chains of injustice
>   and untie the cords of the yoke,
> to set the oppressed free
>   and break every yoke . . .
> to share your food with the hungry
>   and to provide the poor wanderer with shelter—
> when you see the naked, to clothe him,
>   and not to turn away from your own flesh and blood.
>
> (Isa. 58:6-7)

The shalom perspective incorporates but goes beyond the creation perspective of the Amsterdam school. At the same time, it incorporates but goes beyond the salvation perspective of the liberation theologians.

Chapter IV

The Rich and the Poor

In a now-famous passage from his *Church Dogmatics,* Karl Barth said this:

> the human righteousness required by God and established in obe-
> dience—the righteousness which according to Amos 5^{24} should pour
> down as a mighty stream—has necessarily the character of a vin-
> dication of right in favour of the threatened innocent, the oppressed
> poor, widows, orphans and aliens. For this reason, in the relations
> and events in the life of His people, God always takes His stand
> unconditionally and passionately on this side and on this side alone:
> against the lofty and on behalf of the lowly; against those who
> already enjoy right and privilege and on behalf of those who are
> denied and deprived of it. [1]

As we read these powerful and influential words, let us retain our historical
perspective and remember that Barth was by no means the first to speak of
God as taking sides with the poor and oppressed. Some forty or fifty years
before, in his 1891 speech to the Christian Social Congress in Holland, Abraham
Kuyper had said the same: "When rich and poor stand opposed to each other,
[Jesus] never takes His place with the wealthier, but always stands with the
poorer. He is born in a stable; and while foxes have holes and birds have nests,
the Son of Man has nowhere to lay His head." And again, "both the Christ,
and also just as much His apostles after Him as the prophets before Him,
invariably took sides *against* those who were powerful and living in luxury, and
for the suffering and oppressed." [2]

But can that be right? Does God take sides among human beings?
Central in the Calvinist consciousness, and present in the consciousness of other
Christians as well, is the conviction that God has chosen or *elected* certain human
beings. But this is fundamentally different from the idea that God takes sides
among us. Can it be true that God both *elects* and *takes sides*? And if he takes
sides, can it really be said that he takes sides with the poor against the rich, with
the oppressed against the oppressor? Would it not be much better to say that
he takes sides with the righteous against the unrighteous, or perhaps with those
in authority against those who flout authority? No doubt God condemns the
sin of tyranny and no doubt he condemns the sin of greed. But that is quite
different from saying that he takes sides with poor people against rich people,
with oppressed people against oppressing people. When it comes to persons
before God are we not *all* poor, are we not *all* oppressed?

Having laid the groundwork in the three preceding chapters, I want in this and the following two chapters to consider some of the issues that ought to be on the agenda of the Christian as he faces the modern social order. And since, as we saw in Chapter II, the economic dimension of our modern social world profoundly shapes the whole of it, it is there that I propose to begin.

Many are the ills perpetrated upon us by our economic arrangements and practices: work for millions of people is boring rather than fulfilling, the physical context within which we live is at many places corrupted to the point of being injurious to health, the benefits of our world economy are distributed with gross unevenness, and so on. But one great issue supersedes all others in importance: the issue of poverty. Something on the order of 800 million people in this world are poor to the point of scarcely being able to sustain existence. According to the 1978 *World Development Report* of the World Bank, "the past quarter century has been a period of unprecedented change and progress in the developing world. And yet despite this impressive record, some 800 million individuals continue to be trapped in . . . absolute poverty: a condition of life so characterized by malnutrition, illiteracy, disease, squalid surroundings, high infant mortality and low life expectancy as to be beneath any reasonable definition of human decency."[3] Of course, it is not the sheer fact of massive world poverty that is a scandal to the church and all humanity; the scandal lies in the fact that this abject poverty is today not an unavoidable feature of our human situation, and even more so in the fact that the impoverished coexist in our world-system with an equal number who live in unprecedented affluence. Poverty amidst plenty with the gap becoming greater: this is the scandal.

Before we address any of the other evils perpetrated by our economic order, we must speak to this issue of poverty amidst plenty, because unless people have the means to sustain themselves, they cannot work at all, meaningfully or not; they cannot breathe at all, whether pure air or polluted. It is especially the problem of poverty in the Third World that we must face, for though there is poverty in the core areas of our world-system as well, the vast majority of the poor of the earth subsist in the periphery.

For all its enormity, Third World poverty is something of which we in the West have only recently become fully aware—only since the Second World War. Admittedly, we were vaguely aware of it during the colonial era, but we in the colonizing countries offered ourselves self-serving explanations, meant to relieve us of responsibility, which caused us to put the phenomenon out of mind. Poverty, we said, was a natural condition for certain kinds of people; it was impossible to change, or at least there was nothing *we* could do to change it. "It was taken as established by experience that peoples in backward regions were so constituted that they reacted differently from people of European stock," writes Gunnar Myrdal. "Their tendency toward idleness and inefficiency, and their reluctance to venture into new enterprises and often even to seek wage employment, were seen as expressions of this lack of ambition, limited economic horizons, survival-mindedness, carefree disposition, and preference for a leisurely life."[4]

After World War II all this changed. *Development* became the byword, and suddenly was thought to be within the reach of all alike. All that was needed was technology and capital; both of these could be painlessly supplied by us. A new self-serving explanation! But development has not occurred as we expected. The poor are with us in greater numbers than ever before. And now we can no longer ignore their existence. Their cries reach our ears:

> The scandal of poverty in a world of abundance is crying out. Development decade after development decade passes by, but the poor are still dying. They die from starvation, from deprivation, from oppression. But it is their life and labour which create the wealth of the few.
>
> In a world of scarcity in which everyone is in want, poverty would be a common challenge to everybody. But in a world of abundance in which many people are poor in order that a few others may stay rich, poverty—or better, wealth—is an infamy. Where the rich refuse to give up their privileges and share their plenty, their situation asks for reproach.[5]

But why care? Why not simply teach the poor to cope? Why not praise the virtues of poverty? Why not preach a gospel of consolation as the church has done for centuries?[6] Why try to change things? Why should poverty be on the agenda of the Christian, or of anyone else?

Well, could it be that *God* cares? Could it be that God has taken the side of the poor?

> And Mary sang:
> "My soul praises the Lord and my spirit rejoices in God my Savior, for he has been mindful of the humble state of his servant. . . .
> He has brought down rulers from their thrones but has lifted up the humble.
> He has filled the hungry with good things but has sent the rich away empty."
>
> (Luke 1:46-53)

Jesus went to Nazareth, where he had been brought up, and on the Sabbath day he went into the synagogue, as was his custom. And he stood up to read. The scroll of the prophet Isaiah was handed to him. Unrolling it, he found the place where it is written:
> "The Spirit of the Lord is on me,
> because he has anointed me
> to preach good news to the poor.

He has sent me to proclaim freedom for the prisoners,
   and recovery of sight for the blind,
to release the oppressed,
   to proclaim the year of the Lord's favor."
Then he rolled up the scroll, gave it back to the attendant and sat
down. The eyes of everyone in the synagogue were fastened on
him, and he said to them, "Today this scripture is fulfilled in your
hearing."

(Luke 4:16-21)

Looking at his disciples, he said:
"Blessed are you who are poor, for yours is the kingdom of God.
Blessed are you who hunger now, for you will be satisfied."

(Luke 6:20-21)

John's disciples told him about all these things. Calling two of them,
he sent them to the Lord to ask, "Are you the one who was to
come, or should we expect someone else?". . . .
   At that very time Jesus cured many who had diseases,
sicknesses and evil spirits, and gave sight to many who were blind.
So he replied to the messengers, "Go back and report to John what
you have seen and heard: The blind receive sight, the lame walk,
those who have leprosy are cured, the deaf hear, the dead are raised,
and the good news is preached to the poor. Blessed is the man who
does not fall away on account of me."

(Luke 7:18-23)

If we consider Jesus to be God incarnate, and these teachings from
the book of Luke to be God-authorized, as I certainly do, then we cannot but
conclude that God has taken sides with the poor. God is not on the side of
Dutch-speaking people versus those who do not speak Dutch; on that he is
even-handed. God is not on the side of football players versus those who do
not play football; on that, too, he is even-handed. But the poor are different.
It is against his will that there be a society in which some are poor; in his
perfected Kingdom there will be none at all. It is even more against his will
that there be a society in which some are poor *while others are rich*. When that
happens, then he is on the side of the poor, for it is they, he says, who are being
wronged.* He is not on the side of the rich, and he is not even-handed. But

---

*A wealth of Old Testament passages attest the validity of this contention.
I would here just cite two from Isaiah:
   The Lord has taken his place to contend,
     he stands to judge his people.
   The Lord enters into judgment
     with the elders and the princes of his people:

on the other hand, the poor are not romanticized: they are not praised; they are *blessed*. And, yes, they can turn aside the blessing. Blessing is pronounced on those who hunger and thirst for righteousness. Not all the poor do so.

How are we to understand the thrust of all these words in which Jesus places himself (and is placed by Mary) on the side of the poor? I suggest that we do so by placing them in the context of the song sung by the old priest Zechariah in anticipation of the Messiah:

> Praise be to the Lord, the God of Israel,
>   because he has come and has redeemed his people . . .
> to guide our feet into the path of peace.
>
> (Luke 1:68-79)

To guide our feet into the path of *peace,* of *shalom*: that is what the presence of Jesus in our midst means, that is the significance of his declaration in the synagogue and to John's disciples—that in him the word of the prophet Isaiah is being fulfilled. For Isaiah was speaking of the day of shalom. In shalom there are no blind; all see. That is the significance of Jesus' healing of the blind. In shalom there are no lame; all walk. There are no lepers; all are well. There are no deaf; all hear. There are no dead; all are alive. And there are no poor; all have plenty. To limp is to fall short of shalom. To be impoverished is to fall short of shalom. *That* is what is wrong with poverty. God is committed to shalom. Jesus came to bring shalom. In shalom there is no poverty.

In shalom there is also no disease. But let us not fail to note that poverty is significantly different from, say, leprosy. The poor man in Jesus' day was deprived of what was *due* him—as he is in ours. He was deprived of his *rights*. He was deprived of *justice*. Of the leper that was not true. In a society of both rich and poor, the recognition of poverty as a lack of shalom involves *taking sides*. A recognition of leprosy as a lack of shalom calls only for searching for a cure (unless the cure is already available and is being unjustly held back from some). As the prince of shalom, Jesus could not avoid taking the side of the poor against the rich.

In the Interlude preceding this chapter we saw that shalom requires

---

> "It is you who have devoured the vineyard,
>   the spoil of the poor is in your houses.
> What do you mean by crushing my people,
>   by grinding the face of the poor?"
>
> (Isa. 3:13-15)

> Woe to those who decree iniquitous decrees,
>   and the writers who keep writing oppression,
> to turn aside the needy from justice
>   and to rob the poor of my people of their right. . . .
>
> (Isa. 10:1-2)

the presence of right relationships among human beings. Let us now expand upon this point by turning to some of Calvin's comments on the significance of the image of God in man, taking note also of the application he makes of what he says concerning the issue of poverty. Our investigation will yield the additional benefit of reminding us that whatever may be the indifference of later Calvinists to the issue of economic justice, certainly there was no such indifference in Calvin himself.

Fundamental to Calvin's reflections on poverty was his conviction that every human being has been made in the image of God. Thus we share with each other the most fundamental unity of nature. It is this fact—that we are each made in the image of God, mirroring him, rather than the fact that we each have some sort of inherent dignity—that is fundamental in determining what our attitude toward each other ought to be. "We are not to consider what men deserve of themselves but to look upon the image of God in all men, to which we owe all honor and love," Calvin declares.[7] "God Himself, looking on men as formed in His own image, regards them with such love and honour that He Himself feels wounded and outraged in the persons of those who are the victims of human cruelty and wickedness."[8] An act of injury to my fellow human being is an act of injury to God.

The commandment to love one another is grounded on this common sharing in the image of God—on the fact that my fellow human being is, in Isaiah's words, of my "own flesh and blood." "Whenever I see a man, I must, of necessity, behold myself as in a mirror."[9] Every human being is, in this deep sense, my neighbor. Indeed, says Calvin, Jesus' purpose in the parable of the Good Samaritan was to teach "that the word *neighbour* extends indiscriminately to every man, because the whole human race is united by a sacred bond of fellowship."[10] The fact that we are all created in the image of God determines the "order of nature" according to which society should be structured. Unless we live in peace and concord with one another, unless we render assistance to one another, we pervert this order of nature. This is the basis of our duty to love: "To love one another is to act with humanity in recognition of our common humanity."[11] And so it can be said that the very fact that you and I are human beings means that "we cannot but behold our own face as it were in a glass in the person that is poor and despised, which is not able to hold out any longer, but lies groaning under his burden, though he were the furthest stranger in the world. Let a Moor or a Barbarian come among us, and yet inasmuch as he is a man, he brings with him a looking glass wherein we may see that he is our brother and neighbor."[12]

What follows from this for society is what Calvin sometimes called "mutual communication": each is to contribute what he or she can to the enrichment of the common life. "It is not enough when a man can say, 'Oh, I labor, I have my craft,' or 'I have such a trade.' That is not enough. But we must see whether it is good and profitable for the common good, and whether his neighbors may fare the better of it."[13] Calvin regards both the exchange of goods on the basis of money and the division of labor in society as concrete manifestations of this mutual communication. But it is not *true* communication if exchange is conducted in violation of the order of nature. If some are poor and others are wealthy, then it is not in fact an exchange of *good offices*: "since God has united men in the bonds of mutual society, hence they must mutually perform good offices for each other. Here, then, it is required of the rich to succour the poor, and to offer bread to the hungry."[14] And again, "the Lord commends to us . . . that we may, in so far as funds allow, help those in difficulties that there may not be some in affluence and others in want."[15]

It should now come as no surprise to hear Calvin thundering against the rich in his sermons. In one of them he describes certain wheat-cornering operators as "murderers, savage beasts, biting and eating up the poor, sucking in their blood,"[16] and in another he sends a warning to the rich in his own congregation: "if the poor souls that have bestowed their labor and travail and spent their sweat and blood for you be not paid their wages as they ought to be, not succored and sustained by you as they should be—if they ask vengeance against you at God's hand, who shall be your spokesman or advocate to rid you out of his hands?"[17] It is our duty, he insists, not only to avoid the evil but to seek the good: "those who have riches, whether inherited or won by their own industry and labour, are to remember that what is left over is not meant for intemperance or luxury, but for relieving the needs of the brethren."[18]*

Some of these same themes were restated by Kuyper at the beginning of the neo-Calvinist movement in the Netherlands. "God has not willed," he said in the 1891 speech to the Christian Social Congress to which I referred at the outset of this chapter,

> that one should drudge hard and yet have *no bread* for himself and
> for his family. And still less has God willed that any man with hands
> to work and a will to work should suffer hunger or be reduced to

---

*Many passages might also be cited from the writers of the ancient church, such as this one from St. Basil: "What is a miser? One who is not content with what is necessary. What is an exploiter? One who takes another's possessions. Aren't you a miser, a plunderer, when you use for your own benefit something which has been given to you to be administered? He who takes another's coat is a thief; do you deserve any other name if you do not help to clothe the naked? The bread which you keep for yourself although you do not need it belongs to the hungry; the cape hanging in your wardrobe should cover those whose clothes are in shreds; the shoes you spoil should be for those who are barefoot; in the same way, the money you have buried should be given to the needy. You commit as many injustices as there are people with whom you avoid sharing what you have" (quoted by Santa Ana, *Good News to the Poor*, pp. 68-69).

the beggar's staff just *because* there is no work. If we have "food and clothing" then it is true the holy apostle demands that we should be therewith content. But it neither can nor may ever be excused in us that, while our Father in heaven wills with divine kindness that an abundance of food comes forth from the ground, through *our* guilt this rich bounty should be divided so *unequally* that while one is surfeited with bread, another goes with empty stomach to his pallet, and sometimes must even go without a pallet.[19]

Where Kuyper goes beyond Calvin is in his analysis of the roots of the social misery of his day and in his insistence that charity is not sufficient. The social misery that he was witnessing, of which poverty was but the most tragic manifestation, was attributed by Kuyper to a laissez-faire political system arising from the Enlightenment, coupled with an economic system motivated by profit seeking.* The result was a class struggle. And here Kuyper's analysis becomes strikingly similar to that of Marx:

On the side of the *bourgeoisie,* there was experience and insight, ability and association, available money and available influence. On the other side was the rural population and the working class, bereft of all means of help, and forced to accept any condition, no matter how unjust, through the constant necessity for food. Even without prophetic gifts, the result of this struggle could readily be foreseen. It could not end otherwise than in the absorption of all calculable value by the larger and smaller capitalists, leaving for the lower strata of society only as much as appeared strictly necessary to maintain these instruments for nourishing capital—for in this system, that is all the workers are held to be.[20]**

*The French Revolution, says Kuyper, "could not but become the cause of deep-seated *social need*. This followed from the double and intrinsic characteristic; first, to represent possession of *money* as the highest good, and second, in the struggle for money, to set every man against the other. . . . Now add the loosening of all social organization, followed by the proclamation of the mercantile gospel of 'laissez faire,' and you understand how the *struggle for life* was announced by the *struggle for money,* so that the law of the animal world, dog eat dog, became the basic law for every social relationship. The thirst and the chase for money, the holy apostle taught us, is the *root of all evil*; and as soon as this angry demon was unchained, at the turn of the century, no deliberation was sharp enough, no cunning sly enough, no deceit shameful enough in order, through superiority in knowledge, position, and basic capital, to acquire money and ever more money at the expense of the socially weaker" (*Christianity and the Class Struggle,* trans. Dirk Jellema [Grand Rapids, Mich.: Piet Hein, 1950], pp. 34-35).
**Kuyper adds that in this struggle of classes, the wealthy and powerful have not hesitated to bend the state to their purposes: "The ineradicable inequality between men gave the stronger an advantage over the weaker, and as though an animal rather than a human society were involved, produced a world in which the fixed rule prevails that the stronger devours the weaker; and the stronger, almost without exception, have always known how to bend every usage and magistral ordinance so that

Only if we once again see society not as a heap of souls on a piece of ground, but as a God-willed community, as a living human organism, can there be a cure to the misery of poverty. And that, says Kuyper, is "the socialist path"—"I do not shrink from the word," he says, provided one not identify socialism with the program of the Social Democrats. A program, though, is indeed necessary—a program of social reform. Piety and charity are not sufficient, for it is a *social* question we are dealing with; and furthermore,

> this one thing is necessary if a social question is to exist for you: that you realize the *untenability* of the present situation, and that you realize this untenability to be one not of incidental causes, but one involving the very *basis* of our social association. For one who does *not* acknowledge this and who thinks that the evil can be exorcised through an increase in piety, through friendlier treatment or kindlier charity, there exists possibly a religious question and possibly a philanthropic question, but not a *social* question. This does not exist for you until you exercise an *architectonic* critique of human society itself and hence desire and think possible a different arrangement of the social structure. [21]

Implicit in what I have said about shalom, as it is in what Calvin and Kuyper are saying, is that we as human beings have *sustenance* rights. We have a claim on our fellow human beings to social arrangements that ensure that we will be adequately sustained in existence. No doubt this right, like others, can be forfeited; perhaps it is forfeited if a person refuses to work when decent work is available. And no doubt, as with other rights, there are social situations in which the right is abrogated—as, for example, when there are no arrangements that other parties can make to ensure our sustenance. But the deepest answer to the question "Why care about the poor?" is that if we do not, we are violating the God-given *rights* of the poor person.

We might consider four kinds of rights (without suggesting that this is in any way an exhaustive list): (1) rights to protection, as, for example, the right to protection against assault on the street; (2) rights to freedom, as, for example, the right to free speech; (3) rights to voice or participation, as, for example, the right to a voice in selecting the officials of one's government; and (4) rights to sustenance. We in the modern West have been great defenders of

---

the profit was theirs and the loss was for the weaker. Men did not literally eat each other like the cannibals, but the more powerful exploited the weaker by means of a weapon against which there was no defense. And whenever the magistrate did come forward as a servant of God to protect the weaker, the more powerful class of society soon knew how to exercise such an overpowering influence on the government that the governmental power which should have protected the weaker became an instrument against them" (*Christianity and the Class Struggle*, p. 22).

the rights of protection, freedom, and voice—more consistently in theory, admittedly, than in practice—but not even in theory have we in general acknowledged the rights of sustenance. Although our century has seen the rise of the welfare state in all our countries, that has not been because the right to sustenance has been incorporated into our fundamental bills of rights or because it belongs to the liberal ideology that gave rise to our systems. The classic liberal's prescription for the good life is just: do your own thing, but do not interfere with your neighbor. I think I do not speak too cynically when I say that the rise of the welfare state occurred because an increase in the buying power of the laboring force expanded the market of the owners of capital, and because here and there the poor managed to exert some power. With the political transformation presently taking place in the United States, I hear a great deal of talk about various rights to freedom and protection, but I hear nothing about rights to sustenance, nothing about the rights of the poor.[22]

The churches have not helped the situation. All too often when commenting on the rise of the welfare state they have spoken of the distribution of welfare as an act of generosity on the part of the government. Some have then insisted that the government had no business engaging in acts of generosity, that it should confine itself to ensuring rights of protection, freedom, and voice. Others have praised this new development in which the government acts generously toward its citizenry. I want to say, as emphatically as I can, that our concern with poverty is not an issue of generosity but of rights. If a rich man knows of someone who is starving and has the power to help that person but chooses not to do so, then he violates the starving person's rights as surely and reprehensibly as if he had physically assaulted the sufferer. Acknowledging this truth may make us uncomfortable, but it is a conclusion we must draw from our reflections on shalom and the solidarity of all humanity in the image of God.[23]

Furthermore, sustenance rights are *basic* rights, in the sense that they essay to guarantee life itself—without which, of course, all other rights are meaningless. In that way they are more fundamental than most of the rights on which we in the Western democracies have focussed our attention. Freedom of speech is important for the attainment of much that is good in human life, but one can enjoy a large number of rights without enjoying freedom of speech: it remains contingent upon the more essential rights of sustenance.

To clarify this point, perhaps I ought to say a bit about what I take a right to be. I take it that a person has a right to some good if (1) he or she has a *morally legitimate claim* that (2) the *actual enjoyment* of that good be (3) *socially guaranteed* against *ordinary, serious, and remediable threats*. Let me say a few words about each of these components in the concept of a right.

First, a right is a morally legitimate claim on others. One person's right places an obligation, a responsibility, on others. Rights are grounded in responsibilities—they are the opposite of undeserved generosity—and responsibilities I take to belong to the very essence of what it is to be human. What distinguishes us human beings from God's other earthly creatures is that we alone were given responsibilities. Although not all responsibilities involve rights, all rights involve responsibilities. The American philosopher Joel Feinberg speaks eloquently of the significance of the fact that rights are claims imposing obligations:

> Claim-rights are indispensably valuable possessions. A world without claim-rights, no matter how full of benevolence and devotion to duty, would suffer an immense moral impoverishment. Persons would no longer hope for decent treatment from others on the ground of desert or rightful claim. Indeed, they would come to think of themselves as having no special claim to kindness or consideration from others, so that whenever even minimally decent treatment is forthcoming they would think themselves lucky rather than inherently deserving, and their benefactors extraordinarily virtuous and worthy of great gratitude. The harm to individual self-esteem and character development would be incalculable.
>
> A claim-right, on the other hand, can be urged, pressed, or rightly demanded against other persons. In appropriate circumstances the right-holder can "urgently, peremptorily, or insistently" call for his rights, or assert then authoritatively, confidently, unabashedly. Rights are not mere gifts or favors, motivated by love or pity, for which gratitude is the sole fitting response. A right is something that can be demanded or insisted upon without embarrassment or shame. When that to which one has a right is not forthcoming, the appropriate reaction is indignation; when it is duly given there is no reason for gratitude, since it is simply one's own or one's due that one received. A world with claim-rights is one in which all persons, as actual or potential claimants, are dignified objects of respect, both in their own eyes and in the view of others. No amount of love and compassion, or obedience to higher authority, or noblesse oblige, can substitute for those values.[24]

Second, a right is the claim to the *actual enjoyment* of the good in question—not a claim to being promised the good in question, and not a claim to the legal proclamation of the good in question, but the claim to its actual enjoyment. If the law says that you and I have the right to freedom of speech, whereas in fact there is some threat imposed on me whenever I seek to obtain that good, then my right to free speech is being violated no matter what the law says. The law in that case is hollow.

Third, a right is the claim to one's enjoyment of the good in question

being socially guaranteed against ordinary and serious, but remediable, threats—
against *ordinary* threats because of course there are all sorts of threats to our
enjoyment of various goods that are so rare or unpredictable that one cannot
reasonably ask that social arrangements be implemented to take account of
them; against *serious* threats because some threats are too trivial to spend time
on; and against *remediable* threats. What is remediable changes of course from
time to time: today leprosy is remediable, whereas previously it was not.

A right, then, is a claim to a social arrangement that will ensure that
one will not be deprived of the enjoyment of the good in question by ordinary,
serious, or remediable threats. Rights always involve social structures of one
sort or another.* They consist in a claim on one's fellows to the effect that
society be structured in such a way as to give reasonable assurance that the good
in question can in fact be enjoyed.**

Seeing that rights are claims to guarantees against threats makes clear
that rights are God's charter for the weak and defenseless ones in society. A
right is the legitimate claim for protection of those too weak to help themselves.
It is the legitimate claim of the defenseless against the more devastating and
common of life's threats which, at that time and place, are remediable. It is the
claim of the little ones in society to restraint upon economic and political and
physical forces that would otherwise be too strong for them to resist.

Before leaving this topic of rights, we should consider the *duties*
correlative to rights. Those duties, I think, can typically be divided into three
types: (1) duties to *avoid depriving* people of the good in question, (2) duties to
help protect them from deprivation, and (3) duties to *aid* the deprived in the
event that deprivation does occur. When Calvin thundered from his pulpit
against the rich in his city who were victimizing the poor, he was emphasizing
the first sort of duty, the duty to avoid depriving people of sustenance. When
Kuyper said that our duties to the poor go beyond charity and that we must

*Thus there is an intimate connection between architectonic (i.e., struc-
tural) critique of society, and concern with rights.

**"Being socially guaranteed is probably the single most important aspect
of a standard right, because it is the aspect that necessitates correlative duties. A right
is ordinarily a justified demand that some other people make some arrangements so
that one will still be able to enjoy the substance of the right even if—actually, *especially*
if—it is not within one's own power to arrange on one's own to enjoy the substance
of the right. Suppose people have a right to physical security. Some of them may
nevertheless choose to hire their own private guards, as if they had no right to social
guarantees. But they would be justified, and every one else is justified, in demanding
that somebody somewhere make some effective arrangements to establish and maintain
security. . . . Usually, perhaps, the arrangement will take the form of law, making
the rights legal as well as moral ones. But in other cases, well-entrenched customs,
backed by taboos, might serve better than laws—certainly better than unenforced
laws" (Henry Shue, *Basic Rights: Subsistence, Affluence, and U.S. Foreign Policy* [Prince-
ton: Princeton University Press, 1980], p. 16).

concern ourselves with oppressive structures, he was emphasizing the importance of duties of the second sort, duties to help protect people from deprivation
of sustenance.

My main contention now is this: among the minimal claims that all
of us make on our fellow human beings are social arrangements that will reasonably ensure our sustenance in the face of ordinary, serious, and remediable
threats. This includes, as I see it, the right to food, clothing, and shelter that
are adequate for sustaining health and making it possible to contribute to society;
the right to water and air that are not injurious to health; and the right to
elementary health care.* Naturally we can debate about what constitutes elementary medical care, about the degree of pollution in water and air that is
injurious to health, about the amount of food that is necessary for sustaining
health and making it possible to contribute to society. The fact is, however,
that by anyone's definition of these things, hundreds of millions of people in
modern society are being deprived of these goods while at the same time that
deprivation is in good measure remediable. Their rights are being denied them.

No doubt the most promising and dignity-respecting way of secur-
ing the sustenance rights of those impoverished masses in the non–core areas
of our world-system is not to give them doles, but to uncover the causes of
their systemic poverty and then work at eliminating those causes. I wish to say
a few words about those causes; but let me first say that even if we fail to
understand those causes very well, or even if we understand them but find that
there is relatively little that we can do to eliminate them, nonetheless we still
have a duty to the impoverished of the world—the duty to aid them. The rich
man who does not know how to prevent poverty and uses that as an excuse
for not aiding the poor is nonetheless trampling on the rights of the poor man
and thereby, as Calvin would say, violating God himself in his image. The
United States in its fiscal 1981 budget proposed to spend $160.4 billion on
armaments for itself and $6.2 billion on economic aid to other countries (this
is not to mention the armaments it disperses around the world in the form of
military aid to its friends). Of the economic aid, in turn, a good deal goes not
to alleviate mass poverty but to assist already well-to-do nations; for example,
$800 million was earmarked for Israel. All this is a violation of sustenance rights
of such enormous proportions as to cry out to heaven for recompense.

During the period from the end of World War II until just recently,

*Cf. Article 25 of the Universal Declaration of Human Rights of the
United Nations: 'Everyone has the right to a standard of living adequate for health
and well-being of himself and of his family, including food, clothing, housing and
medical care and necessary social services, and the right to security in the event of
unemployment, sickness, disability, widowhood, old age or other lack of livelihood
in circumstances beyond his control.''

the dominant view among people in the West as to the causes of mass poverty in the Third World probably went something like this: poverty or near–poverty is more or less the normal state of mankind. However, we in the West over the past few centuries have constructed a modernized society which has eliminated, or is capable of eliminating, poverty among us. The Third World has been more or less untouched by these developments and thus remains in the state normal for mankind. The crucial stimuli for modernization are technology and capital. Accordingly, if we make these available to the Third World and achieve their participation in a world-wide system of trade, their development will begin and they will eventually catch up with us.

This, I say, was the popular belief until recently. Today ordinary individuals are under the impression that although the United States and its allies have given a great deal of aid in the form of technology and capital to the underdeveloped countries, nothing much has come of it. They hear, indeed, that the income gap is *widening*.* They do not know what to make of this; they are hesitant to fall back on the old explanations which allege some sort of character fault in people of the Third World, but they no longer know what else to think. Perhaps the underdeveloped nations just need more private enterprise!

I submit that these views concerning the roots of mass poverty are almost entirely mistaken and that their popularity among academics and the general public can only be attributed to the fact that it serves our self-interest to hold them. I shall here have to confine myself to sketching in broad outline the points at which they go wrong.

In the first place, the mass poverty of the Third World is for the most part not some sort of natural condition that exists independently of us; quite the contrary, a good deal of it is the result of the interaction of the core of the world-system with the periphery over the course of centuries. In many areas there has been a development of underdevelopment, and we in the core have played a crucial role in that development. Underdevelopment has a history, a history inseparable from ours.

Here I shall have to confine myself to a single illustrative example: Bangladesh, which has perhaps the greatest concentration of mass poverty in

*On this point they are correct: "In 1850 today's rich countries accounted for 26 per cent of the total population of the world and for about 35 per cent of its total income. In the 1960s the rich countries accounted for 28 per cent of the population (not much changed from 1850) but 78 per cent of the total income. The difference between the per capita incomes of the poor and rich countries increased from 70 per cent in 1850 to 900 per cent in 1960" (Hans W. Singer and Javed A. Ansari, *Rich and Poor Countries* [Baltimore: Johns Hopkins University Press, 1977], p. 34). And this, of course, takes no account of the discrepancies within the poor countries between rich and poor.

the world. Other cases differ in their details, but the same dynamics are operative in all. To begin with, we must realize that Asia was not impoverished when the European traders first came into contact with it. A historian of Indonesia remarks that "when the first Dutch merchants and sailors had come to the island world of the Indies, they had been amazed by the variety of its nature and civilization, and the more observant among them had recognized that southern and eastern Asia were far ahead of western Europe in riches as well as in commercial ability and mercantile skill."[25]* The letter from the Emperor of China to King George III of England in 1793, already cited in an earlier chapter, is also relevant here: "As your Ambassador can see for himself, we possess all things. I set no value on objects strange or ingenious, and have no use for your country's manufactures." The subcontinent of India was similarly prosperous, with a stable mixture of agriculture and small-scale manufacture.

In the late 1700s, the British, after gaining control of the whole Indian subcontinent by force of arms, began deliberately to alter its economic and social structure. In the area of Bangladesh, the land was being worked by peasants who paid an annual tribute to an overseer class of *zamindars,* who in turn passed some of it on to the Mogul rulers of the area, retaining the remainder for themselves. The bond between peasant and zamindar was far more than merely economic, however, The zamindars guaranteed protection to the peasants in return for rights of authority over them. For example, the peasants could not be arbitrarily dispossessed of their land so long as they paid the annual tribute. The zamindar had powers of both civil and criminal law in the territory, and the rights of both classes were mainly hereditary.[26]

This system was totally destroyed by the East India Company. The British, represented by traders and missionaries, felt that the institution of private property was insufficiently developed in Bangladesh.** In addition, tney

---

*Another historian of Indonesia, speaking of the beginning of the sixteenth century, has this to say: "Local emporia were the equal of anything Europe had to offer: indeed Malacca was at that time regarded by Western visitors as the greatest port for international commerce in the world, clearing annually more shipping than any other" (Malcolm Caldwell, *Indonesia,* Modern World Series, no. 16 [Oxford: Oxford University Press, 1968], p. 39). By the mid-1800s, however, famines were already wracking the region.

**It might be beneficial to remind ourselves here of the opinion of some members of the early church concerning private property. The great preacher of Constantinople John Chrysostom, for example, said in his sermon on 1 Tim. 4:13 that God has "made certain things common, as the sun, air, earth, and water, the heaven, the sea, the light, the stars; whose benefits are dispensed equally to all as brethren. We are all formed with the same eyes, the same body, the same soul, the same structure in all respects, all things from earth, all men from one man, and all in the same habitation. . . . He hath made common . . . baths, cities, marketplaces, walks. And observe, that concerning things that are common there is no contention, but all is peaceable. But when one attempts to possess himself of anything, to make it his own, then contention is introduced, as if nature herself were indignant, that when God

wanted a simple system of taxation and an upper class loyal to themselves. So they undertook to alter this quasi-feudal hereditary arrangement of mutual obligations into one based on private ownership and monetary relationships, with all land rights up for sale in the marketplace. In the Permanent Settlement of 1793, the zamindars were declared to be owners of the land from which they had been collecting tribute and were given full right to dispose of the land on the market. At the same time, all their official responsibilities were taken away from them and given to European civil servants. The peasants, correspondingly, became landless workers, and their traditional and permanent right to occupy and farm the land was taken away from them: the only relation left between peasant and zamindar was a purely economic one. The consequence of this destruction of all traditional social bonds was the exploitation of the peasants. They "were not only compelled to pay taxes, but also rents, which demographic development soon made outrageous; some peasants took to running away. A new law gave the *zamindars* the right to catch them, and this completed the dismemberment of traditional rural society. On the one hand, great landowners; serfs on the other; the former with no incentive to improve the land; the latter with no means to do so."[27]

But this was only the beginning. The production and weaving of cotton among the Bengalis had gained international fame; their cotton cloth was said to be the best in the world. This entire cotton industry was destroyed by the British, first by monopolistic contract arrangements executed by the East India Company, then by duties on imports of cloth from Bengal into England of about forty-four percent, and lastly by the flooding of the Bengal market with cheap manufactured goods after the industrial revolution was in full swing in England (with the capital financing the industrial revolution gotten in large measure from the plunder of the colonies). Similar things were done to the other industries of Bengal: self-sufficient agriculture was replaced by cash-crop farming; the traditional artisan skills were destroyed by heavy duties on exports and floods of cheap, mass-produced imports; and a transportation infrastructure (roads, railroads, etc.) was developed entirely for the purposes of foreign trade and imperial control. The British wanted from Bengal a cheap, competition-free source of raw materials and a monopolistic market for their

---

brings us together in every way, we are eager to divide and separate ourselves by appropriating things, and by using those cold words 'mine and thine.' Then there is contention and uneasiness. But where this is not, no strife or contention is bred. . . . Things necessary are set before us in common; but even in the least things we do not observe a community. Yet those greater things He hath opened freely to all, that we might thence be instructed to have these inferior things in common" (*A Select Library of the Nicene and Post-Nicene Fathers of the Christian Church*, ed. Philip Schaff [Grand Rapids, Mich.: Eerdmans, 1956], vol. 13, *St. Chrysostom: Homilies on Galatians, Ephesians, Colossians, Thessalonians, Timothy, Titus, and Philemon*, p. 448 [Homily 12]).

own manufactured goods, and they got what they wanted. In the process they pushed Bangladesh decisively into the pit of underdevelopment. Today Bangladesh is almost entirely dependent on one cash crop for its export earnings; in 1975-76, jute and jute products accounted for eighty-two percent of the value of its exports.

Speaking of India in general, Jawaharlal Nehru said this in 1946:

> Nearly all our major problems today have grown up during British rule and as a direct result of British policy: the princes; the minority problem; various vested interests, foreign and Indian; the lack of industry and the neglect of agriculture; the extreme backwardness in the social services; and, above all, the tragic poverty of the people. . . .
>
> A significant fact which stands out is that those parts of India which have been longest under British rule are the poorest today. Indeed some kind of chart might be drawn up to indicate the close connection between length of British rule and progressive growth of poverty.[28]

Fundamentally the same tale could be told for almost all the other areas of the world that today experience mass poverty. At some point each area came into intimate contact with the core of the world-system, and its economy was altered to benefit the Europeans rather than the natives.[29] The social structure was upset and replaced by one in which there were few if any bonds of obligation tying the upper class to the lower.[30] And all of this was accomplished initially by the use at "suitable" points of force of arms. "Europe did not 'discover' the underdeveloped countries; on the contrary, she created them. . . . Some of the peoples with whom the Europeans came into contact were, of course, relatively primitive. But nearly all of the people encountered in today's underdeveloped areas were members of viable societies which could satisfy the economic needs of the community. Yet these societies were shattered when they came into contact with an expanding Europe."[31]

In their book *Global Reach*, Richard J. Barnet and Ronald E. Müller give a vivid description of what, as the result of their interaction with the core areas, one finds today when one visits one of the poor countries of the Third World:

> What a curious contradiction of rags and riches. One out of every ten thousand persons lives in a palace with high walls and gardens and a Cadillac in the driveway. A few blocks away hundreds are sleeping in the streets, which they share with beggars, chewing-gum hawkers, prostitutes, and shoeshine boys. Around the corner tens of thousands are jammed in huts without electricity or plumbing.

Outside the city most of the population scratches out a bare sub-sistence on small plots, many owned by the few who live behind the high walls. Even where the soil is rich and the climate agreeable most people go to sleep hungry. The stock market is booming, but babies die and children with distended bellies and spindly legs are everywhere. There are luxurious restaurants and stinking open sew-ers. The capital boasts late-model computers and receives jumbo jets every day, but more than half of the people cannot read. Govern-ment offices are major employers of those who can, but the creaky bureaucracy is a joke except to the long line of suppliants who come seeking medical help or a job. (For suppliants with money for a bribe the lines shorten miraculously.)

Nationalist slogans are prominent, but the basic indus-tries are in the hands of foreigners. The houses behind the walls are filled with imported cameras, TV's, tape recorders, and fine furni-ture from the United States or Europe, but the major family in-vestment is likely to be a Swiss bank account. There appear to be three groups in the country distinguishable by what they consume. A tiny group live on a scale that would make a Rockefeller squirm. A second group, still relatively small in number, live much like the affluent middle class in the United States—the same cars, the same Scotch, the same household appliances. The vast majority eat pic-turesque native foods like black beans, rice, and lentil soup—in small quantities. The first two groups are strong believers in individual development for themselves and their family, but they see no so-lution for the growing plight of the third group. So they fear them, and their walls grow higher. For the third group disease, filth, and sudden death are constant companions, but there is an air of resig-nation about them. Life has always been full of pain and uncertainty and it always will be.[32]

Once a country such as Bangladesh has fallen into the pit of mass poverty, it is almost impossible, in our modern world, for it to get out. Among the factors that keep it there are the following: most of the poverty in the Third World is rural poverty, simply because that is where most of the population is to be found. In the United States less than ten percent of the population is rural; in India, about seventy percent is. This large rural labor force is grossly under-used. One would expect labor-intensive farming; instead, one finds labor-*extensive* farming. Many people work only part of the year; when they do work, it is typically only for part of the day—and during that part of the day, they work inefficiently. In part this is due to the fact that little work is avilable; in part, to the fact that the laborers are often so poorly nourished that they lack the energy to do superior work.

The introduction of better nutrition and of appropriate forms of labor-intensive agricultural technology would immediately raise the level of agricultural production, but to this there are obstacles. Most of the poor are illiterate, and few have any savings to invest in technology; all they acquire must be consumed for sustenance. But the decisive block to improvement is that the poor are a virtually landless labor force working for wealthy and powerful landowners, often on plantations growing cash crops for export. Since the poor have few hopes that their plight will change, they have little motivation to improve the yield of their labor (and the landowners, in any case, have very little motivation to improve the yield of their land). In short, the social inequity of the landowning institution produces a certain attitude, the so-called "culture of poverty": since the workers see no hope of improving their condition, they adopt a quite reasonable thoroughgoing indifference. "I draw the conclusion," says Gunnar Myrdal in his classic *Challenge of World Poverty,*

> and find it confirmed by a great number of intensive studies which have been made, that in South Asia the sharecropping system stands as the cause of a complex of inhibitions and obstacles which work effectively against any attempts to improve technology and increase labor utilization and yields: such a system "constitutes [an] all-but-insuperable disincentive to vigorous participation in development by the rural masses and not only an affront to social justice."

He goes on to say that he has a less thorough personal experience of the Latin American system of landowning and farm labor, but that,

> according to what I have read and the few observations I have been in a position to make, that system—which also often contains elements of the sharecropping system—is equally inimical to technological advance which would raise labor utilization and yields.[33]

In short, *"greater equality is a precondition for lifting a society out of poverty."*[34]*

I have spoken of the "culture of poverty," by which I mean a type of character formation prominent among the poor whereby they do not even try to escape from their poverty. Thinkers such as Michael Novak have in recent years taken to suggesting that this type of character formation is in fact the decisive cause of mass poverty, and that religion is, in turn, the decisive

---

*Compare this passage from a report of the Secretariat of the Economic Commission for Latin America: "The bulk of the rural population has no surplus income and not even enough land to permit an increase in investment, while those who own most of the land and income are seldom interested in developing their property, stepping up production and raising productivity, or have the capacity to do so. The profits made on large estates are hardly ever ploughed back into the land; instead they are spent on urban investment and luxury consumption, or sent out of the country. Under the existing tax systems, the State is unable to collect a large enough proportion of these profits to increase its investment in agriculture" (quoted by Gunnar Myrdal, *The Challenge of World Poverty: A World Anti-Poverty Program in Outline* [New York: Random House-Vintage, 1970], p. 102).

cause of the character formation. (In this there is of course a strong echo of the Weber thesis.) Novak, himself a Catholic, has criticized the Catholic church of South America for inculcating attitudes that perpetuate poverty, and others have criticized Hinduism for doing the same in Asia.

No doubt it is true that where one finds the character formation of poverty, one also typically finds that character formation undergirded by religion. And it cannot be doubted that the character formation of poverty and the religious attitudes intertwined with it will have to change if the people are to emerge from their poverty. But the thesis of Novak *et al.* has at least two fatal flaws. In the first place, it ignores how the great impoverished areas of the modern world became impoverished; it is one more ahistorical version of modernization theory, which simply looks at a segment of the world *now* and then locates the causes of its poverty in factors *internal* to that area. I have argued, on the contrary, that in very many cases, the mode of interaction between the core and the periphery over the years has contributed significantly to the development of impoverishment. In the second place, the thesis fails to face up to what is necessary to escape from impoverishment. One can try preaching a "Protestant" capitalist work ethic to the impoverished masses of the world; one can even undergird one's preachments with religion. But those preachments will be in vain until this "ethic" has some social plausibility—and I have argued, as has Myrdal, that in the absence of social and economic structural reforms it will have no such plausibility. The truth is surely that not only does a religion of acquiescence in poverty undergird the character formation of poverty and thereby perpetuate poverty itself, but also that poverty from which one can see no escape is a powerful stimulus to the emergence and maintenance of the character formation of poverty and to the acceptance of a religion of acquiescence in poverty. Not only does religion shape society, but society shapes religion.

Incidentally, the liberation theologians share with Novak *et al.* the conviction that the culture of poverty must be broken and that a new character formation which they call "conscientization," must be shaped. But they are persuaded that an awareness of domination and exploitation as contributing to poverty, and a determination to throw off these shackles must be components of this conscientization. I think it would be a gross misreading of what they are saying and doing to suppose that they do not also see that new and positive attitudes toward economic initiative are required. Novak wants them to remove the "revolutionary" component from their program of conscientization. Their replay is that in the absence of social reconstruction, the character development required for "development" is impossible.

Everyone who has studied the matter agrees that the pressure of population is also a decisive factor in the perpetuation of mass poverty. The mortality rate in Third World countries has improved, mainly as the result of the distribution of the benefits of modern hygiene and medicine, but the birthrate has not declined. The result is an extraordinarily rapid increase in population, putting ever greater demands on the agricultural production and at the same time making it ever more impossible for the worker to accumulate savings for investment.

Myrdal cites one more factor as contributing decisively to the perpetuation of mass poverty—namely, what he calls the "soft state." Characteristic of the Third World countries, as the legacy of their interaction with the Europeans, is a serious lack of social discipline and effective administration. Laws are passed but never enforced, plans are approved but never implemented, regulations are instituted but never administered, and corruption is rampant. It takes little insight to see that it is the wealthy and powerful and not the poor who benefit from this sort of social anarchy.

It should be evident that if these are the dynamics perpetuating mass poverty in the Third World, an infusion of aid in adequate quantities might alleviate the poverty but would do nothing at all toward undoing its perpetuation. Even an insertion of labor-intensive agricultural technology is pointless in the face of inequities that deprive workers of all incentive to increase their productivity, deprive them of virtually all education, and make them constantly the victims of the wealthy and powerful who manipulate the soft state to their advantage.

What is needed is land reform, about which Myrdal says that *"the one requirement any type of land reform should meet is that it should create a relationship between man and land that does not thwart his incentives to work and to invest—if nothing else, to invest his own labor.* This will regularly require greater equality if the incentives are not to be operative only among a very small upper-class group."[35] What is also needed is control of the birthrate. The First World, for its own reasons, likes to treat mass poverty as if it were a problem of capital and technology; in fact, it is at bottom a *social/political* problem, and it proves to be to our economic advantage to act in collusion with the oligarchies of the Third World, rather than to act in solidarity with the poor. The one thing needful we refuse to do.

More must be said about our support of these Third World oligarchies, but first let us consider a question that naturally comes to mind: Does not the ultimate solution to the problem of Third World poverty lie in the introduction of more industry so that this huge labor force can be drawn away from the land? To this answer is yes—provided that the industrialization is of the right sort and provided that it draws enough laborers away. In fact, however, the form of industrialization that has been growing most rapidly in the Third World is exactly of the wrong sort—enterprises set up by producers and merchants from the core in order to make quick profits that make their way either out of the region altogether or into the coffers of Third World oligarchies, but scarcely at all back to those in greatest need.

Though the motivation governing the activities of the producers and merchants from the core in the periphery and semiperiphery of our world-system remains what it was in former centuries—*profit*—the general character of their activities in the semiperiphery has changed. As in times past, the areas outside the core still supply raw materials and foodstuffs to the core and still provide a market for some of the finished products of the core industries, but both of these are diminishing in importance in the semiperiphery.* One of the main developments since the Second World War has been the sale of technology and capital equipment in the semiperiphery, but even more important, the production of finished goods for consumption in the core has been moving from core to semiperiphery, in good measure under the aegis of multinational corporations. Volkswagens are now being made in Mexico, Zenith television sets in Hong Kong.

A number of factors have brought about these shifts from the core to the semiperiphery. The owners of capital have been confronted with rising labor costs in the core (though very recently these costs have been declining). On the one hand, this presents the owners of capital with an increasing market for their goods, since more people can afford to buy what is produced; but on the other hand, it increases their production costs and provides an incentive to seek out areas with lower labor costs. The semiperiphery is particularly attractive in this respect because it presents a significant industrial base as well as relatively cheap labor. There will usually be other advantages in this move as well: no strikes, lower taxes (since the states involved have at best minimal social welfare programs), and so on. For these reasons, the semiperiphery is most inviting to labor-intensive industries, but it is also beginning to attract some enterprises that are relatively capital-intensive. And in any case, if the production of a certain product is moved from the core to the periphery or semiperiphery, it is in general not produced in a more labor-intensive manner there than it was in the core. Volkswagen produces cars in Mexico in just as capital-intensive a manner as it does in Germany. This seems surprising, until

*The terms of the historical patterns of trade between the core and non-core areas has seldom been to the equal advantage of both of the trade partners (see Myrdal, *Challenge of World Poverty*, pp. 275-309, and Andre Gunder Frank, *Dependent Accumulation and Underdevelopment* [New York: Monthly Review Press, 1979], pp. 92-139). Nevertheless, I am not trying to make any general claims to the effect that the core has always had the advantage over the non-core in its trading arrangements, nor indeed that unequal advantage always implies unjust exploitation of one of the partners by the other. Furthermore, I am not suggesting that, all things considered, the non-core areas would have been better off had they been spared all interaction with the core. My concern is simply with examining the origins and perpetuation of poverty.

one reflects that the production technology which Volkswagen has developed over the years is a capital-intensive technology.

The result of these dynamics is that these new industries moving into the semiperiphery use only a very small proportion of the native labor force, and they buy that labor at suppressed—often at *extremely* suppressed—wages. Since the products produced are meant for the core (and for the wealthy minority in the periphery), the wages paid to the workers function purely as cost; they are not viewed as enabling the workers to purchase the goods produced:

> The motto now is to work for the world market rather than for the internal market. Effective demand on the national market is not, and is not intended to be, the source of demand for national production; demand on the world market is, and is intended to be, the source of market demand. Therefore there is no reason to raise the wages of the direct producers, because they are not destined to purchase the goods that they produce. Instead the goods are supposed to be purchased on the world market far away. An important exception is the small local market of the high-income receivers, which is supposed to expand. Thus, there is a polarization of income, not only between developed and undeveloped countries on the global level, but also on the national level, with the poor getting poorer and the rich getting richer.[36]

The profits from these enterprises do not entirely return to the core.[37] They are shared with the investors and administrators from the middle and upper classes in the semiperiphery—among whom are to be found the land-owners of whom we spoke earlier. Accordingly, it is also in their interests to keep labor costs down in their own countries, to prohibit strikes, to see to it that social welfare programs that require increases in taxation on business are not introduced, etc., since insofar as the living conditions of the labor force in these areas begin to resemble those of the labor force in the core, these enterprises will no longer find it profitable to move from core to non-core areas. The dynamics of the system actively prevent the gap from narrowing. Naturally such policies require political repression.[38]

There is, then, an alliance of interests between business enterprises from the core and oligarchies from the non-core.[39] And once one sees this, then many otherwise puzzling actions of governments from core countries become clear—especially in the case of the American government. It is obvious to all that around the world today, the United States supports repressive regimes that declare themselves in favor of free enterprise and prove hospitable to American businesses. While United States citizens themselves enjoy great freedom of speech and action, their government effectively undermines these freedoms for many others by combatting opposition to the oppressors in friendly periphery states.

The curious behavior of the United States, then, is partially attributable to a simple protection of its business interests in non-core areas.[40] But beyond this, there are also serious political motivations for its support of repressive Third World regimes: ofttimes these states are perceived to be battlegrounds for superpower ideologies—specifically, they are seen to pose the threat of the incursion of Soviet communism. The United States feels compelled to support avowedly anti-communist regimes even in the face of evidence that they are oppressive if the alternative would be a communist takeover that would bring yet worse oppression. The international left regards this anti-communist dogma of the United States to be nothing more than an opportunistic screen for crass economic protectionism, and indeed such cynicism is significantly widespread beyond its ranks as well. But it must also be taken into consideration that the people of the United States do have a genuine, deep-seated abhorrence of communism as they find it in the world today, and particularly as it has been realized in the Soviet Union and its East European satellites. That abhorrence is entirely justified: these are tyrannies such as the world has seldom seen. I would suggest that American opposition to Soviet communism is both genuine and right.

In this regard, two points must be made, however. First, the opposition to oppression in the Third World today has, in most cases, nothing at all to do with Soviet communism. It is sheer gullibility to believe the self-serving tales of the Third World regimes to the contrary. If there were no Soviet communism on the face of the earth, there would still be such opposition—*and ought to be*. In addition, it should be noted that the United States conducts its opposition to communism in such a way that the oppression it supports in the Third World mirrors the oppression that the communist states wreak on their own citizens. This irony is coupled with another: in *their* pursuit of profit in the Third World, *the communist states* mirror the behavior of the American businesses.[41] Double irony! What the poor and oppressed of the Third World see of the actions of these two superpowers makes them almost indistinguishable from each other.

I do not doubt that the United States would much prefer that the governments it supports be less repressive, more "moderate." The hard truth, however, is that it cannot both give blanket support to the interests of its businesses and also find nonrepressive regimes to support in the Third World: *its policy is self-contradictory*. In their Third World ventures, American businesses seek low wages, low taxes, and freedom from strikes. The evidence is abundant, and particularly convincing to the poor, who are being bombarded with evidence that others manage to amass wealth, that it is impossible to achieve these goals apart from the employment of political repression. The repressiveness of Third World politics is not accidental, and as a responsible party, the United States must choose whether it will take the side of the poor and oppressed of the world or whether it will support the activities of its businesses and their allies in the Third World. It is an illusion to think it can do both, although it has nursed that illusion for twenty-five years, saying that poverty was just a problem of capital and technology and that, accordingly, it was not necessary to take sides. The illusion is now shattered.

But what do the people in the First World who acknowledge the claim of the poor on them do in our present situation? Well, they do not, in my judgment, spend their time putting forth proposals for a New International Economic Order. Economists and others have thrown up a flood of proposals over the past fifteen years for alleviating the plight of the poor.[42] Some of them, if implemented, would undoubtedly help. But it would be a waste of time to spend much time with any of them, since many have already been presented by the Third World to the First in a long series of conferences, and all but the most trivial have been rejected. The situation is not that we in the West (and the East!) want to help the poor but do not know how; the situation is that we know how but do not want to. It is now clear that mass poverty is not the normal situation of mankind, nor is it the consequence of the actions of a few aberrant individuals. It is in good measure the effect of our world-wide economic system and of the political structures that support it—of the unregulated and unqualified pursuit of profit by enterprises from the core, of systems of land ownership in the Third World that deprive workers of all incentive, of repressive governments in the Third World supported by those of the core, of aid programs designed not to help the poor but to win skirmishes in the contest of the superpowers. It has become clear that the First World does not want to change these institutions and these practices. After fifteen years of plans we are back at the starting gate.

What must be done is elementary: we must work patiently and persistently to show people the causes of mass poverty, and we must do what we can to convince them that one of the fundamental criteria by which all political and economic institutions and practices must be tested is just this: What do they do to the poor? If they perpetuate poverty, they fail the most important test of legitimacy, and in that case we must struggle to alter them. In God's Kingdom of shalom there are no poor and there is no tyranny. We must work for the day when practices that perpetuate poverty will have lost their legitimacy in the eyes of the people. When that day comes, we can talk of plans. Until that day comes, plans are mere daydreams. As we set out on this new path, those of us who are Christians will be able to learn much from our fellow Christians in the Third World—if we are granted the humility to listen.

Let me close by quoting some passages from "An Open Letter to North American Christians," signed by thirteen Christians from Latin America, most if not all of whom are leaders in the Protestant churches there:

Our Brothers and Sisters:

. . . Can you comprehend the reason for our preoccupation [with your election of a new president]? [It] is due to the fact that we—with the exception of Cuba—are trapped in the same system. We all move within one economic-political-military complex in which one finds fabulous interests of [the] financial groups that dominate the life of your country and the creole oligarchies of our Latin American nations. Both groups, more allied today than ever, have held back time after time, the great transformations that our people need and desperately demand. . . .

Today, we Latin Americans are discovering that, apart from our own weaknesses and sins, not a few of our misfortunes, miseries and frustrations flow from and are perpetuated within a system that produces substantial benefits for your country but goes on swallowing us more and more in oppression, in impotence, in death. In a few words: Your precious "American Way of Life"—the opulence of your magnates, your economic and military dominion—feeds in no small proportion on the blood that gushes, according to one of our most brilliant essayists, "from the open veins of Latin America." . . .

All this, our brothers and sisters, is carried out in the name of "democracy," in the name of "western Christian civilization," on the backs of our people, and with the benediction and the support of your government, of your armed forces, without which our dictators could not maintain themselves in power for much time.

Friends and fellow Christians, it is time that you realize that our continent is becoming one gigantic prison, and in some regions one vast cemetery; that human rights, the grand guidelines of the Gospel, are becoming a dead letter, without force. And all this in order to maintain a system, a structure of dependency, that benefits the mighty privileged persons of your land and of our land, at the expense of the poor millions who are increasing throughout the width and breadth of the continent.

. . . This letter seeks to be an anguished, fervent call to your conscience and to your responsibility as Christians.

If in the past you felt it to be your apostolic duty to send us missionaries and economic resources, today the frontier of your witness and Christian solidarity is within your own country. The conscious, intelligent and responsible use of your vote, the appeal to your representatives in the Congress, and the application of pressure by various means on your authorities can contribute to changing the course of our governments toward paths of greater justice and brotherhood or to accentuate a colonialist and oppressive policy over our people. In this sense you must ask yourselves if you will or will not be "your brother's keeper" in these lands of America, from which the blood of millions of Abels is clamoring to heaven.

We, between tears and groans, are interceding for you in order that you may respond with faithfulness to the historic responsibility that as citizens of one of the great contemporary powers and as disciples of Jesus Christ it falls on you to assume. . . .[43]

Chapter V

Nation Against Nation

In searching out the root causes of injustice and misery in the modern world, we will inevitably be brought face to face with the fact that profit seeking is able to enlist great power in its service for the exploitation of the weak and helpless. But in addition to the economic sources of injustice, there is another pervasive and malignant force at work: again and again we are confronted by misguided and excessive loyalty to nation.

Keeping in mind the distinction we made in Chapter II between *nations* (peoples) and *states* (discrete ultimate political authorities), we would note that oppression within a state is often a result of the aggrandizement by the state of one of its constituent nations at the expense of its remaining citizenry not belonging to the favored nation. Similarly, we often discover that a given state will terrorize its neighbors with subversion and a buildup of armaments because its single highest priority is to protect the interests of its own nation.

It is to the dynamic of loyalty to nation that I now turn, with the understanding that it is not merely one more dynamic that I address: the practices involved with the pursuit of profit and loyalty to nation are not independent of one another; they are intimately intertwined. The consequences of the pursuit of profit can be seen to intensify loyalty to nation again and again, and loyalty to nation can be seen variously to restrain and energize the pursuit of profit in different circumstances. Between these two vastly compelling dynamics the modern state, with all its powers for violence, is caught.

Many nations and many states, but one economy—that is what characterizes the social system in which we find ourselves today: it is a *world*-system. A world-system, you will recall, is by definition a social unit that has one "ecumenical" economy straddling a diversity of nations; more specifically, it is a world-economy, because its single integrated economy straddles not only a diversity of nations, but a diversity of states as well. In earlier ages, nation, state, and economy were tightly unified, but in the modern world they have pulled loose from one another, and the economy has expanded to integrate diverse nations and states into one system. Indeed, that economy has expanded to the point that it now encircles the entire globe. In the preceding chapters we have focussed principally on the structure and dynamics of the *economy* in our world-system, but now we shall turn to a consideration of the role of *nations* in this world-economy.

The social analysis that I have to this point pursued has close affinities to the "radical" tradition of social analysis. From here on, however, our paths sharply diverge. From the radical tradition one gets no worthwhile analysis of the role of nations in our social order. That is no accident. The radicals doubt that loyalty to nation is a significant force in the shaping of the modern social world. They think that the lure of profit and resistance to perceived exploitation are significant forces, but that devotion to nation comprises nothing more than a cluster of feelings and sentiments that serve as a way of escaping from and coping with the painfulness of social reality, including economic reality. They hear the head of the Chilean state appealing to all good Chileans, and they hear the head of the American state appealing to all good Americans (though they tend not to hear the head of the Polish state appealing to all good Poles); but they write off such appeals as ideological, as appealing to and reinforcing a false system of beliefs which, in the minds of those who consent to hold them, justify the exploitation they suffer or execute. Correspondingly, the radicals see the states of the West as *bourgeois* states rather than *nation* states. (And when they look at Eastern Europe, they think they see classless states, or perhaps proletarian states!) In contrast, I wish to argue that human beings do in fact act out of loyalty to nation in the modern world—vastly more than out of loyalty to class—and that one cannot understand our modern social world without seeing the presence of this dynamic within it.

The Basques are a nation, or a people—I shall use the words inter-changeably; the Frisians are a people; so too are the Germans. When we think of a nation, we think of a group of persons biologically continuous through time. The members of a nation, for the most part, are *born into* the nation. I think Martin Buber is right when he remarks that "kinship is not the *sine qua non* for the *origin* of a people. A people need not necessarily be the fusion of kindred stems; it can be the fusion of unrelated stems as well. But the concept 'people' always implies unity of fate. It presupposes that in a great creative hour throngs of human beings were shaped into a new entity by a great molding fate they experienced in common"; but as he goes on to remark, once a people has been formed, it "survives by dint of the kinship established from this moment on. . . ."[1] Persons who are not descended from members of the people can be incorporated into the nation, but the basis of a people's identity through time and across space consists in the fact that the paradigm members of the people are descended from persons who were themselves members of the people.

Kinship only provides a general basis for national unity, however. Cultural affinity is a tie that binds more strongly. A nation is bound together by shared practices—a common lifestyle which enables the members of the nation to work together and to communicate with one another on a broad spectrum of issues. Usually a common language is an important part of these shared practices. Although each new generation of a nation contributes to the formation of its lifestyle, all such formation is nothing more than a revision of a lifestyle bequeathed to it. What also binds together the members of a nation is their sharing certain *foci* of their existence: they jointly and severally hold in memory certain events and leaders, regard certain places as sacred, give allegiance to certain of their members, and so forth. The shared memories, in combination with the members' awareness of having received the basic outlines of their lifestyle from their predecessors, serve to make them conscious of their affinities with one another through time as well as across space. A nation is a complex biologico-historico-cultural grouping.

Of course there are other such groupings—clans and tribes, for example—and it is extraordinarily difficult to say what differentiates nations from these other generically similar groupings. (I shall make no attempt to do so.) But in any case, a nation is neither a territorial grouping nor a political grouping; it is defined neither as the people who live in a certain territory nor as the people who live under a certain government. Accordingly, nations can migrate from place to place on the earth, as so many of them have done, without thereby losing their identity. Likewise, they can be subjected to diverse states, as so many of them also have been, without thereby losing their identity. Migrations through territories and states characteristically intensify a nation's sense of its nationhood; indeed, it is often such migrations that first meld a group into a nation.

There is yet another feature of great importance to notice about nations: they are self-defining in the sense that their members characteristically maintain a distinction between who is a member and who is not. That means that the members have a concept of the group as such, vague though that concept may sometimes be. Frisians have a concept of their—i.e., the Frisian— nation; that concept does not have to be introduced to them. Not only do Frisians have and feel affinities for one another in the ways already indicated, but they have a concept of that *unit* which is the Frisian people, and they feel themselves to be members of it. Thus, the grouping of persons into nations is not first done by anthropologists for research purposes. The members of nations group *themselves* into nations; the question the anthropologist faces is only whether such self-defining social entities are worth his or her notice. What makes the identification of nations often so slippery is that different nations use different features to ground their self-definition (for some it is a shared language, for others it is custom or religion, etc.), and that they may shift from one feature to another over a period of time.

The fact that nations are self-defining is at the basis of two other phenomena that are of great importance for understanding the role of nations in the modern world. For one thing, it is characteristic of the members of nations to incorporate the fact of their membership into their understanding of their own personal identity, into their *self*-identification. They will of course do this with varying degrees of pride or embarrassment, joy or anger, dominance or recessiveness. Secondly, the fact that nations are self-defining makes it possible for members of a nation to be loyal to the nation as such—to be concerned for, and to work for, its welfare. This particular form of loyalty-to-one's-own should be seen for the remarkable thing it is.

In the modern world, loyalty to one's family amounts to little more than devotion to its immediate members. We no longer have a sense of a family line to which we can be loyal by seeing to it that it is perpetuated, by avenging insults to it, and so forth. Loyalty to nation, by contrast, has (often) survived the acids of modernity. Such loyalty is not devotion to the *members* of the nation, since most of these one does not know; rather, it is loyalty to the group as such, to this "abstract entity"—to the Frisian *people,* to the German *nation.* Of course, such loyalty is mediated by the concrete—by artifacts such as flags and national anthems, by rituals such as national celebrations, by recitations of episodes in the nation's history. But it should also be noted that one cannot understand the significance of national flags, anthems, and celebrations without grasping the concept of that abstract entity which is one's nation and apprehending the relation of these concrete items to that entity.

Now, I think that Christians will naturally feel some tension in their souls when they discover the presence there of feelings of loyalty to nation— as in an earlier day they would have felt tension when they discovered the presence there of such antecedents as loyalty to tribe, clan, city, and so on. As Christians, we are members of, and feel loyalty to, the church, which itself is a "holy nation" in the words of the first letter of Peter, but one that transcends and relativizes all ordinary, natural nations. In my judgment, the peculiar dividedness that this produces in the consciousness of the Christian has never been so well expressed as in one of the documents of the early church, called "The Epistle to Diognetus":

> the distinction between Christians and other men, is neither in country nor language nor customs. For they do not dwell in cities in some place of their own, nor do they use any strange variety of dialect, nor practice an extraordinary kind of life. . . . Yet while living in Greek and barbarian cities, according as each obtained his lot, and following the local customs, both in clothing and food and in the rest of life, they show forth the wonderful and confessedly strange character of the constitution of their own citizenship. They dwell in their own fatherlands, but as if sojourners in them; they share all things as citizens, and suffer all things as strangers. Every foreign country is their fatherland, and every fatherland is a foreign country.[2]

Here, unfortunately, we cannot linger to probe further this tension. Let me simply say that it seems to me that for most Christians today, loyalty to nation is more powerful than loyalty to church.

Indeed, I think it can be said that in the modern world nations have no strong competitors for loyalty except the family. Most of those groupings to which human beings once gave their loyalties have been destroyed by the dynamics of our world-system; between family and nation there is nothing. The pervasiveness of the profit motive in the public arena and of the pleasure motive in the private, coupled with the diminution of ascriptivism and the increase of free associationism, means that people are willing and able to pull up stakes and break all their concrete human ties for the sake of greener pastures elsewhere. We pick and choose among groups and organizations on the grounds of whether they serve our individual goals; we do not give our loyalty to *them* and serve *their* goals. Many of us in fact think it would be wrong to do so. We can live without them; they do not define our identity. The great exceptions remain family and nation. Let me quote Isaiah Berlin on the matter:

> The destruction of traditional hierarchies and orders of social life, in which men's loyalties were deeply involved, by the centralisation and bureaucratic 'rationalisation' which industrial progress required and generated, deprived great numbers of men of social and emotional security, produced the notorious phenomena of alienation, spiritual homelessness and growing anomie, and needed the creation, by deliberate social policy, of psychological equivalents for the lost cultural, political, religious values on which the older order rested. The socialists believed that class solidarity, the fraternity of the exploited, and the prospect of a just and rational society which the revolution would bring to birth, would provide this indispensable social cement; and indeed, to a degree it did. Moreover, some among the poor, the displaced, the deprived, emigrated to the New World. But for the majority the vacuum was filled neither by professional associations, nor political parties, nor . . . revolutionary myths . . . , but by the old, traditional bonds, language, the soil, historical memories real and imaginary, and by institutions or leaders which functioned as incarnations of men's conceptions of themselves as a community, a *Gemeinschaft*—symbols and agencies which proved far more powerful than either socialists or enlightened liberals wished to believe.[3]

In short, if one grants that in human beings there is the impulse, resistible perhaps but nonetheless strong, to give one's loyalty to some group, then the modern social order places us constantly before the threat that loyalty to nation will exceed its proper bounds, since it has almost no competitors.

The features of nations to which I have been pointing come in degrees. The lifestyles of the members of a nation may be more or less similar. The concept that the members have of their nation may be more or less clear, and more or fewer may have a relatively clear concept. Thus nationhood itself comes in degrees: a given group may be more or less of a nation. There is another feature of nations that is realized to different degrees in different nations; unlike the other features, however, it is entirely missing in some nations. I am referring to the conviction of some nations that they have a special role to play in the unfolding of history, some unique contribution to make to the destiny of mankind. In such a case, loyalty to one's nation may well become more than merely loyalty to one's own; it may become a passion that demands respect from all nations for this instrument for the improvement of the whole human race. There are no better examples of this than the conviction of the American people that they are "a light on a hill," and of the Jewish people that they are the moral elite of humanity.

At certain points in the life of some nations a new phenomenon arises—*nationalism*. Nationalism is best understood, I think, as a nation's preoccupation with its own nationhood. Instead of its members simply living their life together as a nation, they become preoccupied with their national existence—rather like the man who constantly checks his pulse rather than simply going about his tasks and letting his heart do its work. It is possible for this self-preoccupation to be stirred up by members of the people who, in one way or another, have come to the conviction that there is something lacking in the national life. More customarily, however, nationalism is the response of a nation to its conviction that it has been wronged, that an injustice has been done it, that it has not received its due. In the words of Isaiah Berlin, it is customarily the result of "the infliction of a wound on the collective feeling of a society, or at least of its spiritual leaders."[4] In any case, whatever its origins, the function of nationalism

> is to indicate disease. Bodily organs do not draw attention to themselves until they are attacked by disease. Similarly, nationalism is at bottom the awareness of some lack, some disease or ailment. The people feels a more and more urgent compulsion to fill this lack, to cure this disease or ailment. The contradiction between the immanent task of the nation and its outer and inner condition has developed or been elaborated and this contradiction affects the feeling of the people. What we term nationalism is their spiritual reaction to it.[5]

The wound that provokes nationalism comes in many different varieties. The context of our discussion makes it especially important to notice that colonialism has proved to be one of those wounds: in seeing this, we begin to see some of the connections between nation and economy in our modern world-system. The surge of nationalism after the Second World War was the response of the nations of the Third World to the exploitation and oppression and humiliation that they suffered at the hands of their colonial masters.

It will be evident that economic exploitation and political oppression can be the wounds that provoke nationalism. Let me emphasize that humiliation and paternalism—being treated without respect—can also be the wound. And we know enough about colonialism to say that the colonial masters invariably regarded their colonial subjects as inferior human beings, if indeed they noticed them at all—for typical of colonialism is a curious ambivalence between regarding the conquered land as empty and regarding it as inhabited by inferior races. One sees this ambivalence in the European description of America, in the Afrikaner description of Southern Africa, and, yes, in the Jewish description of Palestine.[6] Sometimes the native inhabitants of the land are invisible to the conquerors—"a land without people for a people without land," in Herzl's famous apothegm; sometimes they are noticed but scorned. Either way, colonialism entails a denial of respect.

Understanding that the denial of respect may itself constitute the wound that provokes nationalism will enable us in the West to understand what is otherwise so perplexing to us—namely, the fact that over and over in the modern world a people will react against even a relatively enlightened colonialist paternalism and will tolerate as its replacement an authoritarian regime led by one of its own members. It will also help us to understand the response of the blacks to the Afrikaners. Of course the paternalism of the Afrikaners is by no means enlightened. But paternalism it is. The Afrikaners think and speak of the blacks in their midst as children who must carefully—and oh so slowly—be nurtured into adulthood. This is part, but by no means the whole, of the wound they inflict upon the blacks. The Afrikaners are baffled, or say they are baffled, by the fact that these children in their midst do not appreciate all the good things dispensed to them. After all, they say, the blacks have it better in South Africa than anywhere else in Africa. But do they not see that when they treat the blacks as children, they inflict on them a deep wound? Do we not all prefer at some time in our lives to be delivered from the suffocating benefactions of parents and to be on our own—even if that means going hungry for a while and living in cold attics?

Perhaps he exaggerated, yet there was deep truth in what Kant said when he remarked that "paternalism is the greatest despotism imaginable." Better that one be ruled by one's own, even if the rule be harsh and the food be less, than that one's whole people be treated insultingly as children. For now at least one is recognized as a human being. As Berlin remarks in his "Two Concepts of Liberty,"

I may feel unfree . . . as a member of an unrecognized or insufficiently respected group: then I wish for the emancipation of my
entire class, or community, or nation, or race, or profession. So
much can I desire this, that I may, in my bitter longing for status,
prefer to be bullied and misgoverned by some member of my own
race or social class, by whom I am, nevertheless, recognized as a
man and a rival—that is as an equal—to being well and tolerantly
treated by someone from some higher and remoter group who does
not recognize me for what I wish to feel myself to be.[7]

Until we in the West understand these dynamics, until we understand what
treating a people paternalistically and not acknowledging their adulthood is
itself, apart from whatever else we may do to them, to inflict a deep wound on
them, our contemporary world will continue to baffle us.* Of course, the
Afrikaners do understand, despite the fact that they prefer to put it out of their
mind: they themselves rejected the relatively generous paternalism of the British
for the harshness of independence.

A nation may be anywhere along the spectrum from a barely dawn-
ing sense of nationhood to an intense conviction of self-importance; the particular form its nationalism takes will depend not only on the nature of that which
provokes its self-preoccupation, but also on where it stands along that spectrum.
A nation that already has an intense feeling of its own significance will, when
it senses that some injury has been done it, have few options apart from either
flailing out aggressively so as to right the wrong or at least show that it is not
merely a paper tiger, or, alternatively, nursing its wounds in self-pity. The
behavior of the United States after the Viet Nam war seems to me a prime
example of this form of nationalism. By contrast, the effect of nationalism on
a nation that has only a weak sense of nationhood will first of all be to strengthen
that sense. One sees this happening among the blacks in South Africa today

---

*A striking example of the insistence on national self-respect can be found
in this passage from a speech of Fidel Castro, in which he criticizes the tendency of
some Cubans to rely on socialist aid for rescue whenever hostile countries apply pressure: "Imagine that one day there would be a total blockade, through which no fuel,
through which nothing could pass. I am sure, I have absolutely no doubt, that the
people would be able to withstand such a situation . . . a situation where fuel would
be reserved for the tanks, the lorries, for transporting the army and the armed services.
And the population of the cities? We would all move to the country, and work by the
side of the farmers, driving the oxen and digging with hoe, pick and shovel. And we
would win through. This means that we have the right to hold our heads high, the
right to speak our own opinions and ideas; the right to be an example to any of the
small countries of the world, to any of the underdeveloped countries dominated by
imperialism or colonialism in any part of the world. And this also means that we are
committed to gain a place in world history" (speech delivered 2 Jan. 1965, quoted by
Denis Goulet, *The Cruel Choice: A New Concept in the Theory of Development* [New
York: Atheneum, 1971], p. 46).

and among the Palestinians in the Near East. Indeed, one of the surest ways to intensify a group's feelings of national identity, where those are weak, is to wound the group. If the Palestinians were not a nation, as so many Jewish leaders have insisted, they have certainly become one. And though the blacks of South Africa were many nations, they are well on the way to achieving unity.

The most interesting and also the most common cases, however, are those of wounded nations that fall between these two extremes. If leaders of such a people arise in the time of its sorrows, they will invariably engage first of all in a wide-ranging attempt to build up the nation's self-respect—that is, to increase *pride* in one's identification as a member of the nation and to increase *loyalty* to the nation as such. They will do so by seeking to recover "authentic" elements from the nation's past, by seeking to "purify" the nation's life of "foreign" elements, and by promoting the expansion of this recovered and purified cultural heritage. And they will try to persuade the members of the nation as well as all those looking on from outside that this history and this culture are glorious and worthy. They will sing its praises.[8]

I said: *if* leaders of the people arise in the time of its sorrows; the attainment or recovery of its self-respect is not the automatic response of a nation to a wound. Leaders are needed who have some vision concerning where the glory of the nation lies. But even before those leaders can have such a vision, something else must often happen. When a nation is wounded by being denied self-respect, it characteristically *internalizes that denial*. It comes to believe that it is not *worthy* of self-respect. Its members come to loathe themselves—on account of being black, on account of being native American, on account of being Arab. In that case, what is first of all necessary is that there be leaders who overcome that self-loathing. I think there is nothing more powerful for effecting this step than the conviction that God says to every human being whatsoever: you bear my image. When this word is genuinely heard, self-loathing is no longer possible. And when self-loathing has been overcome, then the next step can occur: something significant and worthy can be seen in the history and culture of one's people.

Afrikanerdom is a paradigm of the intermediate form of nationalism of which I have been speaking. As T. Dunbar Moodie makes clear in his book *The Rise of Afrikanerdom*, the Afrikaners before the twentieth century had no particular sense of self-importance. Indeed, their sense of national identity was not even particularly intense. Today, as the result of more than fifty years of nationalism, the situation is profoundly different. The wound to the people was of course the oppression and cultural humiliation inflicted by the English on the Afrikaner. In the time of its sorrows, the necessary leaders, especially intellectual leaders, arose among the Afrikaner people, and they self-consciously set about raising their people's self-respect. They did so in the classic way, by refining and intensifying the Afrikaners' awareness of their history and culture (including their language), and by singing the glories thereof—in addition, it may be added, to working for Afrikaner self-determination, both cultural and political. The result is an extraordinarily intense loyalty of Afrikaners to their nation and an extraordinarily intense pride in their identification as members of the nation.

I spoke just now about the Afrikaner's struggle for self-determination. It is very nearly inevitable that nationalism, if it does not take the form of a nation licking its wounds, will incorporate a struggle for the nation's right to determine its own form of life on significant points. In its essence, this is a struggle for *cultural* self-determination, yet it invariably has political significance as well. It is true that the struggle need not involve the goal of political *independence,* since it is possible for a nation to enjoy all the cultural self-determination it desires without having political independence, but as we shall shortly see, there are dynamics in the modern world that often thwart that eventuality. And in any case, the political significance of a nation's strengthening sense of nationhood and its rising sense of self-respect is evident to friend and foe alike. It is no accident that in the occupied territories Israel is doing all it can to suppress Palestinian cultural consciousness. It is likewise no accident that the Afrikaner is doing all he can to suppress black cultural consciousness.

Nationalism, I have suggested, is a nation's preoccupation with itself, provoked by its sense of a deficiency in its existence. It is the indication of a nation's perception of itself as diseased or injured. Often the effect of a nationalist episode in a nation's life is that its disease is cured, the pain of its injury salved. Nationalism has then functioned as a restorative antibody, as a healing ointment. Post-colonial nationalism in the Third World was, in good measure, a healing phenomenon.

But sometimes nationalism does not go away. Sometimes the preoccupation of a nation with itself continues beyond the correction of the deficiency in its life. Then we are confronted with something not healing but destructive:

> Original nationalism inspires the people to struggle for what they lack to achieve this. But when nationalism transgresses its lawful limits, when it tries to do more than overcome a deficiency, it becomes guilty of what has been called *hybris* in the lives of historical personalities; it crosses the holy border and grows presumptuous. And now it no longer indicates disease, but is itself a grave and complicated disease. A people can win the rights for which it strove and yet fail to regain its health—because nationalism, turned false, eats at its marrow.[9]

A nation can become so preoccupied with itself that its welfare becomes for its members the sovereign good: "*Deutschland über Alles,*" "America first." Then the actions of the nation are no longer submitted to the requirements of justice and peace. They are no longer submitted to normative appraisal. They are no longer tested against the demands of a sovereign Lord. The nation begins to consider itself sovereign. It treats itself as supreme, as ultimate. Loyalty to nation becomes an end in itself. Pride in membership supersedes all other identifications. Legitimate nationalism has then become idolatrous nationalism—idolatrous in the same way that, as we saw earlier, the pursuit of economic growth can become idolatrous. Idolatrous nationalism is not healthful; it is intensely poisonous. When a nation suffers from nationalism unchecked, the life of its members is twisted and distorted, and the nation becomes a menace among nations because it accepts no standards for international peace and justice. It acts solely in its own self-interest, breaking treaties when it sees fit, waging wars when it finds the advantage, thumbing its nose at international conventions and organizations. National self-assertion is its only goal. All that restrains it is a balance of terror.

For the signs of nationalism gone cancerous, the Christian, and everyone else, must be constantly alert; and when we see the signs, we must do all in our power to check the virulent sickness. We in our century have seen, and continue to see, that there is nothing more destructive of shalom than such nationalism. Of this Martin Buber spoke eloquently—presciently—in his address to the Twelfth Zionist Congress in September, 1921:

> Every reflective member of a people is in duty bound to distinguish between legitimate and arbitrary nationalism and—in the sequence of situations and decisions—to refresh this distinction day after day. This is, above all, an obligation imposed on the leaders of a nation and of national movements.
>
> But the criterion which must govern the drawing of this distinction is not implicit in nationalism itself. It can be found only in the knowledge that the nation has an obligation which is more than merely national. He who regards the nation as the supreme principle, as the ultimate reality, as the final judge, and does not recognize that over and above all the countless and varied peoples there is an authority named or unnamed to which communities as well as individuals must inwardly render an account of themselves, could not possibly know how to draw this distinction, even if he attempted to do so. . . .
>
> He . . . who regards the nation as an end in itself will refuse to admit that there is a greater structure, unless it be the world-wide supremacy of his own particular nation. . . . He does not meet responsibility face to face. He considers the nation its own

judge and responsible to no one but itself. An interpretation such as
this converts the nation into a moloch which gulps the best of the
people's youth. . . . All sovereignty becomes false and vain when
in the struggle for power it fails to remain subject to the Sovereign
of the world, who is the Sovereign of my rival, and my enemy's
Sovereign, as well as mine.[10]

That form of nationalism which serves to restore a nation to health
can do without explicit articulated justification. Such healing nationalism speaks
for itself. Not so with nationalism gone cancerous; for this, an ideology is
necessary. The ideology that has characteristically been mustered in support of
cancerous nationalism in our modern world was created in the Romantic movement of nineteenth-century Germany. There it was argued, in the first place,
that each individual human being belongs to a particular nation whose way of
life determines the character and life-purposes of the individual members. Thus
the individual cannot be understood apart from his nation. The nation must not
be thought of as a group of self-determining individuals, but rather the individuals must be thought of as parts of the self-determining nation. Secondly,
it was argued that the best way to think of the relation of parts to parts and of
parts to whole in a nation is by analogy to a biological organism: the significance
of the individual is fundamentally that, in interaction with others, he or she
contributes to the functioning of the whole.*

But the assertion that it is the nation that constitutes the larger whole
that defines the character of individuals and demands their contributions begs
the question: why should this larger whole not be humanity at large instead?
To this the reply of the German Romantics was that the struggle of competing
elements is essential to the progress of humanity toward unity. Self-realization
is not a smooth, uneventful process, but the outcome of strife and struggle.
Kant had already made this point in his treatise *Perpetual Peace*: nature, he
said, "employs two means to keep peoples from being mixed and to differentiate
them: the difference of *language* and of *religion*. These differences occasion the
inclination toward mutual hatred and the excuse for war; yet at the same time
they lead, as culture increases and men gradually come closer together, toward

---

*The idea of an organism, says Fichte, "has been used lately with fre-
quency in order to define the different branches of the public authority in its unity;
but not yet, so far as I know, to explain the totality of civil relations. In a product of
nature, no part is what it is but through its relation with the whole, and would
absolutely not be what it is apart from this relation . . .; similarly, man attains a
determinate position in the scheme of things and fixity in nature only by means of
civil association. . . . Between the isolated man and the citizen, there is the same
relation as between raw and organized matter. . . . In an organized body, each part
continuously maintains the whole, and in maintaining it, maintains itself also. Similarly, the citizen with regard to the state" (quoted by Elie Kedouri, *Nationalism*, 2d
ed. rev. [New York: Praeger, 1961], pp. 39-40).

a greater agreement on principles for peace and understanding."[11] The progress of civilization and the attainment of ultimate harmony demand distinct peoples in competition with each other.

The contention that the struggle of nation with nation is essential to historical advance has consistently been coupled with a fourth theme—the importance of diversity among nations. Writers such as Schleiermacher viewed each nation as a natural division of humanity, having a peculiar character which it is the duty of its members to preserve and enhance: "Every nationality," he says, "is destined through its peculiar organization and its place in the world to represent a certain side of the divine image. . . . For it is God who directly assigns to each nationality its definite task on earth and inspires it with a definite spirit in order to glorify himself through each one in a peculiar manner."[12]

The conclusion drawn by the nineteenth-century German theorists from the interweaving of these four themes of self-determination, organicism, struggle, and diversity was that nations are separate natural entities ordained by God, in loyalty to which individuals find the meaning of their lives, and that the right political arrangement is one in which each nation is self-determining. Only in such an arrangement, they said, would the peoples of the earth fulfill their unique destinies, each making its particular contribution to the whole, and only by sinking themselves into the greater whole of their nation would individuals find freedom and fulfillment; furthermore, the struggle resulting from an international order thus arranged would advance the cause of humanity. It was this ideology that was self-consciously imported into South Africa by the Afrikaner intellectuals in the early part of this century. They adapted it to the South African situation by arguing that it had an Old Testament basis and that one of the defining features of the Afrikaner *volk* is that its religion is Christianity. What has emerged is a strange amalgam that the Afrikaners themselves call *Christian nationalism.*

I have been offering a general account of nationalism, and along the way I have indicated how this general account fits certain specific cases, including the United States. Yet there are also important peculiarities in the case of the United States, and before we move on to some of the ways in which nations interact with states and with the economic order in our present world-system, we might consider some of these peculiarities. We can approach the matter by asking why contemporary American intellectuals are so reluctant to sing the glories of their nation's history and culture. The Afrikaner intellectuals have not hesitated to bend their efforts toward the advancement of their nation and to hymn the glories of its accomplishments. And up through the first quarter of this century the American intellectuals readily did the same for their country. But now, silence—or even bitter attack. Why so?

Well, for one thing, what can the intellectual do? Undoubtedly

America feels wounded by the experiences of the last decade, but there is here no weak sense of nationhood. Nor does America have an insufficiently developed sense of its unique significance in the history of mankind which the scholar can then work to overcome. If anything, its sense of significance has for a long time been inflated. Consider, for example, these words spoken in the first decade of this century, not by some odd crank, but by William Rainey Harper, the noted Old Testament scholar who became the first president of the University of Chicago:

> Another great period is just being ushered in, which promises to eclipse its predecessor even as that predecessor eclipsed those that preceded it. . . . What Babylonia was in the first period, what Syria was in the second, what England was in the third, all this and more America will be in the fourth. . . .
>
> [The] idea of individualism, of the paramount dignity of the individual, has expressed itself, more clearly and more specifically, in every advance of civilization. . . .
>
> But, now, these ideas have been demonstrated only "piecemeal, and incoherently, in separated times and places." However clearly they may have been taught in the New Testament, they have not yet received their perfect demonstration in human history. The question of individualism as a whole is still on trial. . . . The arena in which the great trial shall be conducted is America. The old countries with their traditions and institutions which obstruct their performance of full human functions by the masses, cannot work out the problems which confront us.
>
> . . . Here in this great country, provided by God himself with all the facilities needed, preserved in large measure by God himself from the burdens and trammels of dead institutions and deadly traditions, the consummation of Christian life and thought will be realized. This is the message written on every page of our nineteen centuries of history. It is a wonderful and significant message.
>
> . . . If, now, our faith is sure that there has been committed to us this great mission, shall we not purify ourselves? Shall we not organize ourselves as a nation for the work that lies ahead?[13]

This flamboyant expression of American importance should by no means be seen as merely an expression of Harper's personal opinion. When these words were spoken, almost all Americans would in substance have agreed with them. Many still would. And let us recall that the sense of national self-importance to which Harper was giving expression had been carefully nursed and promoted by American intellectuals throughout the eighteenth and nineteenth centuries. I submit that when a nation with this highly developed sense of self-importance feels wounded, there is little that the intellectuals can do to restore its sense of self-respect—other than to persuade it that it need not feel wounded. They have already done all they could.

But to understand fully the alienation and anger of contemporary American intellectuals, one must also consider the peculiar character of their nation's sense of self-importance. From the eighteenth century on, America's sense of self-importance has always been connected to the understanding it has of its relationship to those great universalistic Enlightenment goals of liberty, equality, and fraternity. Americans insisted that it was in this land that those great ideals were first being realized, and that from this land they would spread throughout the world. America was not just a nation among nations, not even just a *significant* nation among nations. In America was being created a new nation out of fragments of many nations to be a model for all nations. The Romantic ideology with its emphasis on the unique contribution of each nation never enjoyed favor among Americans. America was every nation's future. And part of its frustration during the past fifty years is that it finds itself in the world with another social group whose leaders believe a similar destiny has been entrusted to their nation—namely, the Soviet Union.

Our world today is a world of failed ideals. Not many Russians believe that in their land a new age of equality and participation is being ushered in. No longer do many Americans believe that in their land a new age of liberty and equality has arrived. The diplomats of America now pursue a policy exclusively of self-interest. It bothers them little that self-interest requires the support of regimes around the world that suppress liberty. For a brief period during the Carter administration there was talk of America being the protector of human rights around the globe. That brief flash has vanished into the dark night of shoring up business interests and opposing communism.

I suggest that when the intellectuals in a nation or group once inspired by this peculiar sense of universalistic importance are confronted by failed ideals, by the reality that their group is no longer an effective, devoted agent of those universalistic goals, they will become alienated. Most will convey their alienation in expressions of diminished loyalty: a few will resort to bitter attacks. A few neo-conservatives only will shout shrilly that the glories of the group are as great as ever, that the ideals have not failed, but that disloyal people only *say* they have.

It is time to return to the contention with which I opened this chapter: if we probe into the *causes* of the deprivation of rights and the perpetuation of misery in the modern world, again and again we shall find excessive and misguided loyalty to nation at work. When nationalism produces a morbid preoccupation of a nation with itself, it is bad enough, but when it produces a loyalty that considers the existence and aggrandizement of the nation to be the ultimate social good, then we are dealing with an idolatry that is enormously destructive of shalom. Sometimes this loyalty manifests itself in the aggressive, self-interested, terroristic treament by one state of other states and their citizens. Sometimes it manifests itself internally in the way in which the state treats its own citizens. I do not know which of these manifestations is more injurious, but to give some indication of how loyalty to nation produces injustice, let me focus on the second.

It is often said that characteristic of the political composition of the modern world is the fact that states are nation-states. Surely that is false if the suggestion is being made that the citizenry of most states belong to a single nation; rather, what is true is that the world is now constituted by those tightly defined entities that are our modern states and that one of the most important factors accounting for the differentiation of these states is the insistence of nations that they have a state of their own. Of course, nations have always struggled for *cultural* self-determination; what is peculiar to the modern world is the degree to which nations have struggled for *political* self-determination—and the degree to which those struggles have been successful. The principle of *each nation its own state* has come to seem obviously correct as a principle for assigning sovereignty. At Versailles the old political map of Europe was torn apart and pasted together again on this principle.

I suggest, however, that if we allow our reflections on this principle to go beyond its initial attractiveness, we shall be forced to the conclusion that never in the modern world is it acceptable, inasmuch as it always leads to injustice and conflict. The crux of what goes wrong is that states are of course territorial entities, and nowhere in the modern world are the inhabitants of the territory belonging to a state the members of just one nation. Consequently, when one nation has a state of its own, there will nevertheless always be citizens of that state who are not members of the nation, and these people will be left with only two choices: either to emigrate, under varying degrees of duress, or to accept the status of second-class citizens, with varying degrees of deprivation of rights and of repression. *There is never any other choice.*

The insistence of the Afrikaners that they have a state of their own— along with their insistence that whether they like it or not the black tribes shall also (eventually) have states of their own—lies at the bottom of the grievous injustices that the South African state wreaks on the blacks. The dynamic behind apartheid is not racism in a straightforward way; it is cancerous nationalism (though indeed a racist species of that): loyalty to nation supersedes all. This loyalty leads the Afrikaner to embrace the principle of *my nation its own state,* and to this principle the requirements of justice and peace are subordinated. The actions of the state are judged by whether they serve the cause of the Afrikaner people, not by whether they serve the cause of justice.

In public Afrikaners will often insist that the legal structure of apartheid is not some ultimate good, but that it is in principle only a dispensable *means*. What they have in mind when they say this, however, is not that the structure of apartheid is the means for achieving a society of *justice,* but that it is the means for achieving the goal of *my nation its own state*—and, more generally, for the goal of the *self-determination of the Afrikaner people.* They cannot conceive of the social good as not including the full self-determination of their own people: their *nation,* not justice, is the ultimate social commitment. The speeches they make to their compatriots in private make this clear. In 1970 Dr. Piet Meyer, chairman of the Broederbond, had this to say: "We must never accede to any demands to scrap or water down our policy of separate development and anti-communism . . . All forms of integration in our country must be fought and rejected on all fronts—in the churches, and in the social, cultural, economic and political spheres."[14] And in 1975 the Executive of the Bond said that "measures necessary to keep political control of the white man's future in his own hands must not disappear. Thus no form of political power-sharing with non-white nations is acceptable."[15] I submit, however, that in a multinational and economically integrated society such as South Africa, the principle of *the Afrikaners their own state* is incompatible with the demands of peace and justice.

A nation may have "its own state" in many different ways. In South Africa we see one form of ethnic state. Since the blacks are a large majority there, the centerpiece of Afrikaner policy is to deprive them of all voice in the affairs of state and to force as many as possible into homelands. In Israel we see a different form of ethnic state. For one thing, in Israel proper, Palestinian Arabs are allowed to vote. Yet Israel is a Jewish state. And if we ask what it is that accounts for the injustices that Israel has wreaked and continues to wreak on the Arabs, the conclusion is inescapable that it is in good measure the principle of *the Jewish nation its own state.**

Zionism arose in the context of nineteenth-century European nationalism. The Israeli editor Gershom Schocken has remarked that "Zionism

---

*There are other factors to be considered concerning the Israeli treatment of the Palestinian Arabs as well. As early as 1891—fifty-seven years before the Jewish people had acquired their own state—the well-known Jewish writer Ahad Ha-am warned that the Jewish settlers ought not to arouse the wrath of the natives with ugly actions, but ought instead to meet them in the friendly spirit of respect. "Yet what," he asked, "do our brethren do in Palestine? Just the opposite! Serfs they were in the lands of the diaspora and suddenly they find themselves in freedom, and this change has awakened in them an inclination to despotism. They treat the Arabs with hostility and cruelty, deprive them of their rights, offend them without cause, and even boast of these deeds; and nobody among us opposes this despicable and dangerous inclination" (quoted by Hans Kohn, "Zion and the Jewish National Idea," in *Zionism Reconsidered: The Rejection of Jewish Normalcy,* ed. Michael Selzer [New York: Macmillan, 1970], p. 195).

could not have arisen without the national movements which altered the face
of Europe during the nineteenth century, without the discovery by the Russian
narodniki of the spiritual wealth of the simple people and their needs and problems, and without German romanticism. Kurt Blumenfeld, the important ideo-
logue of German Zionism, said with good reason: Zionism is the gift of Europe
to the Jewish people."[16] Having imbibed the spirit of European nationalism,
the Zionist claimed that since the Jews are a distinct people, and since every
people is entitled to its own land and its own state, the Jews are so entitled as
well. Already in 1900 an orthodox rabbi of Eastern Europe lodged a bitter
attack on Zionism on the ground of its being inspired by nationalism and not
by Judaism. "For our many sins," wrote the rabbi,

> strangers have risen to pasture the holy flock, men who say that the
> people of Israel should be clothed in secular nationalism, a nation
> like all other nations, that Judaism rests on three things, national
> feeling, the land and the language, and that national feeling is the
> most praiseworthy element in the brew and the most effective in
> preserving Judaism, while the observance of the Torah and the com-
> mandments is a private matter depending on the inclination of each
> individual. May the Lord rebuke these evil men and may he who
> chooseth Jerusalem seal their mouths.[17]

Of course the early Zionist leaders did not merely stake their case
on the claim that the Jews constitute a distinct people and as such deserve their
own state; they also undertook to point out the evil consequences of violating
the principle of each nation its own state in this case—or, conversely, the advantages of respecting it: only by granting the Jews their own state, they argued,
could the "Jewish problem"—that is, rampant anti-Semitism—be solved (and
let me just say here that this widespread virulent hatred and discrimination
against Jews remains an important issue today). In addition, they argued that
only by granting the Jews their own state could "the problem of Judaism"—
that is, the problem of the erosion of Jewish identity—be solved. The alliance
of Zionism with European nationalism enabled its leaders on the one hand to
combat the modernists, who expected the progress of emancipation and enlightenment to solve "the Jewish problem," but who had no answer to "the
problem of Judaism"; and on the other hand, it allowed them to combat the
traditionalists, who saw the preservation of their traditional enclaves as the
solution to "the problem of Judaism," but who had no solution to "the Jewish
problem."

To understand fully how the principle of *the Jews their own state* has
worked itself out in Palestine, we must add one more thing: the fact that the
Jewish leaders have traditionally seen the Jewish people as the *only* nation in
Palestine. In this way they differ from the Afrikaners, who see themselves as

dwelling with many other nations on the tip of Africa. The Palestinians, insists the Jew, do not constitute a people. It was this insistence that lay behind these remarkable words of Golda Meir:

> How can we return the occupied territories? There is nobody to return them to. . . . There was no such thing as Palestinians. . . . It was not as though there was a Palestinian people in Palestine considering itself as a Palestinian people and we came and threw them out and took their country away from them. They did not exist.[18]

Meir knew, of course, that there had been Arabs living in Palestine before the formation of the Israeli state, and she knew very well that they had been dispossessed of their land, but they were not a people in her view, and so consequently she saw no substantial issue of rights. That there are human beings with blood that runs and tears that flow among nations other than one's own is scarcely visible to the person blinded by nationalism.

In his book *Zionism and the Palestinians*, Simha Flapan traces in detail the attitudes of the Jewish leaders toward the Arabs living in Palestine. Few indeed there were who sought in Palestine anything other than a state of their own for the Jewish people; and of that large majority who sought an ethnic state, only Dr. Nahum Goldmann among the top Zionist leadership saw clearly that a state of their own for the Jews raised profound issues concerning the rights of the Palestinians. "One of the great oversights," Goldmann said on one occasion,

> in the history of Zionism is that when the Jewish homeland in Palestine was founded, sufficient attention was not paid to relations with the Arabs. Of course, there were always a few Zionist speakers and thinkers who stressed them. . . . And the ideological and political leaders of the Zionist movement always emphasized—sincerely and earnestly, it seems to me—that the Jewish national home must be established in peace and harmony with the Arabs. Unfortunately these convictions remained in the realm of theory and were not carried over, to any great extent, into actual Zionist practice. Even Theodor Herzl's brilliantly simple formulation of the Jewish question as basically a transportation problem of 'moving people without a home into a land without a people' is tinged with disquieting blindness to the Arab claim to Palestine. Palestine was not a land without a people even in Herzl's time; it was inhabited by hundreds of thousands of Arabs who, in the course of events, would sooner or later have achieved independent statehood, either alone or as a unit with a larger Arab context.[19]

Goldmann's awareness of the existence of an emerging Palestinian people did not carry the day. Instead, Zionist and Israeli policy was determined by such individuals as David Ben-Gurion, who remarked in 1936 that "there is no conflict between Jewish and Palestinian nationalism because the Jewish nation is not in Palestine and the Palestinians are not a nation."[20] The standard view of the Zionist leaders has always been that although there is an Arab people, there is no Palestinian people, and that since Palestine constitutes only a bit more than two percent of the total area occupied by the Arabs in the Near East, there is no good reason why they should not be willing to give up that small part of their territory to the Jews, who need it more than the Arabs do, and who will use it better.[21] It is the legacy and perpetuation of these attitudes that feed the Palestinians' justified sense of grievance.

The die was cast in 1944, when the American Zionists, the largest section of the World Zionist Organization, unanimously resolved to demand a "free and democratic Jewish commonwealth . . . [which] shall embrace the whole of Palestine, undivided and undiminished."[22] A *Jewish* commonwealth. An ethnic state. The result for the Arabs has been what it always is in our modern world when one nation claims a state for its own: they could either emigrate from their ancestral homes under some form of duress or be demoted to second-class citizenship that would be enforced with some degree of repression. *There is never any other choice.* Let me allow a member of the Jewish people, one of the fathers of Zionism, make the point. In 1953 Moshe Smilansky, in response to the Israeli parliament's passage of the "Land Requisition Law of 1953," made this statement:

> When we came back to our country after having been evicted two thousand years ago, we called ourselves "daring" and we rightly complained before the whole world that the gates of the country were shut. And now when they [Arab refugees] dared to return to their country where they lived for one thousand years before they were evicted or fled, they are called "infiltrees" and shot in cold blood. Where are you, Jews? Why do we not at least, with a generous hand, pay compensation to these miserable people? Where to take the money from? But we build palaces . . . instead of paying a debt that cries unto us from earth and heaven. . . . And do we sin only against the refugees? Do we not treat the Arabs who remain with us as second-class citizens? . . . Did a single Jewish farmer raise his hand in the parliament in opposition to a law that deprived Arab peasants of their land? . . . How does sit solitary, in the city of Jerusalem, the Jewish conscience![23]

We have looked at just two cases, but the point has been made: it is justice and shalom that determine the legitimacy of a state, not the principle of national self-determination. Does the state protect the rights of those who dwell there? Does it deal equitably with them? Does it establish peace? Those are the questions to be asked, not whether some nation has its own state. Nation must bow before justice. A state is to be the state of *all* its citizens, not the state of some nation *among* its citizens. [24] What unites us as bearers of the image of God is more important than what divides us as members of nations. In their dispensing of justice, the states of the world must always make their ethnic diversity secondary to their essential human unity rather than the other way around. In the modern world this means that there can be no ethnic state, because such a state inevitably wreaks injustice. The evidence is all about us; as George Orwell once remarked, "The nationalist not only does not disapprove of atrocities committed by his own side, but he has a remarkable capacity for not even hearing about them." [25]

As Christians struggle to diminish the conflict of nation against nation in the world today they will not forget the life of that other nation to which they belong, that "holy nation," in Peter's words, the church of Jesus Christ— "elect from every nation, yet one o'er all the earth." After Pentecost God's chosen people on earth no longer excludes the members of any natural grouping—neither Greek nor Jew, female nor male, slave nor free. It does not exclude them because it transcends them. Without destroying all those old loyalties, it transforms them: they become enrichments of this one new nation. So at least it was meant to be. And here and there, now and then, that is how it is. Yet in the modern world, loyalty to nation has bitten so deeply into the life of the church that most Christians in America feel themselves less united as members of one holy dedicated nation with those in Russia, in Vietnam, in Germany, or in El Salvador than they feel themselves divided from them as Americans in distinction from Russians, from Vietnamese, from Germans, from Salvadorans. And so American bombs are dropped by Christians on the cathedral in Hanoi just as German bombs were dropped by Christians on the churches in Rotterdam.

Can that change? Can the church live up to its inner nature? Can it become consistently a sacrament, an effective sign of God's Kingdom of shalom in which no longer shall a nation build but not inhabit, plant but not eat (Isa. 65:22)? For in that Kingdom "nation shall not lift up sword against nation, / neither shall they learn war any more" (Isa. 2:4).

ADDENDUM:
The Rise of the National Security State

In this chapter we have looked at a few of the many complex forms of interaction between nations on the one hand, and states and economy on the other, in the modern world-system. We have seen, for instance, how loyalty to nation can contribute to the creation of injustice, and we have also touched briefly on the relation between the dynamic of loyalty to nation and the dynamic of profit-seeking that has been revealed in the nationalism generated out of the colonial exploitation of the Third World nations. It will be worthwhile at this point to look at one more mode of interaction between these two crucial dynamics which has arisen in the period since the collapse of classical colonialism in the Third World, and which lies at the root of many of that region's present miseries.

From the standpoint of the state, the great advantage in having a single most-favored nation among its citizenry is that it can appeal to feelings of national loyalty in this group when it needs to muster support for its actions, rather than having to demonstrate that its policies secure the rights and promote the welfare of *all* of its citizens. Of course, this advantage is obtained only at the cost of the restlessness of those who do not belong to the nation in power, and sometimes that cost is very high. Yet much of the power of the contemporary state results from its ability to appeal to national loyalty.*

In recent years this appeal of the state to feelings of national loyalty has been regularly used in the Third World to gain support for policies that amount to the economic exploitation of some members of the regnant nation *by other members of that same nation* in cooperation with enterprises from the core. In our last chapter we noticed that upon the demise of classical colonialism after the Second World War, a new pattern of economic relationships between the core and the noncore began to emerge. Enterprises manufacturing goods for consumption in the core moved to the noncore, often under the aegis of multinational corporations and in cooperation with members of the elite in the host country. The principal goal in making these moves has been to diminish the cost of labor. Accordingly, it has been in the interest of the Third World elite to suppress labor costs and keep the labor force quiescent. Repression has proved necessary to achieve these goals. In recent years this repression has often been accomplished by the military taking over the state and then working in harmony with the elite. But usually those who hold power in such states belong to the

---

*According to Marxist theory, communist states should no longer depend to any significant degree on appeals to national loyalty, but in actual fact they have not gotten away from doing so. Consider, for example, these words of Kim Il Sung, the leader of the People's Democratic Republic of Korea (unofficially, North Korea): "The homeland is a veritable mother for everyone. We cannot live or be happy outside of our homeland. Only the flourishing and prosperity of our homeland will permit us to go down the path to happiness. The best sons and daughters of our people, all without exception, were first of all ardent patriots. It was to recover their homeland that Korean Communists struggled, before the Liberation, against Japanese imperialism despite every difficulty and obstacle" (quoted by Immanuel Wallerstein, *The Capitalist World-Economy* [Cambridge: Cambridge University Press, 1979], p. 59).

same people as those persons they repress. Thus we are not dealing here with a direct counterpart to the old colonialism; rather, some members of the regnant nation use the state to repress other members of the same nation.

Such rulers typically attempt to engender acceptance of the repression they create by playing on the people's feelings of national loyalty and attempting to enlist this loyalty in support of the state. Obviously this can be a precarious enterprise.* In order to make it less precarious, the strategy is regularly adopted of seeking to convince the nation that it is under attack, that the state is its protector, that in this "state of emergency" all must cooperate in supporting the state, and that the inequities and infringements of liberty that the people experience are unavoidable in their state of siege. Enormous investments are made in armaments, thereby further impoverishing the people. Never trusting its own persuasive powers, the state takes the final step of passing so-called "security legislation," ostensibly to protect the people against subversion, but in fact to stifle internal dissent. This whole complex has been aptly called the *national security state.*

The strategy and philosophy as a whole have perhaps never been so forthrightly and articulately stated as by General Augusto Pinochet Ugarte of Chile, in his Presidential Message of September 11, 1976:

> National security thus understood emerges as a concept destined not only to protect the national integrity of the state, but very specially to defend the essential values that make up the national soul or tradition, since without them national identity itself would destroy itself. And from this firm pedestal, national security projects itself dynamically to the field of development, thus focussing not only on the material plane, but on harmony and at the service of the spiritual progress of man. National security, including the authentic tradition and national development, spiritual as well as material, thus appear as the integral elements of the common good of a particular community. . . .

What, exactly, does this enemy consist of in the world of today? Marxism is not a doctrine that is simply wrong, like so

---

*I think one can formulate a sort of "law" for the contemporary state at this point: the more injustice a state tolerates or perpetrates, the more it finds it necessary to appeal to (and cultivate) feelings of national loyalty in order to maintain a consensus that its policies are indeed legitimate; roughly speaking, the more gross the injustice, the more excessive the nationalistic appeals must be. We have already seen that national loyalty, when it goes beyond proper bounds, makes the nation a threat to all other nations. Thus social injustice and national conflict hang intimately together—just as, conversely, justice and peace hang intimately together. Some years back, states tolerating or perpetrating substantial injustice attempted to legitimate their actions not so much by appealing to feelings of national loyalty, but by arguing that these were necessary steps to a better tomorrow. One hears this sort of argument less and less frequently these days, as the sense of failed ideals becomes ever more pervasive.

many others in history. . . . It is also a permanent aggression, that today is at the service of Soviet imperialism. . . . This modern form of permanent aggression produces a nonconventional war in which territorial invasion is replaced by the attempt to control the state from within. To that end, communism uses two tactics simultaneously. On the one hand it infiltrates the vital nuclei of the free societies, like the university and intellectual centers, the media, the labor unions, the international organizations and, as we have seen, even the church sectors. On the other hand, it promotes disorder in all its forms. . . .

Therefore the new institutionality is conceived on the basis of a new democracy that is capable of defending itself actively and vigilantly from those that try to destroy it. . . . The Constitutional Acts that we promulgate today make all acts of a person or a group that challenges these values illegal and to be punished judicially. . . .

The fact that our peoples are victims of a permanent aggression imposes the duty on us to have vigorous and efficient emergency regimes to defeat communist subversion and to neutralize those who ease the way for it. . . . It is the fruit of the preceding analysis that it is also understood that in the face of a Marxism that is converted into permanent aggression, it is absolutely necessary to root power in the Armed Forces and the Police, since only they have the organization and the means to confront it.[26]

When we put these words together with what is actually happening in Chile, the pattern becomes clear: the rulers support the exploitation of the people by the elite. They attempt to secure acceptance of these policies by appealing to the feelings of national loyalty among the people. And to intensify those feelings they follow the classic strategy of seeking to persuade the nation that it is under attack.

It is difficult to imagine a more gross abuse of the feelings of loyalty to nation. This repetitive appeal to the dangers of Soviet imperialism is a cynical distraction from the issues at hand—and one can say this without being at all naive concerning the reality of Soviet expansionism: as I suggested in the preceding chapter, there would be revolutionary movements in the Third World today if there were no communist states anywhere on the face of the earth. And there ought in fact to be revolutions there—profound restructurings of these inequitable and oppressive social orders. The injustices suffered are vastly greater than those that were experienced by American colonists at the hands of the British when they fought their own revolution. It is sheer cynicism to label every move for reform a communist plot. The lesson to be learned from the restlessness of oppressed people is that injustice must be rectified, not that repression must be instituted.

One may also notice the irony that these states which seek to legitimate themselves by arguing that the actions they take are for the sake of the security of the people are themselves profoundly insecure. The mighty wind of security legislation and armament buildups sweeping across the world today produces only more insecurity. Does that not confirm the profound truth of the Old Testament prophetic vision, that the state that does not follow the way of the Lord and pursue justice will not find security? Uneasy sleeps the tyrant. One cannot preserve privilege and at the same time enjoy security. The path to security is justice.

Chapter VI

A City of Delight

In the West there have been two or three major traditions of reflection on the nature of the good life. In one of these, going back to Aristotle, *happiness* is the fundamental, organizing concept. In a second, going back to the Enlightenment, *freedom* plays that role. And perhaps we ought to acknowledge that there is a third tradition of such reflections organized around the concept of *order* and going back to Plato.

Of these three, the freedom tradition has been far and away the most prominent in the modern world. It is my own conviction, however, that this tradition inevitably comes to an impasse. Freedom, understood as autonomy, cannot be the ultimate goal of humanity; it cannot be the fundamental qualifier of the good life. It is an illusion to suppose that we human beings can be, in any fundamental way, autonomous. So my own reflections in this book have been centered within the happiness tradition. I am persuaded that it is in this direction that our reflections must turn if we want to find the new directions that we so badly need.

Yet I trust I have made it clear that our struggle for the good life must be understood in such a way as to incorporate within it the struggle for liberation. Naturally when I speak here of "the struggle for liberation" I do not mean the struggle for autonomy in some all-embracing sense; rather, I connect liberation directly to injustice, to the deprivation of rights: the struggle for happiness must incorporate the struggle for justice. In my discussion of rights in Chapter IV, I argued that rights are always grounded in duties, in responsibilities, in obligations. It follows, then, that happiness must be understood in such a way that the enactment of responsibilities is one of its fundamental components.

I suggested that the biblical concept of shalom meets precisely these requirements. A community of shalom, for one thing, is a responsible community: where shalom exists, there we enact our responsibilities to one another, to God, and to nature. But shalom is more than that. It is fully present only where there is *delight* and *joy* in those relationships. It is possible that even if all of us would carry out our responsibilities to each other, to God, to nature—and, yes, to ourselves—delight might yet be missing in important ways. Suffering might remain, for of course not every form of suffering is the result of irresponsibility on someone's part. I suggested that this is one of the areas in which our increasing mastery of nature properly enters the picture: such mastery makes it possible for us to push back some of the sorrows of human existence.

By virtue of embedding this discussion within the happiness tradition of reflection on the good life, I have not only placed myself in opposition to our modern Enlightenment and post-Enlightenment tradition; I have also thereby allied myself with the medieval Christian tradition of such reflections. For at the center of the medieval reflections on such matters was the concept of beatitude, *beatitudo*. Yet I must immediately add that the shalom understanding of happiness is profoundly different from that of the medievals: the fact that in the discussion of beatitude among the latter, injustice never enters the picture, nor, accordingly, the need for liberation from injustice, is one indication of the fundamental differences.

Beatitude, to the medieval understanding, is an *intellectual* experience, an activity of the mind; specifically, it consists in the contemplation of God. Aquinas is a fit representative of the medieval vision, and we could scarcely do better than allow him to introduce the concept in his own words: the true end of man, he says, is happiness, and "man's happiness consists essentially in his being united to the Uncreated Good"; thus, "the ultimate and principal good of man is the enjoyment of God. . . ." The essence of this union with God that constitutes man's ultimate happiness "consists in an act of the intellect"—specifically, in the intellectual act of knowing God in his essence, "in the contemplation of Divine things. . . . Therefore the last and perfect happiness which we await in the life to come, consists entirely in contemplation. But imperfect happiness, such as can be had here, consists first and principally in contemplation, but secondarily, in an operation of the practical intellect directing human actions and passions. . . ." And so, although "perfect and true happiness cannot be had in this life," nevertheless, "a certain participation of Happiness can be had in this life": "in so far as a man gives himself to the pursuit of wisdom, so far does he even now have some share in true beatitude."[1]

But if the essence of human happiness consists merely in an intellectual contemplation of God, is there then no ultimate need for human companionship in our lives? And does our life in nature not contribute to our fulfillment? Is the existence of a just and happy community dwelling in harmony with nature irrelevant to man's ultimate happiness? Perhaps not *irrelevant,* Aquinas would suggest, but certainly not necessary.

Here in this life the happy individual needs friends and such things as will sustain the body, but this is not the case when he or she has attained perfect happiness. In the intellectual contemplation of God, Aquinas insists, there is no lack whatsoever: "If we speak of perfect Happiness, which will be in our heavenly Fatherland, the fellowship of friends is not essential to Happiness, since man has the entire fulness of his perfection in God." Should we find ourselves in the presence of other human beings, love for them will result from love for God, but the absence of human companionship does not imply a deficiency in fulfillment. Likewise, the person who when disembodied has knowledge of God experiences no deficiency: "Since man's perfect Happiness consists in the vision of the Divine Essence, it does not depend on the body. Consequently, without the body the soul can be happy." The persons who know and love God will eventually receive new bodies at the resurrection, and will then experience an increase in the *extent* of their happiness. They will, however, experience no increase in its *intensity*. And it should be added that their new bodies will be "no longer animal but spiritual. Consequently [the] external goods [of our present bodies] are nowise necessary for that Happiness, since they are ordained to the animal life. . . ."[2]

Obviously this understanding of the content of man's true happiness is profoundly different from the shalom understanding with which I have been working. Let me make it clear that I do not reject this medieval understanding on the specious ground that it comes from the adolescence of the human race, whereas our own thinking represents man having come of age. To think thus is a mark of our own childishness. For me the ultimately decisive reason for rejecting that theo-monistic understanding of happiness is that it is not adequately biblical; so far as I can tell, *shalom* is more genuinely the content that the biblical writers give to the destiny appointed to us by God: our appointed destiny incorporates living in human community in the midst of nature.

In the preceding two chapters I have explored some of the implications of this concept of shalom for our treatment of our fellow human beings. But I did not do so in the abstract. Rather, I took two pervasive features of our modern social order—mass poverty and the deprivation of rights caused by nationalism—and held them up against the criterion of shalom. In this chapter I wish to explore some of the implications of the shalom vision for our relationship to physical reality, and again I will do so in a specific context.

In searching for some fundamental feature of our relation to nature to hold up to the light of shalom, the phenomena of the pollution of our planet and the exhaustion of its resources spring immediately to mind. But, without at all suggesting that I regard those phenomena as unimportant—for most emphatically I do not—I would like instead to consider the *created* environment within which almost all of us live or work—namely, the city. More specifically, I would like to consider the *ugliness* of so much of the contemporary city. One of the most important consequences of the workings of our modern social order is that people are compelled to move from country to city and town. The capitalization of agriculture, which is the dynamic behind this process, has already gone so far in the United States that less than ten percent of the population remains engaged in agriculture.³ They leave the farm for the city, and there they are immersed in ugliness.

In his marvelous book *The City in History,* Lewis Mumford remarks that the Amsterdam of the seventeenth century was one of the finest, most humane cities ever constructed by mankind. And to this day people come from far and near to enjoy the beauty of what remains of it. But I do not suppose that very many of them come to enjoy the new Amsterdam, those parts of the city built since World War II; I do not suppose, for instance, that anyone comes from far *or* near to the corner of de Boelelaan and van der Boechorststraat* to drink in the beauty of the urban scene. Does that matter? Does that represent an impoverishment of human life, a diminution of shalom? The cries of the poor and the tyrannized touch the heart of God. Do the cries of those depressed by the ugliness of the shantytowns of Rio de Janeiro, the slums of Manhattan, or the squatters' quarters of Capetown also touch his heart?

Throughout this discussion our focus will be on the physical dimension of the city. To proceed we must establish a way of thinking about that dimension. It is customary to view the city simply as a large collection of buildings in close proximity to one another, each more or less self-contained and possessed of its own degree of architectural distinction. I propose in this reflection to break away from that sort of atomistic way of thinking, however, and view the city instead as an integral entity in which the individual buildings are abstracted parts.

Adopting the holistic perspective, we see the city as a unit orchestrating paths and partitions to establish gathering places for human beings on a given amount of the earth's surface. On acreage where once people could gather and travel more or less as they wished, the city introduces confinements, restrictions, barriers. The gathering places are the houses, the offices, the factories, the stores, the plazas. The paths are the roads and walkways—plus, in Holland, the bicycle paths. The city imposes these restrictions on the face of the earth in order to create an environment—a *shared* environment, I might emphasize—in which its dwellers can perform such activities as they find desirable or unavoidable. Thus, fundamentally a city is a shared environment for human activity.

The city shapes space. In part it shapes *interior* space inside factories, offices, houses, concert halls, etc.; but, just as importantly, it shapes *exterior* space—*urban space* we may call it—with buildings, trees, and other objects that confine our view when out of doors. Though people sense urban space and feel its varying qualities, customarily they take no conscious note of it. But to see

*This intersection is the location of the main buildings of the Free University of Amsterdam, where the material in this book was initially presented as a series of lectures.

that there is indeed such a thing as urban space, think for a moment of a room in which the walls, ceiling, and floor together shape space in a certain way. Now, even if the ceiling of the room, its "lid," were removed, space would nonetheless be shaped by the walls and floor, though indeed less completely so, for space would "leak out" the top. So too, then, the buildings and other objects of a city give definite characteristics to the spaces among them, characteristics that we note and feel as we move about in those spaces. The beauty or ugliness of the shared public dimension of a city is determined mainly by the character of its exterior, urban space, by the character of the facades and other features that together shape that space, and by the light that enters it.

Within the context of a definite configuration of technological possibilities, it is mainly the actions that city dwellers find to be necessary and desirable that determine their indoor/outdoor environment. And since these actions differ to some extent from city to city, each city is an expression of, a causal consequence of, the lifestyles of its residents—or, actually, of the lifestyles of its current residents plus generations of their predecessors. A city, like a work of art, is value and rationality embedded in sensory material. To a trained eye the physical characteristics of a Dutch city can tell a great deal about the Dutch style of life, both present and past.

It is important to realize that this causal efficacy operates in the reverse direction as well: not only is the city an expression of the lifestyle of its residents; it also *shapes* that lifestyle, making some activities attractive and convenient, and rendering others almost impossible to perform. The lifestyle of the Dutch is different from that of Americans in part because they live in different kinds of cities. Cities are in fact moral agents, just as buildings are moral agents. The industrial cities of nineteenth-century England twisted and distorted human life as few cities ever have. The black townships of South Africa, the shanty-towns of South America, the slums of the United States, are doing the same today. Such cities have tragically mislaid Aristotle's famous dictum that "the city comes into existence in order that men may live; it persists that they may live well."[4] And, for better or worse, the American suburbs also shape the lifestyle of American suburbanites, and the huge blocks of flats in the new Dutch cities shape the lifestyle of the contemporary Dutch.

I think we would miss something of great importance, however, if we understood the connection between a city and its inhabitants to be no more than a matter of the development of a serviceable physical environment for the performance of a given set of activities; there are also certain quite independent demands that we place on this physical environment. Traditional Muslims, for example, require of their cities that they be expressive symbols of the richness-within-unity which is Allah. And I am persuaded that all of us subconsciously ask that there be a fittingness between the overall character of our cities and the fundamental convictions and attitudes of their inhabitants—in the same way that there is a fittingness between a jagged line and the emotion of agitation.[5] The expressive quality of central Paris is very different from the expressive quality of central Amsterdam: the former is expressive of royal pomp and pride; the latter, of bourgeois *gezelligheid*.

For these reasons, to experience a city is to absorb some sense of what it has been like to be human in this place on the earth's surface. Also, of course, to experience a city is to perceive the memorials—the Rembrandt house, the Washington Monument—to persons and events from the past, and thus to have brought into one's own awareness some of the decisive shapers of the identity of these people here. In short, a city not only provides places in which we can gather with our contemporaries; its stones and bricks and timbers and tiles bring us into contact with our fellow human beings from the past. When a city obliterates the traces of its past, it attentuates the temporal dimension of human community.

But important as all this is, my concern here is not with a city's potential for building—or destroying—human community; it is rather with our experience of the city itself, with the aesthetic excellence of the shaped public space, of the facades and other features that shape this space, and of the way light pervades this space. Does *this,* I want to ask, have anything to do with happiness, with shalom?

The tradition of reflections on the significance of the aesthetic is of course a long one. Such modern-day thinkers as Clive Bell and Mikel Dufrenne see in aesthetic experience an apprehension of the ultimate reality of things, transcending our ordinary commerce with objects. The Muslims and the Byzantine Christians saw the situation in just the opposite way: for them aesthetic excellence, identified with beauty, was a reflection of deity. I have already alluded to the fact that Muslims, in particular, applied this belief to their reflections on the city—indeed, they applied it to the *construction* of their cities. For them, the beauty of the city inhered in its being an expressive symbol of the richness-within-unity of Allah. In my judgment there is no parallel to the profundity of the Muslims' manner of fitting their understanding of the city into their understanding of reality and life as a whole. We would do well to pay attention to it even though we shall not want to imitate it. By contrast, those in our society who place *freedom* at the center of their reflections on the good life have had nothing to say about the city—much about works of art, but nothing about the city. Is this an indication of the poverty of that line of thought?

In spite of my admiration for the profundity of the Muslim reflections on the city, aesthetic excellence is not for me the transcendental phenomenon that it is in the Byzantine-Muslim line of thought, nor do I find aesthetic experience the transcendental phenomenon that it is in the Bell-Dufrenne line of thought. And so I do not fit the aesthetic of the city into the pattern of Christian thought generally by saying, for example, that the city must be an expressive symbol of God. For me, the core of aesthetic excellence is what the main tradition in the West has always said it is: that which gives pleasure upon perceptual apprehension. As Aquinas says, "beautiful things are those which please when seen"[6] (to which I would add, "or *heard*"). For me, then, the link between shalom and the aesthetic of the city has to occur in the phenomenon of delight—specifically, delight in sensory experience. The fundamental issue has to be whether such delight is an authentic component in shalom. I find it impossible to conclude anything other than that it is.

Shalom incorporates our right relationship to—and more than that, *our delight in*—the physical. As a sign of God's Kingdom of shalom, Jesus did not just forgive sins and relieve religious anxiety; he healed *bodily* infirmities. Such healing was consonant with the prophetic vision of shalom which included banquets with rich red wine. And surely the wine of which the prophets spoke was no more some sort of nonmaterial, spiritual wine than the bodies that Jesus healed were nonmaterial, spiritual bodies.

The Genesis account supports the conclusion that shalom is in large measure the eschatological counterpart of creation. Surveying everything that he had made, including this besouled creature, man, who was made of dust but given that ultimate prize of responsibility, God saw that it was very good. Now surely in this affirmation of success and delight that God pronounces on his handiwork we must likewise hear his affirmation that the physical world that embraces us is *fit for* our fulfillment—is in fact meant to serve our fulfillment. For after all, the God who placed us here and pronounced approval of his work of creation is the God of love for this human being of his. We must then share with him in pronouncing our approval of the physical world as the arena of our fulfillment. "The earth God has given to the sons of men" (Ps. 115:16); and he has given it to us for our use *and for our delight*. In the garden of Eden, says the writer of Genesis 2, "the Lord God made to grow every tree *that is pleasant to the sight* and good for food" (Gen. 2:9).

It is impossible to speak on these matters without taking account of the intense pain that the artist has been given to suffer by several of the traditions of Christianity, including the Reformed, or Calvinist, tradition. This is not to suggest that I intend this discussion to be a reflection on art; in fact, I have very deliberately avoided taking that path, because I am profoundly convinced that if we are concerned that our fellow human beings should find some sensory refreshment in their lives, then it is the city that we must first of all pay attention to, and not those isolated objects that we call works of art. I say this as one who loves the arts intensely; yet I have nothing but abhorrence for our modern practice of constructing cities that are deserts of aesthetic ugliness and then sprinkling about within them as small oases our concert halls, museums, etc., in order to salve an aching conscience. Among the reprehensible features of modern society, this must be counted high. It is *the city* that is the *all*-embracing environment of almost *all* of us.

So I have not been discussing art. Yet in discussing the aesthetic of the city, my comments have been intensely relevant to the arts, and that is why they will bring to the surface the pain of which I spoke. Of course it is true that to some extent modern art is in conflict with every religious tradition and community, since it is itself an intensely religious phenomenon,[7] but there is more to the pain than that. Within the Calvinist tradition, the pain is often induced by the rampant intellectualism characteristic of modern Calvinism. By their very nature, artists express their ideas and values in images rather than in rationally analytical discourse, and the modern Calvinist, much enamored of analytical reasoning, too often approaches their work with suspicion, if not censure and suppression. On an even deeper level than that, many modern Calvinists hold *obedient action* to be the basic category: they perceive God solely as lawgiver and contend that we are to spend our lives in the activism of obedience, engaged in ever-vigilant battle with the ever-present Evil One. They tend, accordingly, to be cautious utilitarians, dubious of the value of aesthetic delight.

This constitutes yet another area in which modern Calvinism has departed from its origins. Consider, for example, this striking passage from Calvin's *Institutes,* in which, after explicitly repudiating the suggestion that we should allow ourselves to use physical goods only so far as necessity requires, he has this to say:

> Let this be our principle: that the use of God's gifts is not wrongly directed when it is referred to that end to which the Author himself created and destined them for us, since he created them for our good, not for our ruin. . . . Now if we ponder to what end God created food, we shall find that he meant not only to provide for necessity but also for delight and good cheer. Thus the purpose of clothing, apart from necessity, was comeliness and decency. In grasses, trees, and fruits, apart from their various uses, there is beauty of appearance and pleasantness of odor. . . . For if this were not true, the prophet would not have reckoned among the benefits of God, "that wine gladdens the heart of man, that oil makes his face shine." . . . Scripture would not have reminded us repeatedly, in commending his kindness, that he gave all such things to men. And the natural qualities themselves of things demonstrate sufficiently to what end and extent we may enjoy them. Has the Lord clothed the flowers with the great beauty that greets our eyes, the

sweetness of smell that is wafted upon our nostrils, and yet will it be unlawful for our eyes to be affected by that beauty, or our sense of smell by the sweetness of that odor? What? Did he not so distinguish colors as to make some more lovely than others? What? Did he not endow gold and silver, ivory and marble, with a loveliness that renders them more precious than other metals or stones? Did he not, in short, render many things attractive to us, apart from their necessary use? . . .

Away, then, with that inhuman philosophy which, while conceding only a necessary use of creatures, not only malignantly deprives us of the lawful fruit of God's beneficence but cannot be practiced unless it robs a man of all his senses and degrades him to a block.[8]

One of the most influential interpretations of early Calvinism in our day is of course Max Weber's, in which he called early Calvinism "worldly asceticism" and "ascetic Protestantism." But if what Calvin says here is at all typical of early Calvinism—and it is my own judgment that it at least represents a prominent strand within early Calvinism—then on a central point we must question Weber's interpretation. When Weber looked at the bourgeois capitalist, he was struck by the fact that here was someone who, in what seemed to Weber an utterly unnatural fashion, kept his nose to the grindstone of work, accumulating capital, but seldom enjoying what it could buy, suppressing the natural human tendency to indulge the senses. "The *summum bonum* of this ethic, the earning of more and more money, combined with the strict avoidance of all spontaneous enjoyment of life," says Weber, "is above all completely devoid of any eudaemonistic, not to say hedonistic, admixture. It is thought of so purely as an end in itself that from the point of view of the happiness of, or utility to, the single individual, it appears entirely transcendental and absolutely irrational."[9]

Weber goes on to ask what could have produced such an unnatural form of human being, and suggests that in large measure the culprit was Calvinism, with its notion of the calling and its "idea of the necessity of proving one's faith in worldly activity" (*PE,* p. 121). The sign of one's election by God is to be found in those works which bring glory to God in the practice of one's calling: "however useless good works might be as a means of attaining salvation, . . . they are indispensable as a sign of election" (*PE,* p. 115); "worldly activity . . . could . . . be considered the most suitable means of counteracting feelings of religious anxiety . . ." (*PE,* p. 112).

What followed, argues Weber, was that "the moral conduct of the average man was . . . deprived of its planless and unsystematic character and subjected to a consistent method for conduct as a whole" (*PE,* p. 117); "it was this rationalization," he says, "which gave the Reformed faith its peculiar ascetic tendency . . ." (*PE*, p. 118). Weber's point in calling this rationalization "ascetic" is that, in his judgment, a similar rationalization occurred in the medieval monastery, where "the life of the saint was directed solely toward a transcendental end, salvation. But precisely for that reason it was thoroughly rationalized in this world and dominated entirely by the aim to add to the glory of God on earth" (*PE*, p. 118). Monasticism "had developed a systematic method of rational conduct with the purpose of overcoming the *status naturae,* to free man from the power of irrational impulses and his dependence on the world and on nature. It attempted to subject man to the supremacy of a purposeful will . . ." (*PE*, pp. 118-19). Thus Puritanism can be thought of as taking the ascetic rationalization of the monastery and spreading it out so that it applied to all the members of the holy commonwealth, and to all of their activity within the ordinary social world: "now every Christian had to be a monk all his life" (*PE*, p. 121).

Plausible as this interpretation is, I think that in the light of such passages as the one just quoted from Calvin it will not do. Weber's interpretation is one variant on those interpretations that regard *obedient action* as the fundamental category in early Calvinist thought. But as I argued in the first chapter, that is not accurate. The fundamental category is *gratitude,* and obedient action is only one manifestation of this gratitude. (Furthermore, the connection between action and election is not that by industrious action one proves one's election, but that by obedient action one expresses *gratitude* for one's election.) Another dimension of the expression of gratitude, as is evident from the Calvin passage, is taking delight in the world God gives us.

Thus one does not really find in early Calvinism sensory *asceticism.* Sensory delight, for the monks, was a distraction from that contemplation of God toward which they had bent all their efforts; they longed for the day when the distraction would be removed. Poverty was embraced as an ideal. All this is foreign to Calvinist thought and practice, in which I contend that one finds, instead of sensory asceticism, *disciplined frugality* with respect to sensory delight. Sensory delight is not to be repudiated, but disciplined, so as to be a component within gratitude. The medieval monks in their disciplined asceticism were fighting the allure of all those delights that are inferior to the beatitude that contemplation of God can yield; the Calvinists in their disciplined frugality were fighting the battle with sinful ingratitude. What they share is discipline, not asceticism.

The full history of art and the aesthetic in the thought and practice of the Calvinist tradition remains to be written. What has often misled critics into thinking that early Calvinism was insensitive to aesthetic matters, in spite of the flowering of painting among Calvinists in Holland and the flowering of poetry among Calvinists in England, Holland, and France, is, first, that they have mistaken a sort of aesthetic elegance for aesthetic insensitivity, and second, that they have interpreted the artistic renunciation of the Calvinist church service as typical of Calvinist life in general, when most emphatically it was not. Thus I find the interpretation offered by the contemporary English poet Donald Davie in his recent book *A Gathered Church* much more plausible than Weber's interpretation.

The topic of Davie's book is dissenting movements within the English church in the eighteenth century, movements which were in great measure Calvinist in their inspiration. In one of his chapters he discusses the hymns composed by the Calvinist poet Isaac Watts for his congregation in Southampton—hymns that, as Davie observes, have sunk more deeply into the consciousness of English-speaking people than any other poetry ever composed. At the conclusion of his discussion, Davie suggests that Watts's poetry is almost a paradigm of the Calvinist aesthetic, of what he calls "Calvinist classicism." He goes on to suggest that

> a Calvinist aesthetic exists. "In nothing perhaps has Calvin been more misjudged than in the view that he lacked an aesthetic sense. . . ." It was after all John Calvin who first clothed Protestant worship with the sensuous grace, and necessarily the aesthetic ambiguity, of song; and who that has attended worship in a French Calvinist church can deny that—over and above whatever religious experience he may or may not have had—he has had an aesthetic experience, and of a peculiarly intense kind? From the architecture, from church furnishings, from the congregational music, from the Geneva gown of the pastor himself, everything breathes *simplicity, sobriety,* and *measure*—which are precisely the qualities that Calvinist aesthetics demands of the art-object. . . . And so, even if we admit for the sake of argument that Calvinism denies sensuous pleasure, we encounter time and again the question, when faced with a Calvinist occasion: Do we have here a denial of sensuous pleasure, or do we not rather have sensuous pleasure deployed with an unusually frugal, and therefore exquisite, fastidiousness? It is peculiarly of the nature of Puritan art to pose just this question, though it is by no means the account of it that is usually given.[10]

Old Amsterdam, old Bruges, old Florence, old Capetown, old Boston—these are the cities of delight, all of them old. Why are we in the modern world no longer capable of building cities of delight? What are the dynamics of ugliness? It does no good merely to bewail in idealistic fashion the ugliness of our contemporary cities. If we wish to reshape our social world, and in this case its physical context, we must understand the dynamics that have made it what it is. Allow me then to point to some of the dynamics of urban ugliness in the contemporary world, acknowledging that the power of these various dynamics differs from area to another.

In many places, and certainly in the United States, there is a powerful resistance to the public planning and sometimes even to the public regulation of what is after all our shared public environment; there is an insistence that each person be allowed to plan, with at most minimal regulation, whatever part of the city he or she happens to own. In part this is a result of the private capitalism that has come to consider all such forms of public planning and regulation to be violations of the free market, sometimes necessary perhaps, but always regrettable. It is also the result of the familial privatism that so deeply infects our modern world: we submit to the boredom of wage-labor in order to receive money which we then use to secure necessities and luxuries for ourselves and our families; too often our concern extends no farther.

A sense of civic identity is swiftly passing from the modern world in the face of these potent dynamics. Even where people have a voice in the destiny of their city, the majority neglect to exercise it. They are indifferent to the public environment. Never have I felt this tyranny of the private economy over our cities so keenly as when I first caught sight of the Ieros Odos in Athens, the ancient Sacred Way that led from Athens to Delphi. For years my mind had been filled with pictures of the Sacred Way as a great and beautiful ceremonial route along which processions once moved to the holy places of Delphi. What I saw instead was a dusty, tar-covered street, lined for miles with car repair shops, junk yards, tire stores, and neon signs.

But even in those areas where a considerable degree of public planning and regulation is tolerated, one discovers over and over again that the aesthetic of the public environment is given minimal attention at best. Considerations of economic growth and profit making are consistently given preeminence. If a choice has to be made between economic growth and the destruction of the urban environment, economic growth wins out and the city as a humane environment is destroyed. Often this occurs because powerful economic interests gain effective control of the public regulative and planning agencies and bend them to the service of their own private economic interests.[11]

It must be granted, however, that the results have not been a great deal better when planning agencies and their architectural advisers have given explicit consideration to aesthetic concerns. Twentieth-century architecture, as much as, and perhaps more than, any of the arts, has been a child of the Enlightenment. The city was to be redesigned on "rational" grounds—as in Le Corbusier's elegant but inhumane "Radiant City." Rather than exploring the wellsprings of authentic human life and designing a city to fit, architects have produced a "rational design," into the slots and holes and windswept plains of which human life has been squeezed. The city was meant to be a "machine for living"; our twentieth-century cities are the philosophy of the Enlightenment made concrete—and glass and steel.

Another important factor in the destruction of the city as a humane environment is our commitment to that technological convenience, the private automobile. (Actually the automobile is not merely an*other* factor; it is so crucial to modern metropolitan life that it has become one of the foremost concerns in all aspects of planning and regulating all of the major cities of the world.) In most cities there is a tacit commitment on the part of all concerned to assure the automobile access to within approximately one hundred meters (and preferably closer) of every spot at ground level in the city. One of the results of such planning is that wherever pedestrians go in the city, they are surrounded by belts of mortal danger. Another result is that streets must be widened in order to achieve this accessibility, and the contrast, so wonderful to experience in the old cities of Europe, between narrow streets and wide plazas is everywhere destroyed. Huge bleak parking areas are introduced. And, perhaps worst of all, wide expressways are sent crashing like destructive tornadoes through our cities. Often the destruction is enormous: witness old Boston. But of course, when one is traveling in a car it is in any case almost impossible to get enjoyment out of the public environment of the city. Thus our commitment to the car as our principal means of transportation reinforces our tendency to think of the city not as an integrated public environment for our life together, but as a collection of individual buildings. We race at great speed from one destination to another, paying no attention—indeed, finding it impossible to pay any attention—to what lies along our way, insisting only that the traffic move swiftly and that our various destinations be more or less pleasant oases in the bleak urban desert.

I need not describe for you the results of the workings of these dynamics. We can all see them all around us (although some countries are isolated from the worst of the results; the very livelihood of Holland, for instance, has for centuries depended on public planning). But to give you some sense of what has been lost, let me recount Lewis Mumford's description of the medieval European city:

> In the main . . . the medieval town was not merely a stimulating social complex; it was . . . a more thriving biological environment than one might suspect from looking at its decayed remains. There were smoky rooms to endure; there was also perfume in the garden behind the burghers' houses; for fragrant flowers and herbs were widely cultivated. There was the smell of the barnyard in the street, diminishing in the sixteenth century, except for

the growing presence of horses and stables. But there would also be the odor of flowering orchards in the spring, or the scent of the new-mown grain, floating across the fields in early summer. . . .

As for the eye and the ear, there is no doubt where the balance of advantage goes. The majority of medieval towns in these respects were immensely superior to those erected during the last two centuries: is it not mainly for their beauty, indeed, that people still make pilgrimages to them? One awoke in a medieval town to the crowing of a cock, the chirping of birds nesting under the eaves, or to the tolling of the hour in the monastery on the outskirts, perhaps to the chime of bells in the new bell tower in the market square, to announce the beginning of the working day, or the open-ing of the market. Song rose easily on the lips, from the plain chant of the monks to the refrains of the ballad singer in the marketplace, or that of the apprentice and the house-maid at work. Singing, act-ing, dancing, were still "do-it-yourself" activities.

If the ear was stirred, the eye was even more deeply delighted. Every part of the town, beginning with the walls them-selves, was conceived and executed as a work of art: even parts of a sacred structure that might be unseen, were still finished as care-fully as if they were fully visible, as Ruskin long ago noted: God at least would bear witness to the craftsman's faith and joy. The worker who had walked through the nearby fields or woods on a holiday came back to his stone carving, his wood working, his weaving or gold-smithing, with a rich harvest of impressions to be transferred to his work. The buildings, so far from being musty and "quaint," were as bright and clean as a medieval illumination, if only because they were usually whitewashed with lime, so that all the colors of the image-makers, in glass or polychromed wood, would dance in reflection on the walls, even as the shadows quivered like sprays of lilacs on the facades and the traceries of the more richly carved buildings. . . .

Life flourishes in this dilation of the senses. . . . Though diet was often meagre in the Middle Ages, though many comforts for the body were lacking even for those who did not impose pen-itential abstentions upon themselves, the most destitute or the most ascetic could not wholly close his eyes to beauty. The town itself was an ever-present work of art.[12]

I have been speaking of the dynamics operative in the modern world that have been destructive of the public environment of our cities. Let me now add that the intellectuals of the modern world have done little to resist this destruction. I think, for example, of the Frankfurt School, which as part of its critique of modern culture paid a great deal of attention to art from the 1940s on into the '70s, but said nothing at all of the aesthetics of the city. In that they are typical. The intellectuals in modern society have been intensely interested in the arts, supporting the construction and preservation of symphony halls, opera houses, theatres, art museums, and so forth. But they, too, have been willing to travel through environments of ugliness so as to enter these fine jewel boxes. No more than anyone else have they concerned themselves with the city as the environment experienced by all of us as we travel about to conduct our activities.

On the surface of it this is a very strange combination of attitudes— intense concern with the arts combined with indifference for the aesthetic of the city. After all, most of the residents of a city never enter its art museums, its opera houses, its theatres. And of those who do, certainly not many spend most of their time there. Should not a person concerned with the arts be even *more* concerned with the aesthetic of the city, which is the constant environment of us all?

To understand this paradoxical situation, one must grasp something of the attitude modern intellectuals hold toward the arts. In the first place, they are neither devotees nor promoters of *the arts in general*; they are devotees of *high* art, of *elite* art. When they speak of art, it will often be only this elite art that they have in mind, so much so that they will be led into making generalizations that, though they may be true for the high art of our society, are certainly not true for art in general. Should they acknowledge other "lower" forms of art, they will tend to treat them with unconcealed and unrelieved scorn. This latter attitude characterized the Frankfurt School. They studied in considerable detail what they called "mass culture," but their scorn for it is evident on every page.

This veneration for high art so characteristic of the intellectuals in our society is grounded in their understanding of what it is that the high-art artist does. The concept of *expression* is central: artists do not aim to *represent reality*, as the long tradition of the West held; rather, they aim to *express themselves*—their feelings, their attitudes, their vision of life. And in the case of the authentic artists the vision of reality that they express will be prophetically different from that by which the bulk of their fellow human beings live and which shapes our ambient social world. Thus in art not only do we find an expressive alternative to our heavily rationalized society, but the vision expressed is a critical negation of the vision shaping our social order. One can see then why the intellectuals in our society so often resort to religious language to speak about art. Art for them *is* a religion, a prophetic salvific religion. But it is also easy to see that in these attitudes there is nothing that would lead intellectuals to move on from an interest in art to an interest in the city; instead, they *contrast* art with the city on the grounds that the city cannot under any circumstances be the free expression of the vision of an individual artist who has seen deep into what is amiss in the attitudes formative of our social world.

What serves to perpetuate this attitude of the modern intellectuals is their curious tendency to think of the aesthetic as confined to art. There is, indeed, no current *theory* of the aesthetic that yields the conclusion that the aesthetic dimension of reality is confined to art, and yet the assumption is commonly made that what lies behind art is always an aesthetic intention, and conversely, that the aesthetic does not go beyond art. The aesthetic is thus bound up tightly with art; and the critics' concern with the aesthetic in art never leads them on to where the aesthetic touches almost all of us almost all of the time—in the city.[13]

We have been discussing the relation of the city to shalom. In conclusion let me observe that to all of us acquainted with the biblical message there is yet one more dimension of the relation of the city to shalom that resonates in our consciousness: the image of the biblical writers for our ultimate destiny is that of life in a city—not, be it noted, in a garden. In this respect the biblical vision is almost unique among the great religious visions of human destiny. But what does it mean that our ultimate destiny is imaged with a city? In his provocative book *The Meaning of the City*, Jacques Ellul answers this question vividly. Let me quote some of what he says:

> The Christian conception . . . is the expectation of a new city. And this reveals a very singular myth, which cannot be put on the same shelf with pagan myths of a golden age or the Eden to come. For characteristic of all these myths is the notion that there was at the beginning of time . . . a golden age when there was an equilibrium in everything and in man's heart. Life was natural—in nature—and trouble was brought in by the pride of a Prometheus, for example, or by some other event. Whatever may have happened, from that time on, war and death have been in the world, and man has been in quest of the lost golden age. It is proclaimed to him that he will reach it . . . that the golden age will return to the earth and in the same form. . . . This ancient myth of a new life in nature . . . is found under many forms in every corner of the earth, from the Eskimos to the North American Indians to the Tartars. Everywhere we find the same idealization of nature as bringing peace. . . . And the characteristic of this notion is always man's abandonment of all that he has built to defend himself, to ensure his supremacy, to conquer the earth, by a return to the natural life and a direct relationship with things. . . .
>
> In the common myths we have a backward movement. . . . The essential point . . . is a refusal of the existing order, a denial of man's "progress" in the sense of simple evolution, not of im-

provement. It is a black line drawn through all of history, which is only the history of human degradation. . . . Man must . . . come back to what he once abandoned and destroyed. But the Hebrew notion is completely other: to the extent that this view is centered in the city, it takes in all of man's works and all of his history. Far from advocating a return to the past, it calls for a step ahead; it wants to lose nothing of what man has done. And in this respect Karl Marx was, as many have asserted, directly inspired by Jewish mythology, in which there is nothing to be destroyed from the fantastic adventure of human civilization. Rather, man's history must be transcended. . . . Thus the golden age will be characterized by an acceptance of history, and not by its refusal. This myth is therefore a kind of adoption, the ennobling of man's work, the very opposite of scorn and rejection.[14]

Of course it is also true that when it images our ultimate destiny as life in a city, the Bible speaks of this city, symbolized as Jerusalem, as coming down out of heaven from God (Rev. 3:12, 21:10). Our ultimate destiny is not brought about simply by industrious, rationalized action. It is the creation of God, "as extraordinary, unbelievable and unexpected as the first."[15] Yet in the eschatological image of the city we have the assurance that our efforts to make these present cities of ours humane places in which to live—efforts which so often are frustrated, efforts which so often yield despair—will, by way of the mysterious patterns of history, eventually provide the tiles and timbers for a city of delight.[16]

About ten years ago in my own city of Grand Rapids, Michigan, a very large bright red sculpture designed by Alexander Calder was placed in a newly designed plaza. In my judgment it is among Calder's very finest works. Without the Calder, the plaza would be little more than a dreary open space to hurry across; with the Calder there as the rivetting center of attention, the space of that plaza has acquired a strongly centralized, magnetic quality. By now the Calder is an indelible part of every Grand Rapidean's image of our city. When the purchase of the Calder was being discussed, there were those who suggested that the money should instead be given to the poor. Of course no one had proposed collecting this amount of money and giving it to the poor before the issue of the sculpture came up. The question I have posed in this chapter is this: Could it be that living in a city devoid of sensory delight is itself a form of poverty?

Resistance

We have studied some of the miseries and some of the injustices characteristic of our modern social order. And we have probed the dynamics, the practices, that are at the root of these sorrows and deprivations of rights. We have studied mass poverty and discovered that prominent among its roots is a complex of economic practices and legal prescriptions whereby growth is taken as the ultimate economic and social good, whereby the production and merchandising of goods for sale on the market for profit is only minimally regulated, and whereby the person who provides capital to an enterprise is thereby entitled to a voice in the enterprise while the person who provides labor is not. We have studied the deprivation of civil rights and the terror caused by excessive loyalty to nation. And we have looked at the ugliness of our contemporary cities, perpetuated if not caused by the practice on the part of our cultural elite of revelling in high art while ignoring the life-diminishing qualities of our shared environment.

We have seen that economic growth, loyalty to nation, and the contemplation of high art often receive the status of idols among us: they are regarded as something of transcendent worth and hence raised above all normative criticism, while all other values are subordinated to them; and though we eventually see our lives diminished, we find ourselves enslaved and do not see how to extricate ourselves. Of course there are other sorrows we could have analyzed; of these the most threatening is certainly the massive accumulation of armaments that the states of the world are assembling. The sorrows to which we have addressed our remarks are only a sample, though the dynamics we have uncovered are common to most of the others as well.

We have also looked at some of the ideologies that serve to legitimate these practices in the eyes of so many in our society. I have not suggested that these large-scale practices are the result of people's decisions to implement certain ideas; in fact, for the most part it seems to me that they are not: it is the psychological mechanisms of *modeling* and *conditioning* that secure their perpetuation.[1] Nevertheless, ideas do have consequences. Mainly they work ideologically, by serving to justify these practices in people's eyes—making them seem right and good, often by making it seem that there is no viable alternative. Ideologies serve not so much to *create* as to *sustain* practices.

I have interspersed our discussion with criticisms of the ideologies that sustain the practices on which we have focussed our attention, but my greater interest has been in trying to demonstrate, as forcefully as I could, that these injustices and miseries are violations of the shalom for which we are called to work, and that the practices which lead to them are accordingly unacceptable. Such a line of argument, I am persuaded, is not of merely academic interest, since one way to change practice is to persuade individuals that the practice is wrong. Moral discourse is sometimes effective in action, particularly if those to whom one speaks are persuaded that right and wrong are grounded in the will of God.

I have not—not in much detail, anyway—suggested alternative practices and alternative institutional arrangements and regulations, but naturally we want to know what such alternatives would look like. Partly this is a matter of intellectual curiosity, but it is more than that: we want to know where we can effectively direct our energies. It is my conviction, however, that in good measure we already know the alternatives, or can easily become acquainted with them. There are examples in the world of states that treat all their citizens alike, making no ethnic distinctions among them. There are examples in the world of states that regulate capitalism in such a way that their citizens are not impoverished. And where we do not have examples of alternative practices—as we do not of alternative ways of the core treating the periphery in their economic interactions—we have plenty of suggestions. Our contemporary academics have not been lax in producing suggestions for how things might be handled differently. Over and over the crucial issue proves rather to be this: we are not as a whole persuaded that they *should* be handled differently.

Perhaps I should say that those *with power* in regard to the issues at hand are not in general thus persuaded. Hereby a new and indispensable note is sounded, for these practices do not victimize all of us equally: not only are there *victims* of excessive loyalty to nation; there are also *benefactors*. Not only are there victims of our economic practices; there are also benefactors. Not only are there victims of the elite's practice of turning away from the city to find meaning in high art; there are benefactors as well. And we all know that when the benefactors of such practices are confronted with the argument that those practices are wrong, they are far more inclined than others to reject the argument rather than revise their practice. Self-interest regularly shapes moral conviction.

In that circumstance, what should the victims (and those who side with the victims) do? Should they confine themselves to talk in the hope that somewhere they will find a listening ear? Or should they engage in active resistance and opposition? And under what circumstances, if any, is civil disobedience morally permissible as a component in such active resistance? Further, under what circumstances, if any, is resorting to violence legitimate as such a component?

These questions plunge us into an immensely important cluster of topics which, to my regret, I cannot here treat. Their complexity makes it impossible to treat them briefly. Let me simply remind my readers that there are already long lines of reflection on these matters—and, in particular, long lines of reflection by Christians. An excellent review of such reflections by Lutherans and Calvinists and Catholics at the time of the Reformation is available in the second volume of Quentin Skinner's *Foundations of Modern Political Thought*; his analysis of the nature and sources of the Reformers' doctrine of justified resistance is particularly valuable.

Though there are those in modern society, including Christians, who say that the dictates of the state should always be obeyed, no serious Christian thinker has ever held this. None has interpreted Paul's injunction in Romans 13 to obey the authorities as implying this. All have agreed that if the state asks us to do something that we know to be contrary to the law of God, we are not only permitted but obliged to disobey the state: we are to obey God rather than man.

The situation that aroused the attention of the Reformers was not that of the state asking some person to do something that he or she knows to be contrary to the will of God; rather, it was that of the state itself doing things that subjects of the state know to be contrary to the law of God. Here too, though, there was a substantial measure of agreement: all eventually concluded that if no disobedience to law and no recourse to violence are involved, then one is allowed, perhaps even obliged, to engage in active resistance with the aim of rectifying the situation—whether that involves the replacement of authorities or the reform of laws and institutions.

Eventually a consensus even arose on the issues of disobedience and violence. At first the Reformers were inclined to say that resistance might never take the form of civil disobedience or of recourse to violence: one had to suffer injustice in patience because only the officers of government, they believed, were morally permitted to use violence. But reflection on the situation of persecution eventually led them to conclude that not every person who holds political power does so legitimately. In particular, they concluded that an official who exceeds the bounds of his authority by inflicting "injuries" on the people of an "atrocious and notorious" character has lost his claim to office. Such a person "automatically reduces himself to the status of a felonious private citizen":[2] he no longer has a claim on our obedience. At first the Reformers held that, in such a case, only other persons in political office—the "lower magistrates" or the "magistrates of the people"—were morally permitted to act to restrain the criminal. But eventually the Scotch and English Calvinists concluded that private citizens as well were sometimes permitted both to act in violation of the law and to take up arms against the tyrannical and godless ruler; indeed, they argued that sometimes the citizens were obliged to do so.

It is my own view that the Reformers were certainly right in their conclusion that active resistance to tyrannical government is not only permitted but on occasion obligatory, sometimes even when that involves civil disobedience—though perhaps the reasons they offered for these conclusions need some restatement. The contemporary discussion should now focus, it seems to me, on the other question of whether violence is ever morally permissible as a component in that resistance. We in our age somehow find it vastly easier to excuse governmental violence than the violence of resistance—this in spite of the fact that if we compare the violence perpetrated by resistance movements in our bloody century with the violence perpetrated by governments, the former pales into near invisibility. No doubt this is so because we assume that even the worst of governments still somehow carries authority. To this assumption the reflections of the Reformers come as a jarring challenge: the government that perpetrates injuries of an atrocious and notorious character has lost its legitimacy, and the officers of such a government have only the status of private citizens who have committed criminal acts. If this conclusion is true, then the key question to consider in reflecting on the hostilities between governments and resistance movements will often simply be whether violence in response to violence on the part of private citizens is ever justified.

Will the church, once it sees clearly that its calling is not to turn away from the social world but to work for its reformation, become an active agent of resistance to injustice and tyranny and deprivation? I do not know. But certainly there is nothing else of promise in the world today. The Marxist conviction that the working class would become such an agent has proved to be one of the great illusions of history. Sections of the church are already the principal agents of resistance in South America and in Poland, as they were in Nazi Germany. The actions of the church do not rest, after all, simply on human empathy. They are grounded in the conviction that there is a word from outside our existence that calls us to the actions of love, with the assurance that those actions will not ultimately be unavailing. They are energized by a power from outside our existence that gives courage to people who never knew they had it. They are supported by the experience of a community that transcends nations.

It is nonetheless easy to despair over the church. And let us not suppose that the coming of God's Kingdom of shalom depends solely on what church people do. But through all the dark days of its existence, there is one way in which the church has remained the sacrament of, the effective pointer to, a new day: down through the ages it has been the bearer of the Bible—the Word of God which points to him who is the Word of God, Jesus of Nazareth. The church has borne that Word even when the actual bearers were corrupt. And thereby, often to its surprise and its distress, it has sown the seeds of resistance and of hope—among the blacks of South Africa, among the peasants of South America, and indeed throughout the world.

Chapter VII

Justice and Worship: The Tragedy of Liturgy in Protestantism

A peculiar worry soon begins to haunt the church when the conviction sinks in that discipleship incorporates commitment to struggle for the reform of the social order. Has not the Christian way of being-in-the-world now lost all distinctiveness? Has not the church now become one among other social reform agencies in the modern world? The worry becomes even more acute whenever a program of action is laid out, since almost invariably there will be others who agree with large parts of the program. There are others in the modern world concerned about mass poverty, about the effects of nationalism, about urban blight. So not only is there no distinctiveness in the fact that the Christians' way of being-in-the-world incorporates the struggle for the reform of a corrupt social order, but there does not even seem to be distinctiveness in the particular goals of their struggle. It appears that Christians insert themselves into the social world in fundamentally the same way as the secular socialists, the secular progressives, or whatever. So wherein lies the distinctiveness of Christian existence?

Is it that Christians, though their goals are similar to those of others, have different motivations and a different framework of beliefs undergirding those motivations? Is it that they use Bible and church to energize and direct them, whereas the secular reformists seem to do nicely without these? In short, is it just that they accompany their actions with a different *inwardness*? Is that, ironically, where our line of thought leads us? We began by insisting that Christianity is not merely a gospel of inwardness, but that it asks of us certain actions in the world—specifically, that it asks of us participation in the struggle to reform the social world. If we are now brought back to inwardness as the seat of our distinctiveness, we shall feel disappointed, cheated, let down. Is *this* all it comes to? After this long tour are we back at inwardness?

It is my own conviction that the church, and humanity at large, neglects inwardness at its own peril. And when I here speak of inwardness I do not just mean motivation for social action along with the beliefs that undergird it. I mean contemplation. I mean the cultivation of what in some traditions is called spirituality, and in others, piety. It seems to me that amidst its intense activism, the Western world is starved for contemplation. Likewise it seems to me that the unmistakable witness of the Scriptures is that where genuine piety or spirituality is missing, there life as a whole is deeply wounded. Contemplation, spirituality, piety—these in my judgment themselves belong to authentic shalom, with influences radiating throughout the whole of our existence; furthermore, it is my expectation that in coming years they will be pursued by ever greater numbers of people here in the West. One way to deal with our concerns about the source of our distinctiveness is to confront them forthrightly and say: the inward life is important; not *all*-important, but important.

Others have attempted another answer. They have insisted on backing up a bit and raising seriously the question of whether the social program of the Christian really is substantially like that of anyone else. Is it not as a whole fundamentally different, with different goals and different strategies? The Anabaptists believe that their rejection of violence makes their program significantly different from others; the Dutch neo-Calvinists have tended to believe that their embrace of "sphere sovereignty" does the same thing for their program.

I think that this response also deserves serious consideration. But here I want to explore a different answer to the question of what is significantly distinctive about the Christian's way of being-in-the-world. I want to explore *worship,* worship by way of participation in the liturgy of the church. More precisely I want to explore the possibility that a rhythmic alternation of work and worship, labor and liturgy is one of the significant distinguishing features of the Christian's way of being-in-the-world.

I expect that some of my readers who are Christian will already be feeling acutely disappointed and uneasy. You were hoping that I would mention something important, something significant, something that you could point to without embarrassment when engaged in discussion with, for example, the Marxist, and say: "Here, on this important point of practice we differ." But you would feel embarrassed to mention to the Marxist participation in the liturgy of the church as an important distinctive, because you know that he or she would dismiss it with a wave of the hand as unworthy of consideration by an adult.

One question that ought to be raised here is this: Why should you let the Marxists (or anyone else) determine *your* scale of importance? Why say to them, "You tell me what you think is important, and then I'll see if I can find a difference between us that fits *your* standard of importance." Perhaps one significant difference between you and them lies in different standards of importance. But let that point pass. For in all likelihood, when I suggest that one of the significant differences between the Christian's way of being-in-the-world and the secularist's lies in the fact that the Christian participates in the liturgy of the church, the disappointment that you feel is the result of the fact that *you yourself* do not think this really important.

Deeply embedded in the thought framework of the modern church as a whole, and especially in that of the churches of the Reformed/Presbyterian tradition, is the conviction that the liturgy has no importance of its own, that its importance lies entirely in the benefit it renders to our life in the world—so that if one has the inner strength to live that life without benefit of liturgy, then liturgy can be nicely passed by. The language will vary, but the idea remains that the only point of Sunday is its benefit for Monday through Saturday; that the liturgy is fundamentally nothing more than a refueling stop; that the church is *mission,* this being understood in such a way that ideally the church should never be gathered for worship but always dispersed for work; that going to church is fundamentally going to sermon, and that the function of the sermon is just to build us up for our work in the world; that one ought to spend as little money as possible on a church building, since the liturgy is the last thing worth spending money on; that the decisive question to ask of the liturgy is simply "What did I get out of it?", whereas the question to ask of our work in the world is "How did we do?"; that fundamentally liturgy is issuing marching orders.

But is it true that the whole point of the liturgy is to benefit our life in the social world? Does liturgy have no importance of its own? I want to explore that question, along with another yet more fundamental: Could it be that when participation in the Sunday liturgy of the church is missing, then life as a whole is altered in a certain way? Is it not possible that the liturgy *authenticates* our action in the world?

We tend to think of our responsible work in the world as a solid, complete reality in itself, but we do not typically think of liturgy in this way. It would be difficult to find a book on liturgy written since the Second World War that did not discuss the relation of the liturgy to the Christian's life in the world. On the other hand, it would be easy to find books on Christian social action that say nothing at all about the relation of such action to the Christian liturgy. This situation reflects our conviction that the authentication of liturgy requires that its participants struggle for justice and peace in the world, whereas no similar *liturgical* condition is placed on the authenticity of the struggle for justice and peace. We are by now all accustomed, concerning the former of these convictions, to say that there is a Word from the Lord on the matter: over and over the prophets of the Old Testament affirm that the sacrifices and the solemn assemblies of those who wreak injustice in the world disgust the Lord. They are an offense to him.* But nothing similar is said—so we think—about

---

*Consider, for example, this passage from the book of Amos:
"I hate, I despise your feasts,
    and I take no delight in your solemn assemblies.
Even though you offer me your burnt offerings and cereal offerings,
    I will not accept them,
and the peace offerings of your fatted beasts
    I will not look upon.
Take away from me the noise of your songs;
    to the melody of your harps I will not listen.
But let justice roll down like waters,
    and righteousness like an ever-flowing stream."

(Amos 5:21-24)

the Lord's being disgusted with the industrious social activism of those who refuse or neglect to join with his people in worship. We assume that the asymmetry in our contemporary understanding of the relation of work to worship reflects the very same asymmetry in the biblical message.

That fine theologian of the Orthodox Church Alexander Schmemann defines *secularism* in one of his writings as "a negation of worship": "It is," he says, "the negation of man as a worshiping being, as *homo adorans.* . . ."[1] Perhaps you would wish to define the term differently. But the suggestion that man is meant to be a worshipping being—might there be some profound truth in that? And might it be that a certain inauthentic secularity begins to characterize our work in the world when that truth is denied in practice?

Let us follow the thought of Schmemann a bit farther; for in his writings there are to be found profound and provocative reflections on the place of worship in the life of man and on the place of liturgy in the life of the Christian. It is of course not at all surprising that Schmemann, a great deal of whose effort has been devoted to revitalizing the Orthodox tradition, should speak profoundly of worship. For it is that tradition above all that has kept alive the conviction that, to use the words of the Orthodox liturgy, "It is meet and right to sing of Thee, to bless Thee, to praise Thee, to give thanks to Thee, to worship Thee in every place of Thy dominions. . . ." What is especially appealing in Schmemann's thought is his intense aversion to dividing up reality into the "spiritual" versus the "material," the "sacred" versus the "profane," the "supernatural" versus the "natural."

At creation, says Schmemann, "God blessed the world, blessed man, blessed the seventh day (that is, time), and this means that He filled all that exists with His love and goodness, made all this 'very good.' " To this act of God, he continues, "the only *natural* (and not 'supernatural') reaction of man, to whom God gave this blessed and sanctified world, is to bless God in return, to thank Him, to *see* the world as God sees it and—in this act of gratitude and adoration—to know, name and possess the world." He goes on to say that

> all rational, spiritual and other qualities of man, distinguishing him from other creatures, have their focus and ultimate fulfillment in this capacity to bless God. . . . "*Homo sapiens,*" "*homo faber*" . . . yes, but, first of all, '*homo adorans.*' The first, the basic definition of man is that he is *the priest.* He stands in the center of the world and unifies it in his act of blessing God, of both receiving the world from God and offering it to God—and by filling the world with this eucharist, he transforms his life, the one that he receives from the world, into life in God, into communion with Him. The world was created as the "matter," the material of one all-embracing eucharist, and man was created as the priest of this cosmic sacrament. (*LW,* p. 15)

Thus, say Schmemann, the world is a *sacrament* of God. Both in its totality as cosmos and in its becoming as history, it "is an *epiphany* of God, a means of His revelation, presence, and power. [It] truly 'speaks' of Him and is in itself an essential means both of knowledge of God and communion with Him, and to be so is its true nature and its ultimate destiny"; correspondingly, "worship is truly an essential act, and man an essentially worshipping being. . . . The very notion of worship is based on an intuition and experience of the world as an 'epiphany' of God, thus the world—in worship—is revealed in its true nature and vocation as 'sacrament' " (*LW,* p. 120).[2]

I trust you can see already from these few brief passages why Schmemann will have nothing to do with the suggestion that worship involves a turn away from this so-called profane world to a so-called sacred world. Worship is the response to one's apprehension of the ultimate meaning and nature of *this* world, not of some other world. It is the response to one's apprehension of *this* world as the epiphany of God. Furthermore, worship has nothing to do with the denigration of *this* world and the denial of its worth. It is for one's enjoyment of *this* world that one blesses God. "It is *this world* (and not any 'other world'), it is *this life* (and not some 'other life') that were given to man to be a sacrament of the divine presence, given as communion with God, and it is only through this world, this life, by 'transforming' them into communion with God that man *was to be*" (*LW,* p. 100).

But a fall has occurred. And the essence of that fall, says Schmemann, is that the world has become opaque to man, no longer perceived as sacramental. It has come to seem "natural not to live a life of thanksgiving for God's gift of a world . . . natural not to be eucharistic" (*LW,* p. 16). In short, man has become *secular,* according to Schmemann's definition of the word. The secularist, he says,

> quite often accepts the idea of God. What, however, he emphatically negates is precisely the sacramentality of man and world. A secularist views the world as containing within itself its meaning and the principles of knowledge and action. . . . [He rejects] the primordial intuition that everything in this world and the world itself not only have *elsewhere* the cause and principle of their existence, but are *themselves* the manifestation and presence of that *elsewhere,* and that this is indeed the life of their life. . . . (*LW,* p. 124)

Let me pause here for a moment to express my hesitations about one or two points in Schmemann's thought. It seems to me that he tends to run together our activity of worshipping God with our awed and grateful acceptance of the world as a sacrament of God. I myself would say that worshipping God is but one manifestation, one expression of that acceptance. Another expression is our responsible development of the potentials of the world, and yet another is love of neighbor. Man is indeed *homo adorans,* but he is also *homo laborans* and *homo amans.*

Secondly, Schmemann, so far as I can tell, nowhere expresses any acknowledgment of the pain that so often accompanies what he calls secularism. Not all who see the world as nothing but world are happy in that. Some there are who long to find the world expressive of God, but whose longing goes unsatisfied. They long to find the world an epiphany of the wisdom and power and handiwork of a creator, but they do not find it so. They long to find the Bible a sacrament of the Word of God, but they hear nothing. And some there are whose experience of the world is so painful—in the brickyards of ancient Egypt, in the gulag of Soviet Russia, in the sickbed of a cancer ward—that though they continue to cry out to God for deliverance, they cannot apprehend the world as his sacrament. Their tears blur their vision and their cries obstruct their hearing. They cannot worship.

But that brings me back to Schmemann's main point: worship is grounded in one's apprehension of the world as a sacrament of God. It consists, in awed and grateful response to that apprehension, of blessing God, of praising Him. And this is not to be regarded as something pleasant to do if one just happens to have a taste for it—if one just happens to be "religious"; rather, such apprehension is the recognition of the reality of things: it belongs to man's true nature to respond to that apprehension by worship: worship is ontologically grounded.

It is now easy to see that for the individual who apprehends the world as a sacrament of God, work and the worship are fundamentally connected. Both are expressions of gratitude; together they constitute the two phases of the manifestation of devotion.

Nothing that I have so far said speaks to the uniqueness of Christian worship—nor indeed to the uniqueness of Christian work. That has not been inappropriate inasmuch as the worship of the Christian has continuities with the worship of mankind generally. Yet Christian worship *is* also significantly different, and to grasp the interconnections of worship with work in Christian existence fully, we must move on to discern some of what makes it unique. For that, we must engage in some liturgical theology.

"I am the Alpha and Omega," says God in the book of Revelation, the one "who is and who was and who is coming." The picture of God constructed by the classical theologians was that of a God outside of time, dwelling in eternity, ever-present, with no past and no future, impassive, immutable. The picture of the biblical writers is profoundly different: he is past and future as well as present because his *actions* are past and future as well as present: his actions are located in our history.[3] Central to the character of Christian worship is the fact that the God worshipped is apprehended as engaged in a history that is both his and ours, but a history of which he is Lord and we are not. In this fundamental aspect, Christian worship is revealed to be a descendant of the worship of old Israel.

Recall then the farewell speech of Moses to the tribes of Israel, as we find it in the book of Deuteronomy. Like mighty gongs being struck over and over and over, three themes interweave throughout the speech: *remember, expect,* and *take heed.* Israel is forever to remember that the God who created the heavens and the earth has liberated it from the bondage of toiling in the brickyards of Egypt. It is forever to live in the confident expectation that God will be faithful to his promise to give his people land and to bless them. And in the open space between never-failing remembrance and never-failing expectation, it is to take heed of God's commandments, commandments which are not some imposition of alien duty, but which have been given for the good of its members (10:13), so that they may have life (4:1). In society they shall not pervert justice; justice and only justice shall they follow (16:19-20). And they shall worship before the Lord God, rejoicing in all the good he has given them (26:10-11). What was unique in the life of Israel was that its work and worship were to be its way of keeping faith with the God whose actions of liberation and blessing in the course of history it was forever to remember and expect. As we shall shortly see, the overarching background of Christian work and worship, though different in its content, is identical in its structure. A fully Christian theology will be a theology of hope and of remembering, as well as of keeping faith with the God whom one remembers and hopes for.

From this all-embracing context of the God worshipped being a God who acts in history, we must now move inward to notice that in Israel work and worship are to be done in rhythmic alternation—or rather, work and *rest* are to alternate, with worship occurring in the context of rest. Worship is to take place in the context of a rhythmic temporal structure in our daily existence: "Six days you shall labor and do all your work; but the seventh day is a sabbath to the Lord your God; in it you shall not do any work . . ." (6:13-14). "The seventh day is a sabbath of solemn rest, a holy convocation," one of "the appointed feasts of the Lord" (Lev. 23:2-3).

What is the meaning of this instruction to introduce the rhythm of six-plus-one into their daily existence? Let me divide this question, treating first the meaning of that *rest* with which labor is to alternate, and then treating the meaning of the alternating rhythm itself. Listen to what Deuteronomy says: the significance of the seventh day is that "you shall remember that you were a servant in the land of Egypt, and the Lord your God brought you out thence with a mighty hand and an outstretched arm; therefore the Lord your God commanded you to keep the sabbath day" (Deut. 6:15). The seventh day is the feast of liberation from bond servitude; it is the celebration of freedom from enforced toil. One might ask why the appropriate expression of freedom from bond servitude was seen to be rest, rather than work in which one is one's own master. Part of the answer is that whenever a people is freed from servitude—as the Dutch from the German occupation after the Second World War—it celebrates by halting its work for a while; but the deeper answer lies in the fact that there are other echoes than those of liberation in the day of rest.

Listen to the writer of Exodus, who attached a different—not contradictory, but complementary—significance to the rest of the seventh day: "In six days the Lord made heaven and earth, the sea and all that is in them, and rested the seventh day; therefore the Lord blessed the sabbath day and hallowed it" (Ex. 20:11). The writer apprehended God's work of creation as itself taking time, not being done instantaneously; and the completion of God's creative work was marked by rest. Man's alternation of work and rest is to echo the alternation between work and rest in God's own life. The question then becomes what the nature of God's rest is: Is it the rest of exhaustion from work? Is it the rest of release from the boredom of work? Is it the rest of a necessary period of recreation so that one can go back to work refreshed? Surely none of these. God's rest is the rest of delight in his works.

I think it is inescapable that the fundamental meaning of this component of rest in the rhythmic alternation of six-plus-one in daily existence is that human life is meant to include something more than labor, something more than the industrious struggle for the mastery of the world and the reform of society, even if that struggle is conducted in freedom and not in bond servitude. It is meant to include delight in the works of God and man. The six-plus-one alternation of labor and rest is not the alternation of work with recovery from work so as to be able to go back to work;* it is the alternation of mastery of the natural and social world with thankful enjoyment of the world. The day of rest, the sabbath, "is important precisely in connection with and in opposition to the rush and the lust for a hurried expansion of power that so easily affects history and man's experience of it. The exodus was well-nigh an exodus from bondage to technocratic expansion in Egypt. The subsequent emphatic commandment to remember and observe the sabbath was an eloquent sign against that and a clear indication for wholesome historical life." The institution of the day of rest as a holy day was not the invitation to escape from history for a while into some realm of immutable perfection, but the invitation to "celebrate what is given and, more specifically, to take time to highlight the ordinary as something very worthwhile."[4]

But why the insistence on the *rhythm*? We can perhaps acknowledge

---

*This theme is not wholly missing, however: " 'Six days you shall do your work, but on the seventh day you shall rest; that your ox and your ass may have rest, and the son of your bondmaid, and the alien, may be refreshed' " (Ex. 23:12).

deep wisdom in the call for a balance between mastery and grateful enjoyment in human life. But why the rhythmic alternation of the two? Is it not just as well that each person intersperse the two in his own life as he sees fit?

The first point to be made about this rhythm is a negative point: it is not the reflection of some rhythm of nature. The religions of the world are filled with rhythms of work and festival. Normally the dating of the festivals echoes the rhythm of nature in some obvious way. There are some festivals coinciding with planting time and others coinciding with harvest, some with the shortest day of the year and others with the longest, but this six–plus–one alternation is profoundly peculiar. It corresponds to no natural cycle at all. I know, of course, that some have argued that there is a natural rhythm, albeit a highly subtle one, of needing one day of rest after six days of work. This would be a work/exhaustion cycle. If there is indeed such a cycle, it is strange that most peoples of the world have never recognized it, that indeed many regularly work much longer stretches without rest. But in any case it is clear that even if there is such a natural cycle, the significance for Israel of the rhythm does not lie there. Instead, this rhythm was given to be practiced as a re-membrance, as a memorial of the pattern of God's creative activity and of the pattern of Israel's liberating experience: *the very rhythm of everyday life was to be a liturgical practice.*

We are here confronted with the phenomenon of doing something as a memorial, or as a remembrance. This is a concept foreign to us and difficult to grasp; yet we cannot skip around it, for as Max Thurian, the theologian of the Taize community in France, remarks, "The idea that prayers and almsgiv-ing, like sacrifices, are presented before God *as a memorial* is part of the liturgical theology of Judaism. It is found in both the Old and New Testaments as an everyday fact, and the word to designate it is the equivalent of that which Christ uttered when He said, 'Do this as my memorial.' "[5]

Shortly I will describe what I think the Hebrew meant by doing something as a memorial; but it may help first to take a near analogue from ordinary experience. Once a year, on 20 October, the Free University of Am-sterdam celebrates its *Dies Natalis*. Labor is halted for a few hours and something of the rest of delight is inserted into the lives of members of the University. Free drinks are dispensed, conversation flowers, and the day is climaxed with a festive banquet. But all of this is intertwined with the celebrative remembering of the founding of the University. This is not accomplished by way of everyone being silent for a minute so as to bring to mind that day of 20 October 1880. Rather, it consists in a public *doing in remembrance*: a worship service is held at which songs of thanksgiving are sung, a procession of professors in ceremonial dress takes place, an academic address is delivered appropriate to this body of people by a member of the faculty, and those who stand in the continuity of academic succession with the founders of this institution express in word and gesture their gratitude for and loyalty to the institution and its tradition. I suggest that this is not far from being an example of what the Hebrew meant by doing something as a memorial.

The heart of the Jewish concept of the memorial is that the people bring the object of the memorial to the attention of someone other. To eat the Passover supper as a memorial of Israel's deliverance from Egypt is for Israel to bring to someone's attention that deliverance. So, too, to celebrate the Lord's Supper as a memorial of Jesus is for the church to bring its Lord to someone's attention.

To whose attention is something presented when some memorial action is performed? On the one hand, God is the recipient. The context in which the people presents its memorial to God—a context often explicitly expressed in words—is always that of *thanking* God for his covenant fidelity (of which the memorialized event or person is one indication) and of *interceding* with God for his continued blessing in the future: presenting something before God in the context of thanksgiving and intercession is one side of a memorial action. On the other hand, by doing something in memorial, the people may also bring to *its own* attention the memorialized event or person. The context in which the people presents its memorial to itself is that of *a renewed commitment to obedience*: bringing something to its own attention in the context of renewed commitment is the other side of a memorial action. Memorial actions differ from one another with respect to which of these aspects is dominant, but in most of them there are at least traces of both. The overall context is characteristically twofold, looking both backward and forward, establishing both a remembrance and an expectation.

There is yet another feature of some memorial actions that is of particular interest here: the incorporation of a ritualized reenactment of the central event that is being memorialized. This feature is especially obvious in the Passover celebration, but it is also a significant aspect of the six-plus-one rhythm of work and rest and of some of the Sabbath observances themselves. It is important to note that Israel understood the six-plus-one rhythm to be a life-long recapitulation, a life-long doing-in-remembrance, of God's great acts of creation and delighting in creation, and of liberating his people from the "iron furnace" of Egypt (Deut. 4:20). Each seven-day cycle served not only as a reminder, but as a *reenactment,* of the great cycles of God's creative activity and rest, and of his people's enforced toil in Egypt and subsequent divine deliverance to freedom.

But not only was the six-plus-one rhythm of work and rest that constituted the overall context within which Israel conducted its worship understood as a memorial; the specific activities of worship prescribed for the day of rest were themselves understood by the people—for the most part, anyway—as doings-in-memorial. As Thurian suggests, Israel understood and practiced virtually all aspects of its worship as doings-in-memorial: this is what distinguished its worship sharply from that of its neighbors.

There is no need to show in detail how Christian worship represents a continuity of structure, though an alteration of content, when compared to the worship of old Israel. The church conducts its worship within the context of remembering and expecting as well, but the great event at the center of its remembering is now the resurrection of Jesus, and the great event at the center of its expecting is now the full arrival of God's Kingdom, that Kingdom whose content is shalom. The day of the week on which it rests is now the first day, since that is the day of the resurrection, the day that the early Christians already called "the Lord's Day." Thus the rhythm becomes a one-plus-six rhythm rather than a six-plus-one rhythm. And at the pivotal center of its worship on that day is its celebration of the Lord's Supper as a memorial.

Having completed this rapid excursion through a theology of liturgy, we can now return to our inquiry into the interrelation of work with worship, of labor with liturgy, in Christian existence. Earlier we saw that for one who sees the world and history as a sacrament of God, work and worship have a common root: gratitude. Now we can go deeper. The Christians' way of being-in-society is embraced, along with their manner of worship, within their way of being-in-history. Work and rest are locked together in that one-plus-six rhythm which is the celebration in memorial of God's new creation and our liberation. Thus, when the day of rest is dropped out of life, the memorializing rhythm of life as a whole is destroyed.

In turn, on that day of rest we celebrate in memorial the remembered and expected acts of God, at the center of which are Christ's resurrection and the arrival of the Kingdom of shalom. Whereas our remembering and expecting are the abiding context within which we do our daily work, in worship we celebrate in memorial the very actions remembered and expected. Thus, when we drop worship out of the day of rest, we destroy this practice of bringing to the fore (in memorializing celebration) the actions that constitute the abiding context of our existence. And when that happens, the significance of our work (as works of taking heed that are performed in the context of remembering and expecting) is soon lost from view. Our work itself is altered.

Yet one more connection can be discerned. If the worship is performed, but the works of mercy and justice are missing, then a shadow is cast over the worship, and its authenticity is brought into question. For this very same God whom we are to worship by celebrating his deeds in memorial also requires of us that, in grateful response to those deeds, we take heed of him by doing the works of mercy and justice.[6] But can we not also say that if the works of mercy and justice are performed but the worship is missing, then a shadow is cast over those works, and *their* authenticity is brought into question?* For this very same God, whom we are to heed by doing the works of mercy and justice in gratitude for those deeds of his that we remember and expect, also requires of us that we celebrate in memorial those deeds: work and worship are mutually authenticating.

Bonhoeffer was profoundly right when he said that only he who helps the Jews may sing the Gregorian chant. But will not he who helps the Jews, in the spirit of taking heed to the God whose deeds he remembers and expects, also sing the Gregorian chant? I know that some Christians find themselves at the point of being unable to worship. Though they do the works of justice and shalom in the world, worship is too joyous for them, too confident, too assured. Better then that they should do the works of justice and shalom out of, say, duty, than not do them at all. But something is missing. One is reminded of Nietzsche's devastating indictment that Christians have no joy.

And now at last I come to "the tragedy of liturgy in Protestantism" of which the title of this chapter speaks. I submit that there is a tragedy of liturgy in Protestantism, especially, though by no means exclusively, within the Reformed/Presbyterian tradition. The tragedy consists in there being so little within this tradition of the very thing that we have been discussing: *worship*. The tragedy consists in the fact that within this tradition there is a suppression of the central Christian actions of celebrating in memorial.

When one looks at the actions that constitute the liturgy of the church, one sees that they comprise two different directions, two different orientations. Some are actions directed toward us: God addresses us and we are the recipients. These are the actions of *proclamation,* central to which are of course the reading of the Scriptures and the preaching of the sermon. But there are also actions directed toward God: we address God and he is the recipient. These are the actions of *worship* in the true sense. The Christian liturgy is an interchange between actions of proclamation and actions of worship.

Even a brief glance at the history of the Christian liturgy makes clear how difficult it has been for the church to hold these two directions in balance. The Roman and Orthodox traditions have historically found it difficult to give due weight to the dimension of God addressing us in judgment and grace—in short, to proclamation. The Protestant tradition has historically found it difficult to give due weight to the dimension of us addressing God in love and devotion—in short, to worship. As one might expect, these differences in practice

---

*I am not suggesting that the *sincerity* of those performing such works is brought into question—a person can sincerely work for justice without engaging in Christian worship, after all—but rather that their (Christian) *authenticity* is brought into question.

are reflected in how the members of these traditions think and speak of the liturgy. Often members of the Roman and Orthodox traditions speak of the liturgy as if it were entirely worship. Often members of the Lutheran and Reformed traditions speak of the liturgy as if it were entirely proclamation. No liturgy has ever been entirely one or the other. Yet liturgies *do* differ profoundly in their emphases, and the tragedy of liturgy in Protestantism—and particularly in the Reformed tradition—is that the worship dimension is suppressed, sometimes radically so. The liturgy is no longer "eucharistic," and a fundamental dimension of the life of the church and of the existence of the Christian is thereby stunted.

Do not, however, interpret me as wishing to play down the proclamation dimension of the liturgy or as thinking that everything in the proclamation dimension of Protestant liturgy is all right. In the liturgy, when it is authentic, the people gather as a community around the Word of God and receive from it inspiration, guidance, and consolation for their work in the world. Such gathering is itself one of the actions of the Kingdom, and it is hard for me to imagine Christian action in the world retaining its vitality and its direction without such gathering and listening. What so often happens instead is that in countless ingenious ways the sharp sound of the Word of God is muffled so as to protect the status quo. These points are all worth developing further, but the direction our discussion has taken demands of us that we here focus our attention on that other dimension of liturgy, worship.

The suppression of the dimension of worship in the Reformed liturgy is perhaps especially evident in its peculiar didacticism. Let me illustrate. Already in the second century of our era, and regularly thereafter, there were bits of dialogue in the liturgy that consisted of lines exchanged between the presider and the people. An example is the following, used at the beginning of the eucharist section of the liturgy:

> PRESIDER: Lift up your hearts.
> PEOPLE: We lift them up to the Lord.

This particular bit of dialogue remains a regular part of the Roman liturgy to this day. But in the Reformed liturgy which emerged from the Palatinate it disappeared along with all the other ancient examples of liturgical dialogue. What happened is that the people's words, "We lift them up to the Lord," were taken away from them, were incorporated into a long didactic introduction to the Lord's Supper read by the minister, and were altered from an *expression by* the people of their devotion into an *injunction to* the people to lift up their hearts. This is but one example of a general pattern. I could easily devote an entire chapter to indicating the many points at which ancient expressions of the people's devotion, found yet in the late-medieval Roman liturgy, were recast in the Reformed liturgy into the hortatory mood and spoken by the minister—though indeed an overall assessment of the Reformed liturgy must take due note of that great contribution that the Reformed liturgy has made to the Christian liturgy generally, namely, the singing by the people of the Psalms.

What naturally results from the diminution of the worship dimension in liturgy is that incredible starkness so characteristic of the Reformed liturgy and its setting. So little of the multifaceted richness of our humanity is here manifested! So many renunciations! In the preceding chapter I noted the insistence of the contemporary English poet Donald Davie that aesthetic excellence is not missing from the Reformed liturgy—though it might be overlooked if one were looking for the luxuriance that characterized baroque Catholicism. Davie characterized that excellence with the words *simplicity, sobriety,* and *measure.* I do not contest Davie's claim (although it is worth noting that he made his observation with the liturgy of the *French* Reformed church in mind, a liturgy derived from Geneva and Strasbourg, in which the tendencies that I have been speaking of are much less pronounced than they are in the Reformed churches whose liturgies are derived from the Palatinate). Nevertheless, it is not difficult to predict what will happen when proclamation, centered in the sermon, becomes the overwhelmingly dominant action of the liturgy: all that might distract our attention will be stripped away, up to the point where the congregation sits in silence, lined up in rows in a well-lit white box, listening. That this stark removal of the world can yield, at its best, an awesome sense of transcendence, I do not deny. There is good reason why those great mystical paintings in contemporary art—Rothko, Motherwell, Barnet Newman—are so nearly empty. But how much of what it is to be human is thereby set aside! How much of life is suppressed! By contrast, where proclamation is not allowed to overwhelm the liturgy, where the dimension of *worship* is given its rightful place, there the richness of life will put in its appearance. There color and gesture and movement and space and sound will enter as vehicles of praise and gratitude.

What also results from the suppression of the worship dimension of liturgy is the seriousness, the sobriety, the absence of joy so characteristic of the traditional Reformed liturgy and so contrary to the spirit of the divine rest and people's liberation that we are intended to mirror. When proclamation overwhelms worship in the liturgy, then I think we must expect joy to be diminished. It's true, indeed, that proclamation itself should be received in joy. The Orthodox liturgy manages to do so: in a quite marvelous way it surrounds the reading of the Scriptures with expressions of joyful devotion. And of course the Reformed tradition, just as much as the Orthodox, regards the Scriptures and the reading thereof sacramentally; indeed, it goes on to regard the sermon in a much more sacramental light than the Roman and Orthodox traditions have ever done. Yet experience seems to teach that unless the worship dimension receives due emphasis throughout the liturgy, proclamation will be received with a form of ethical seriousness that excludes joy.

The diminution of the worship dimension in the Reformed liturgies occurred already in the first and second generations of the Swiss Reform, during which the most radical liturgical reform that the Christian church has ever known took place. It is not difficult to understand why the shift away from worship to proclamation occurred there: the Swiss reformers found the people of their parishes profoundly ignorant of the Christian Gospel. Furthermore, it must be remembered that although the late medieval liturgy itself included a significant dimension of worship, the liturgy scarcely served as the expression of the devotion of the people. The laypeople would take books of private devotion to church and go through them while the liturgy was being performed unintelligibly up front. The Swiss reformers then addressed themselves to what they perceived as the great need of the day: instruction and exhortation from the Bible. I certainly do not fault them for that. And as a matter of fact, the people may actually have expressed more of their devotion in the new liturgy than they ever did in the old. Nonetheless, those reforms have meant for their successors a deep suppression of one of the fundamental dimensions of human existence.

It is especially ironic that this should have happened in churches that stand theologically in the tradition of Calvin, because if ever there were a theologian who saw the universe sacramentally, it was Calvin. For him, reality was drenched with sacrality. At the outset of this book I argued that Calvin's reforms meant a radical turn toward the world. But for him, as for Schmemann, the world to which one turns is a sacrament of God. What must be remembered here is that it was not Calvin, but Zwingli, far and away the most radical of all the reformers in liturgical matters, who had the decisive influence on the liturgies coming out of the Palatinate.

In my judgment, the most fateful of all the steps, taken first by Zwingli and then by others after him, was that of making the Lord's Supper no longer a regular part of the Christian liturgy. From its very beginnings the Lord's Supper was the church's great doing-in-memorial and its great expression of thanksgiving. For fifteen hundred years the liturgy of Christians on Sunday, everywhere in the world, invariably included the Lord's Supper along with the proclamation of the Word as its two main components. Then in 1525 Zwingli in his church in Zurich took the fateful step of pulling these two apart, dividing the year into forty-eight preaching services and four communion services. To his dying day John Calvin protested this practice, insisting that the liturgy of the church must include the Lord's Supper each Sunday. Speaking against the medieval practice of the people communicating just once a year, he said, in the last edition of his *Institutes,* "the supper could have been administered most becomingly if it were set before the church very often, and at least once a week"; and again, "the Lord's Table should have been spread at least once a week for the assembly of Chrsitians. . . ."[7] But Calvin's insistence was without avail.

Once again, it is not difficult to understand why Zwingli took the step he did. In addition to certain theological convictions that made him feel at ease with the new arrangement, it was pastoral considerations that were decisive for him. Among other things, he was profoundly convinced that the high point of the Lord's Supper is not the "elevation of the host," but the communion—the actual eating and drinking—and he was persuaded that the faithful congregation as a whole should participate in this, not just the clergy. But for centuries the ordinary members of the church in central Europe had communicated once a year, on Easter, and seldom more than that. Zwingli found it impossible to get them to do so much more often, and since he thought that the celebration of the Supper without actual communion was a charade, he adopted his strategy of pulling the two components apart and putting them into separate services. Perhaps he had no choice. And, indeed, we ought to keep in mind the fact that the people in his parish communicated more frequently than most in late medieval Catholicism. But once again, despite this fact, the consequences have been tragic.

One of the major results of Vatican II has been that the Catholic church has taken a giant step in its liturgy in the direction of Protestantism. Next to the Swiss Reform, the liturgical reform of Vatican II is the greatest in the history of the church. I am profoundly convinced that we Protestants must now take an equally large step in the direction of Catholicism—or rather, in the direction of our common ancient tradition—by reinstituting the Lord's Supper as a regular part of the church's liturgy. This, in my judgment, is the decisive step that must be taken if we wish once again to have a balance of worship and proclamation—if we wish to overcome the tragedy of liturgy in Protestantism. For this is the great feast in which we hold in remembrance Jesus Christ and in which we look forward to the coming of his Kingdom of shalom. This is the great thanksgiving for Creation and for the liberations of Exodus and Resurrection. This is the great circle in which we declare our unity as "a holy people" across all nations.

If worship is balanced with proclamation in the Christian liturgy, and if, in turn, liturgy is set within the rest-of-delight whereby Christians declare, with that one-plus-six rhythm of their daily existence, that the struggle for the embodiment of justice and shalom in the world does not exhaust the true life, then the distinctiveness of the Christian's way of being-in-the-world will not be confined to inwardness. It will be there for all to see.

Chapter VIII

Theory and Praxis

A characteristic feature of the core area of our modern social world is the availability to its members of massive amounts of high culture, most of it now separated by long stretches of time and space from the societies in which it was originally produced, and most of it having at best a minor and indirect function in our own ambient society. The writings of Meister Eckhart, the theories of Copernicus, the art of the Mayan Indians, the music of Notre Dame de Paris of the thirteenth century—all have been pulled loose from their originating societies and made available to us in ours. Many are the scholars who make it their professional occupation to occupy themselves in this towering edifice of culture, exploring its nooks and crannies, developing their responses, making their own contributions here and there, and helping to hand it on to succeeding generations. For some the temptation proves irresistible to go yet farther and make this the concern of their lives, letting society go its own sorry way while they lock themselves away in this abiding, socially transcendent cultural stronghold, acquiescing in society while pursuing *Bildung*. As Rotterdam burns, they study Sanskrit verb forms.

Quite a different characteristic of the modern world is the presence within it of a certain type of *project,* namely, working for the reform of the structure of the social world. Over and over groups of people in the modern world have risen above their participation in society sufficiently to consider its structure. Upon doing so they have come to the conclusion that it both can and ought to be altered. Accordingly, they have committed themselves to work for reform. And just as there are scholars who occupy themselves in that great edifice of culture, so too there have been scholars who have occupied themselves in one or another of these projects of structural reform, making it the governing interest of their theorizing. They have engaged in scholarship of social commitment. Theirs has been praxis-oriented theorizing.

Now suppose a scholar has caught that vision of world-formative Christianity which, so I argued at the outset of this book, first emerged in original Calvinism. Suppose he or she has seen that obedience to Jesus Christ requires that one not acquiesce in the social world as one finds it, turning away whenever possible toward some supposedly higher world of religious truth or cultural delight, but rather that one must struggle for its reform, doing what one can to introduce justice and shalom. What will such individuals, in their capacity as scholars, then do?

Will they not engage in such theorizing as will be of use to themselves and their colleagues in that struggle? Will that interest not govern their science? Will their scholarship not be in the service of that goal? Will they not resist the lure of *Bildung*—even the lure of *Bildung* "in Christian perspective"— and place their theorizing in the service of this eminently concrete struggle for the embodiment of shalom in the world? Will not praxis in that way govern their theorizing? A seesaw battle is taking place in history between the forces that advance and the forces that retard shalom. Is it not the calling of scholars, and certainly of Christian scholars, to participate in that battle?

Consider the pattern of our discussion throughout this book: I have explored normative questions concerning the social order by taking a certain vision of what the social order ought to be like—namely, the shalom vision— drawing out some of the implications of that vision, and setting it within the larger interpretative and legitimating context of the Christian gospel; and I have held up our modern social order against the normative structure to see where it falls short. I have picked out some of those shortfalls, explored the dynamics that have produced them, and asked what, if anything, can be done to alter those dynamics. Is not such a pattern of theorizing the indispensable counterpart of world-formative Christianity? Is it not inevitable that it is exactly such a pattern of theorizing that liberation theologians, who have committed them- selves to the cause of the poor and the oppressed of the Third World, call for and practice?

I do not come to these conclusions easily. I myself was reared in the tradition of those who in their scholarly activity occupy themselves exclusively in that great edifice of culture. Nonetheless, I come to them ineluctably.

Let me make clear that I am not simply saying that scholars are responsible, as members of society, for the way in which theory gets applied. Perhaps the most common notion in the Western world of how scholarship is related to praxis goes something like this: the scholars immerse themselves in high culture in order to contribute to the discovery and formulation of an ever more unified body of laws that will provide us with ever more complete ex- planations of what transpires in our experience. This body of nomological the- ory is then applied by technologists, for whom it constitutes an indispensable resource into which they can dip so as to find what is useful for the purpose of altering our natural, social, and psychological worlds. That, I say, is the com- mon picture: the scientists discover laws, and the technologists make applica- tions. And nowadays most of us would insist that all of us together, including the theorists, are responsible for the uses to which knowledge is put. The scientists are co-responsible with the rest of us for promoting healthful uses of this resource of theory and for opposing destructive uses; they cannot wash their hands of this social responsibility.

But my plea here is not that the scholars recognize their co-respon- sibility for the manner in which nomological theory gets applied; rather, my plea is for the *integration* of social commitment and theorizing—or, more specifically, for the integration of Christian commitment and theorizing, by way of the commitment becoming the *governing interest* of the theorizing. It is indeed possible for scholars to adopt as the governing interest of their inquiries the making of a contribution to the formation of a body of nomological theory. They may do so because someone to whom they owe obedience has told them to do so. Or they may do so because they think that nomological knowledge is of intrinsic worth for human beings and they wish to share in making this good available to humanity. Or again, they may do so because they see that nomological theory is of use in technology, and they wish to contribute to this technological resource. Or they may be entirely free of any such altruistic impulses, doing what they do simply because they find the prospect of being discoverers in the landscape of natural law delightful, even exciting. Whatever their reasons, they can, as I have suggested, adopt as the governing interest of their inquiries the making of a contribution to the formation of nomological theory. But so, too, they can adopt some social goal as their governing interest, and they can in that way integrate commitment and theorizing.

Let me also make clear that I am not calling for the sort of thing that theologians, in their field, call contextual theology. Probably various things have been meant by that; but sometimes the idea is that theologians should emphasize those facets of the Christian gospel and of the theological tradition that are especially relevant to the lives of the people amongst whom they are working. In Argentina their emphases should be different from what they are in Pasadena. They should not try to construct a theology utterly abstracted from social context, shaped only by the interior demands of theological scholarship, and then try to impart it to everybody indifferently on the ground simply that the recipient is a human being. One hopes that the person who contextualizes theology will often be led to emphasize the theme of justice, since for most audiences that will be of special relevance. But my call here is not for theorizing that emphasizes the theme of justice; it is for theorizing that places itself in the service of the cause of struggling for justice. There is an apothegm of Karl Marx that has become so worn with repetition that one is embarrassed to cite it, and yet it puts the point forcefully: *The goal is not to describe the world but to change it.* Contextualized scholarship aims at relevant description of the world; praxis-oriented scholarship aims at changing the world.

In his now-famous essay "Traditional and Critical Theory," Max Horkheimer formulates the program of the Frankfurt School by attaching the name "traditional theory" to nomological theory, and then distinguishing that from the project in which he and his colleagues were engaged, which he calls "critical theory." As described by him and practiced by members of the School, critical theory was shaped by the goal of contributing to the release of human beings from all modes of domination. It was theory shaped by the interest in that mode of social praxis, and so it was a species of what I have called praxis-oriented theory: a normative view of social structure was articulated and set within an interpretative and legitimating context. Our actual social order was held up against that normative structure, and where a significant shortfall was perceived, the dynamics causing that shortfall were analyzed and the question was raised of what, if anything, could be done to alter those dynamics. Of course, the governing vision of the Frankfurt School's analysis was different from the vision I have set forth in this book. That is my reason for not calling what I have done critical theory. For the Frankfurt School, individual autonomy was the social ideal. Theirs was a critique of domination in the service of radical liberation. Mine has been a critique of injustice and deprivation in the service of shalom.

During the past century there has arisen in the Netherlands a neo-Calvinist concept of scholarship in which there is also an intense concern for structural integration of Christian commitment and theorizing. It differs from praxis-oriented theory, however, in its understanding of the point at which the critical link between theory and praxis occurs. A comparison of these two views of linkage and structural integration raises issues of fundamental importance. Before I go on to make that comparison, however, let me insist that at the heart of the neo-Calvinist vision there is indeed a fundamental linkage of praxis to theory—or, more precisely, of *life* to theory. Many of the critics of the neo-Calvinist project of Christian scholarship have castigated the scholarship that has emerged as hopelessly abstract, so far divorced from the real issues of life as to be useless to them. I think there is some merit to that criticism. The roots of the defect pointed to, however, cannot be that in this movement the theoretical activity of the scholar is treated as divorced from his life as a human being. To the contrary, Dooyeweerd never tired of insisting that theory is not, and cannot be, in his word *autonomous*. Theorizing, he insisted, is inescapably shaped by elements in the life of the theorist that lie outside the realm of scholarship.

In the neo-Calvinist concept, the goal of scholarly endeavor (that is to say, the "interest" that governs the direction of the scholar's theorizing) is, for the non-philosophical sciences, to develop a body of nomological theory—a body of laws, abstract, general, integrated—rather than a body of theory useful for the struggle to reform society into more just and healthful structures.* For the praxis-oriented theorist, as we have seen, the decisive link between

---

*Kuyper never tired of insisting that just as the Christian politician ought to work for the reform of social structures with the support of Christian people generally, so in a similar way the Christian scholar ought to work for the reform of scholarship with the support of Christian people generally. Thus, it was *parallelism* of scholarly and social reform that Kuyper stressed, rather than scholarship *in the service of* social reform.

theory and praxis lies at the point where social commitment becomes the *governing interest* of the scholar's theorizing. For the neo-Calvinist, on the other hand, the decisive link occurs at the point where religion functions as the *controlling principle* of the scholar's inquiries.

If one carefully scrutinizes what goes on in scholarship, says the neo-Calvinist, one sees that often the root of what leads scholars to reject a certain theoretical claim is that they more or less consciously perceive that claim to be out of accord with their religious commitment. This is a dynamic operative in all scholars, since everyone has a religion (that is to say, everyone absolutizes something, everyone fixes on something as giving unifying coherence to his endeavors). The thing that makes a body of theorizing *Christian* in character, then, is that the Christian religion is allowed to control the theory acceptance of the scholar. Theoretical claims out of accord with the Christian religion are rejected *on account of* being out of accord, and others are accepted *on account of* their following more or less rigorously from Christian principles. In this way a body of Christian theory emerges. And not only is this true as a matter of fact, but it is entirely right and proper that Christians should practice theorizing thus: it is, in fact, their obligation to do so.

In the praxis-oriented concept and project of scholarship, Christian conviction shapes the *direction* in which scholars turn their inquiries; it determines the *governing interest* of their theorizing. In the neo-Calvinist concept and project of scholarship, Christian conviction shapes the scholars' *acceptance and rejection* of theories; it functions as a *controlling principle* of their theorizing. For the former, the decisive link of theory to praxis lies in what scholars choose to think about; for the latter, it lies in what scholars think on the matters they choose to think about.

Though Kuyper has first claim to being named the originator of the neo-Calvinist concept, it is in the work of Herman Dooyeweerd that it received its classical articulation. I think it will help the discussion if I flesh out just a bit what I have said thus far with some elements of Dooyeweerd's development of this basic vision.

Dooyeweerd argued that what he called the "functions" of things— the properties, the qualities, the actions, and so forth—could be distinguished into some fourteen or fifteen different groupings, which he called *modalities*. One such grouping of functions, for example, constitutes the *physical* modality; another, the *psychic* modality; yet a third, the *aesthetic* modality; and so forth. It was his conviction that the object, the *Gegenstand,* of the theorist's endeavors in the various special sciences, the entity on which the theorist focusses his or her inquiries, is always one such abstract modality. And he held that the goal of the theorist was to formulate laws concerning the interrelationship of the functions belonging to that modality—or, perhaps, laws concerning the interrelationship of entities with respect to the functions they possess within a certain modality. The goal, in short, is the construction of nomological science. Dooyeweerd completes his picture of scientia by describing the business of philosophy as that of giving a synoptic picture of the interrelation of the modalities.

Dooyeweerd then went on to argue that it is inherent in the structure of the special sciences that they make philosophical commitments and, in turn, that it is inherent in the structure of philosophical theorizing that philosophers take something as absolute, that they take something as the interpretative clue for their construction of a general theory of reality. What they take as absolute, as interpretative clue, may either be one of those modalities—in which case their thought will acquire a reductionistic character—or it may be what lies outside the created order—namely, God—in which case there is at least the hope of their escaping reductionism. But when we speak of taking something as absolute, we are, in Dooyeweerd's view, perforce in the realm of religion. Thus, religious commitment is unavoidable for the theorist—though what is sadly true is that scholars may in their theorizing take as absolute something quite different from the God to whom they profess allegiance in their life. In such cases we are confronted with religious ambivalence between theory and life, or at least between theory and profession.

I scarcely need remark that in this particular formulation of the neo-Calvinist vision there are many highly provocative claims. Here I want to set those all aside and concentrate simply on the contrast between that vision itself, on the one hand, and the praxis-oriented vision, on the other. I have formulated the contrast as sharply as possible, for it seems to me that the issues raised by the contrast ought to be at the center of discussion and debate in the community of Christian scholars, inasmuch as they concern the very identity of every Christian scholar. Both visions are far from that old view in which Christianity was seen as something to be superadded to the results of reputable scholarship. In both there is structural integration of scholarship with Christian commitment, but the point of linkage is, as I have been saying, very different.

To get at the fundamental issues, we must dig down to some basic epistemological considerations.[1] I suggest that any reflections on the formation of belief, knowledge, and scientia should begin with the realization that we as normal human beings all possess a variety of *belief dispositions*—that is to say, we possess various dispositions, propensities, inclinations, such that when some event in our experience activates the disposition, a belief is produced, a proposition is accepted. For example, we are all so constituted that upon having certain memory experiences we are disposed to have certain beliefs about past events. Upon having certain sensations we are disposed to believe that we are in the presence of certain physical objects. Upon having certain other sensations we are disposed to believe that we are in the presence of persons. Upon judging that one proposition that we already believe is good evidence for another that we do not (yet) believe, we are disposed to believe that second. And for some propositions (traditionally called *self-evident*) we are disposed, simply upon grasping them, to believe that they are true.

Some of these dispositions would appear to be innate—that is to say, their presence in us is not the result of learning, not the result of conditioning. But clearly others of them are not innate; as the British eighteenth-century philosophers were fond of observing, some are produced by "induction." To take one of their common examples, if my seeing of a coach is "constantly conjoined" with my hearing a certain characteristic sound coming from the coach, then after a while the belief that there is a coach passing by, which was at first induced by the sight of the coach, is later induced by the hearing of that sound. This particular process of acquiring new belief dispositions is clearly a case of so-called classical, or Pavlovian, conditioning.[2]

But so-called *operant* conditioning also works in us to produce new belief dispositions—or perhaps I should say, to revise those with which we are indigenously endowed. For example, it seems to be a feature of us as human beings that we are disposed to believe what we apprehend people as telling us. Probably when we are very young this disposition is unqualified: we believe whatever we apprehend anybody as telling us on any matter. But gradually we discover that some of the things we come to believe in this way are false, and those discoveries serve to modify that original unqualified disposition, so that eventually we no longer believe what certain sorts of people say on certain matters under certain conditions.

What I have been describing so far may be regarded as the foundation of the formation of our human belief structures. To get the full picture we must now add another level—that of the human will. It does seem to me that philosophers have often exaggerated the role of the will in belief formation, suggesting things that would imply that by an act of will you could, for instance, simply decide to give up the belief that you are presently holding a book in your hands—whereas surely you cannot do so. Nevertheless, the will does have a role: we *are* able in various ways to *govern* the workings of our belief dispositions. Perhaps in certain special cases we can indeed decide whether or not to believe something, but beyond a doubt we can work in disciplined fashion to restrain and modify our belief dispositions—just as we can work in disciplined fashion to restrain and modify our other dispositions. For example, we can work at getting ourselves to refrain from coming to conclusions on the truth of the matter in marital disputes until we have heard both sides of the story. Let us call this form of governance *acceptance governance*. We can govern our belief dispositions in such a way that when in situations in which a certain disposition would normally have been activated, we can resist such activation and avoid automatic acceptance of the proposition in question.

But there is another sort of governance that we can exercise over our belief dispositions, which may appropriately be called *direction governance*. Without in any way revising my reasoning disposition—that is, my disposition to infer one sort of thing from another—I can govern what sorts of things I will do my reasoning about. I can decide whether to spend the next year reasoning about aesthetics or about social theory. So, too, without at all revising the workings of my perceptual belief dispositions, I can decide whether to walk around the car to see whether the tire needs air or to forego doing so.

In summary so far, human belief formation (understanding "belief" in such a way that knowledge is a species of belief) has as its foundation our belief dispositions, some of which are innate, and some of which are the result of conditioning. Then as its first floor it has our ability to govern the workings of these dispositions—and here we may distinguish between our capacities for acceptance governance and our capacities for direction governance.

Now with respect to our capacities for the governance of our beliefs, there are, it seems to me, norms, obligations, responsibilities. It is not true that "anything goes" in our treatment of other human beings. And neither is it true that "anything goes" in our believings. With respect to certain propositions we are obliged to take appropriate steps to bring it about that we believe them if true and reject them if false—in that way to get more closely in touch with reality. Our obligations concerning direction governance specify the propositions with respect to which we ought to take such steps; and our obligations concerning acceptance governance specify the steps we ought to take.

Let me emphasize, lastly, that obligations concerning the governance of one's beliefs cannot be determined apart from the totality of one's human obligations in general. I am obliged to do my best to find out the truth on certain matters concerning which you may have no such obligation at all; what accounts for the difference will be any of several features of our distinct human situations. Our obligations as beings capable of governing our dispositions to believe are inextricably connected with our obligations in general.

With this equipment in hand let us now return to the contrast we were considering between the neo-Calvinist's understanding of the link between commitment and scholarship and that of the praxis-oriented theorist. It is now easily seen that one of the main points of the neo-Calvinists is a point about *acceptance* governance and about certain of the obligations that attach to it: they are persuaded that if one takes examples of reputable scholarship of any considerable size, one discovers over and over that these are in tension with authentic Christian conviction. From this observation they go on to make two further points: (1) that often the reason for this incompatibility is that scholars hold to religions other than Christianity and have governed their theorizing so as to assure that what they accept will be compatible with their religion; and (2) that *Christian* scholars are not only fully justified but even obliged to govern their own theorizing so as to assure that what they accept will be compatible with authentic Christian conviction.

Together these contentions constitute a pointed repudiation of the conviction, so deeply ingrained in the post-Enlightenment West, that if ever one discerns conflict between one's religious convictions on the one hand, and the results of reputable science on the other, then one is obliged as a rational person to resolve the conflict by revising one's religious convictions. The neo-Calvinists have had the imagination and courage to ask the provocative and deeply unsettling question of whether it is not sometimes the right and even the duty of rational individuals to restore the harmony by revising their theoretical conclusions. This question sends reverberations throughout our whole understanding of the nature of rationality.

It is my own conviction that the neo-Calvinists are substantially correct in these theses. In putting them forth they have made an important contribution to the discussion concerning the relation of commitment to theory, and in some of my own writings I have tried to formulate and defend them in my own way.[3] Although substantial work remains to be done on these issues, I think that the main outlines of the neo-Calvinist's thought on them is correct.

There is no reason at all for the praxis-oriented theorists to hesitate in granting these points, since clearly theirs is not a point about acceptance governance, but a point about direction governance. Praxis-oriented theorists are committed to certain social goals, and are persuaded that by the pursuit of scientia they can obtain knowledge that will be of service in the pursuit of those goals, so they practice scientia with that goal in mind. It functions as the interest that governs the direction of their inquiries. It serves to establish what is of importance for them to investigate.

Probably the most common protest against praxis-oriented theorizing is that to allow one's inquiries to be governed by social commitment is implicitly to violate the canons of rationality. Scholars ought to do their best to abstract themselves, in their capacity as scholars, from all social commitments. They should aim to make their scholarship value-free, simply describing reality as it is, since to do anything less than this is to fail to live by the norms of rationality. But with our background epistemology in mind, we can easily see that this objection is groundless: praxis-oriented theorists are making no proposal at all about the canons or norms of acceptance governance. In particular, they are not resolving that their criterion for acceptance of propositions ought to be whether or not such acceptance would aid the attainment of their social goals: that would indeed be a wildly mistaken, even perverse, proposal.

They are simply proposing that the *direction* in which we turn our inquiries be governed by the prospective utility of such knowledge for our social praxis. And far from suggesting that scholars be *obliged* to abstract from all social commitments in choosing a direction for their inquiries, they hold that it would be irresponsible for them to do so. As we saw earlier, that on which it is important for a person to discover the truth is determined by the totality of his or her concrete human obligations.

The dispute, then, is over direction governance. The neo-Calvinist has traditionally insisted that the governing interest of scholarship be simply the construction of a body of nomological theory. The praxis-oriented theorist insists that social commitment be allowed as governing interest. It seems to me that exclusivism on either side is out of place. The total realm of scholarship must be pluralistic enough to allow both.

Up to this point in this chapter I have been firmly insisting on the legitimacy, and more than that, on the *need* for praxis-oriented theory: that derives naturally from everything I have said thus far in this book; but I am persuaded that the construction of nomological theory also has its place. Indeed, it seems to me that the knowledge the theorist can provide us is often of *intrinsic* worth. Not every legitimate *logos* is the *logos* of a *praxis*. Understanding, comprehension, knowledge—these too constitute a fulfillment of our created nature. The grasp that the theorist can provide us of ourselves and of the reality in the midst of which we live—of its unifying structure and its explanatory principles—is a component of the shalom that God meant for us. Where such knowledge is absent, life is withered. I am aware that there are those who have argued—Habermas is an example—that there is no interest in human beings that knowledge as such satisfies, that we do not in fact ever regard knowledge as worthwhile in itself, that our pursuit of it is always instrumental. In Habermas's view knowledge is always *instrumental*—either to a technical interest, a practical interest, or an emancipatory interest.[4] It seems to me that this case is far from having been convincingly argued.

It should be noted, though, that even when scholars are not engaged in praxis-oriented theory, social reality will consistently shape their judgments about what is important enough to investigate, thus influencing direction. By refusing to allow considerations of what is useful for some goal of social reform into their assessment of importance, they do not automatically free such assessments from all considerations save those native to the world of scholarship. The prominence that our theologians of the past two centuries have given to issues of epistemology is surely the result of the religious pluralism of our society and the emerging prominence of unbelief: these social trends have rightly made these issues seem important to them. And the importance that philosophers have assigned to themes such as freedom and emancipation is surely a result of the decrease of ascriptivism in our society and the corresponding increase in value generalization—social trends that we discussed in Chapter II. In this way and others, scholarship does and should reflect social reality. It is an illusion to suppose otherwise.

It follows from what I have been saying that scholars, in determining the direction of their inquiries, will have to engage in the difficult and complex task of weighing the need for praxis-oriented theory against the need for non-praxis-oriented theory. They will have to weigh the importance of occupying that great edifice of culture against the importance of entering into some project of social reform. And always they will have to do this weighing in the light of their total, concrete situation. In particular, they will have to do it in the light of the deprivations and oppressions to be found in the social order as it stands. They cannot act as if they were above history.

Indeed, one of the factors they will have to consider is the social consequences of *not* pursuing praxis-oriented theory, if that is what they decide. Always there are dynamics at work in society for the perpetuation, and even the increase, of injustice. Sometimes scholars can make a contribution to the alteration of those dynamics by their development of praxis-oriented theory. If they abandon it—if instead they choose to pursue pure theory—then of course they will be responsible for allowing those dynamics to take their course without intervention. Social responsibility is inescapable for the scholar.

If these reflections are correct, then I think we must conclude that the legitimizing basis that neo-Calvinists give for humanity's pursuit of scholarship must be supplemented. Characteristically they see this pursuit as grounded in the so-called "cultural mandate"—which they interpret as the mandate given by God to mankind to work toward the differentiation of the various social spheres, and then toward developing the potentials within each. That is why they are inclined to resist praxis-oriented theory and favor the pursuit of pure nomological theory: for them it represents letting scholarship "come into its own." But to speak only of the cultural mandate is to give scholars no principle for determining the direction of their scholarship. In particular, it is to give them no principle that relates that determination of direction to human need. Yet only if scholars consider the particular ways in which their society falls short of justice and shalom can they responsibly direct their scholarship. The cultural mandate is insufficient as a grounding for the practice of scholarship. One needs as well the mandate to work for shalom.

The neo-Calvinists have focussed on the fact that Christian commitment involves "a way of seeing reality," and they have reflected seriously on the consequences of that fact for the practice of scholarship. What they have failed to think through—so it seems to me—is the consequences of the fact that Christian commitment also involves a mode of engagement in society. Their understanding of commitment has remained too abstract. What is needed is reflection on the relevance of theorizing to obedient action, not just reflection on the nature of obedient theorizing. In truth, there can be no understanding of the nature of obedient theorizing without perceiving the relevance of theorizing to obedient action, and the need for theorizing to be of service to the action.

And finally, a point of strategy: it seems to me imperative that in our practice of scholarship we do our best to break out of the bondage of our situation as relatively well-to-do members of the First World in order to be able to hear the cries of the deprived and oppressed of humanity. It is of course easy to leave such a remark as this at the level of a slogan. Let me try to give it some depth.

We can begin with some very striking passages from Abraham Kuyper. In his *Encyclopedia of Sacred Theology,* Kuyper included a section that he called "Science and Sin." When read in the light of the epistemological considerations I have introduced, it is clear that what Kuyper is doing in this section is pointing to various *malformations* in our belief dispositions (and to some extent in our acceptance governance of those dispositions)—malformations that he considered to be the consequence of the entrance of sin into our human situation. Further, the malformations to which he points are not odd or incidental; they work in a regular, law-like manner. Among the early modern philosophers the story circulated of the man who believed that his body was made of glass. I do not know whether there ever was such a person, but in any case Kuyper's interest is not in such accidental deformations as that.

The modern philosophers, from Descartes on, have been concerned with law-like malformations in the genesis of our beliefs. They have tended, however, to have an extraordinarily constricted view as to their range. Descartes, for example, on the whole limited his concern to the fact that "our senses sometimes deceive us," that we are often too credulous in believing what people tell us, and too hasty in drawing conclusions. Such familiar phenomena as these are not of any great interest to Kuyper in the matter at hand (though indeed he does not overlook them); he devotes much more attention to points of direct relevance to us here—namely, to the ways in which our social goals, antipathies, and background distort the workings of our belief dispositions (and of our acceptance governance of those dispositions). The dispositions are especially consequential, he thinks, in the development of social theory, although he is aware that their influence often radiates beyond that point.

Here are some of his thoughts on the effects of social background:

> He who has had his bringing-up in the midst of want and neglect will entertain entirely different views of jural relationships and social regulations from him who from his youth has been bathed in prosperity.

And on the effects of social goals, or interests:

> Our outlook upon things is also governed by numerous personal *interests*. An Englishman will look upon the history of the Dutch naval battles with the British fleet very differently from a Netherlandish historian; not because each purposely desires to falsify the truth, but because both are unconsciously governed by national interests. A merchant will naturally hold different views concerning free trade, fair trade and protection, from the manufacturer, simply because self-interests and trade-interests unconsciously affect his views. . . . These are all moral differences, which are governed by self-interests, and which sometimes work consciously and lead to the violation of conscience, but which generally govern the result of our studies unconsciously and unknown to us.

And on the influence of sympathy and antipathy:

> The darkening of the understanding . . . would be better understood if we called it the *darkening of our consciousness*. Over against sin stands love, the sympathy of existence, and even in our present sinful conditions the fact is noteworthy, that where this sympathy is active you understand much better and more accurately than where this sympathy is wanting. A friend of children understands the child and the child life. A lover of animals understands the life of the animal. In order to study nature in its material operations, you must love her. Without this inclination and this desire toward the object of your study, you do not advance an inch. . . . And this is significant in every department of study.[5]

Now it seems to me that there clearly are such phenomena as Kuyper here points to. There are such deformations as these in the dispositions that determine our beliefs. Of course, one would like to have the laws in question formulated with more precision; one would like to have careful empirical confirmation of their presence; one would like to have a theory concerning the operative psychic mechanisms. To the best of my knowledge, the empirical studies of belief formation presently leave us far short of these desiderata. Yet that there are such phenomena as these to be studied seems clear.

It is impossible for us in our day to read these passages without thinking immediately of Marx. Clearly ideology, as Marx identified it, is a specific example of what Kuyper was discussing. In Marx's view, there is a belief disposition in human beings such that, when individuals are aware of enjoying unjust advantages in society, they tend to adopt belief structures of a sort such that, if the beliefs were true, their social position would be justified. Marx called such belief-structures "ideologies," and he held that a characteristically prominent element in ideologies is the belief that the structure of society cannot be altered, or at least cannot be altered for the better. On the one hand, Kuyper's reflections on malformation are of much greater generality than Marx's—and Kuyper sees, as Marx does not, that sin lies somewhere in the background of these deformations;* on the other hand, Marx probed with much greater depth and profundity the particular malformation that gives rise to ideologies.

The main reason Kuyper did not develop further these tantalizing, provocative suggestions of his is clear: he thought that these socially determined deformations of our belief dispositions pale, in the significance they have for the character of our theorizing, when placed alongside religiously determined deformations:

> the chiefest harm is the ruin, worked by sin, in those data, which were at our command, for obtaining the knowledge of God, and thus for forming the conception of the whole. Without the sense of God in the heart no one shall ever attain unto a knowledge of God, and without love, or, if you please, a holy sympathy for God, that knowledge shall never be rich in content. . . . From which it follows at the same time that the knowledge of the cosmos as a whole, or, if you please, philosophy in a restricted sense, is equally bound to founder upon this obstruction wrought by sin.[6]

I think it is deeply regrettable that Kuyper allowed his conviction that the influence of religiously determined deformations in the practice of scholarship is less important than the influence of socially determined distortions to deter him from analyzing further the workings of the latter. The fact that they are *less* important does not make them *un*important. But further—and this is perhaps the most significant point to make here—socially produced deformations have an influence on *religious* convictions and attitudes. These are not independent. There can be little doubt that the religious convictions of Americans and of Afrikaners are shaped by exactly those socially determined deformations to which Kuyper points. With great skill Kuyper and his followers practiced the hermeneutics of suspicion with respect to the workings of religiously determined malformations. It is equally necessary that the hermeneutics of suspicion be practiced so as to uncover the workings of socially produced malformations. The effects of sin on our beliefs go beyond the effects of idolatries.

---

*"It will not do to omit the fact of sin from your theory of knowledge. This would not be warranted if sin were only a thelematic conception and therefore purely ethic; how much less, now, since immediately as well as mediately, sin modifies so largely all those data with which you have to deal in the intellectual domain and in the building-up of your *science*. Ignorance wrought by sin is the most difficult obstacle in the way of all true science" (Kuyper, *Principles of Sacred Theology*, trans. Hendrik de Vries [Grand Rapids, Mich.: Eerdmans, 1965], pp. 113-14).

The trouble with these deformations in our belief dispositions is of course that they introduce unreliability. Too often when these factors are operative, the beliefs that emerge are false. And how, you ask, can we *discover* that they are false? In many ways. But surely one immensely important way is to listen to those who because of their social background or goals or sympathies see the situation differently than we do. It is especially important that we, who see history from the topside, listen to those who see it from the underside: Gentiles listening to Jews, Jews to Palestinians, men to women, rich to poor, South African whites to South African blacks, Dutchmen to Moluccans, North Americans to South Americans, the First World to the Third.

There is yet one more path toward the goal of becoming self-critical, and indeed, it is the most direct of all: it is the path of listening attentively to the prophetic word of the Bible, that great unmasker of self-deceit. Perhaps we shall discover, though, that these paths join: by listening to the cries of the oppressed and deprived we are enabled genuinely to hear the word of the prophets—and of him who did not count equality with God a thing to be grasped at, but took the form of a servant, walking the path of humble obedience to the point even of accepting execution as a despised criminal: the Prince of Shalom.

Postscript

"History is irreversible," says Lucien Goldmann in his *Philosophy of the Enlightenment*, "and it seems impossible that Christianity should ever again become the mode in which men really live and think."[1] The choice for mankind is now between the "bourgeois individualism" of capitalism, which Goldmann sees as spiritually empty in its devotion to morally neutral technical knowledge, and socialism, which he sees as an immanent, historical, and humanist religion committed to the creation of a new community. The choice, he agrees, is a painful one, since the spiritual emptiness of capitalism is balanced by the violation of individual conscience characteristic of socialism as we know it. But the possibility of a transcendental faith shaping history is probably over, and in any case, "the 'judgement of history' has passed Christianity by. Diderot's argument that modern society makes it impossible for anyone to give a genuinely Christian character to his whole life is more valid than ever today. The more sincere and intense the Christian life of modern man, the more it becomes a purely inward, psychological 'private matter' deprived of all influence on life in society."[2]

I have written this book out of the conviction that Goldmann is mistaken, and that our Western secularism is a passing thing. I have seen those Christians of whose existence Goldmann is skeptical. I have seen Beyers-Naudé, and Helder Camara, and the brothers of Taize (France) combining in endlessly creative ways the renewal of the liturgy with a commitment to peace. I have heard the news of bands of Christians around the world saying No to injustice while singing hymns to God the Father and his Son Jesus Christ. I have found the inspiration for my words in these enfleshments of faith, of love, and of hope.

Notes

Preface

[1]Goldmann, *The Hidden God: A Study of Tragic Vision in the "Pensées" of Pascal and the Tragedies of Racine,* trans. Philip Thody (London: Routledge & Kegan Paul; New York: Humanities Press, 1964), p. 264.

[2]For an elaboration of these epistemological hints, see my "Can Belief in God Be Rational if It Has No Foundations?", in *Faith and Rationality* (Notre Dame, Ind.: University of Notre Dame Press, 1983).

[3]Walzer, *The Revolution of the Saints: A Study in the Origins of Radical Politics* (Cambridge: Harvard University Press, 1965), p. vii.

[4]Abraham Kuyper, *Calvinism: Six Stone Lectures* (Grand Rapids, Mich.: Eerdmans, 1931), p. 27.

Chapter I

[1]Walzer, *The Revolution of the Saints: A Study in the Origins of Radical Politics* (Cambridge: Harvard University Press, 1965), p. 12.

[2]Troeltsch, *The Social Teaching of the Christian Churches,* trans. Olive Wyon (New York: Macmillan, 1931), 2:602.

[3]A variant on avertive and formative religions as I have explained them here is that form of religion in which present reality is perceived as acceptable, but the future—after death, say—is regarded as threatening.

[4]This third form is the same as what Lucien Goldmann calls the "tragic vision," which he ascribes to Pascal, Racine, and Kant: "Many forms of religious and revolutionary consciousness have insisted upon the incompatibility between God and the world and between values and reality. Most of them, however, have admitted some possible solution, if only that of an endeavour which can be made in this world to achieve these values, or, alternatively, of the possibility for man of abandoning this world entirely and seeking refuge in the intelligible and transcendent world of values or of God. In its most radical form, tragedy rejects both these solutions as signs of weakness and illusion, and sees them as being either conscious or unconscious attempts at compromise. For tragedy believes neither that the world can be changed and authentic values realised within the framework it provides nor that it can simply be left behind while man seeks refuge in the city of God" (*The Hidden God: A Study of the Tragic Vision in the "Pensées" of Pascal and the Tragedies of Racine,* trans. Philip Thody [London: Routledge & Kegan Paul; New York: Humanities Press, 1964], p. 64).

[5]Claus Westermann argues that in the Bible God is confessed not only as deliverer but as dispenser of blessing, whereas the contemporary church has almost totally ignored the latter: "From the beginning to the end of the biblical story," he says, "God's two ways of dealing with mankind—deliverance and blessing—are found together. They cannot be reduced to a single concept because, for one reason, they are experienced differently. Deliverance is experienced in events that represent God's intervention. Blessing is a continuing activity of God that is either present or not present. It cannot be experienced in an event any more than can growth or motivation or a decline of strength. . . . When the Bible speaks of God's contact with mankind, his blessing is there alongside his deliverance. History comes into being only when both are there together. . . . We can no longer hold that God's activity with his people is

to be found only in his 'mighty acts.' In addition to these acts, experienced in events, God's work with his people includes things manifested not in deeds but in processes that are usually regarded as 'unhistorical'—the growth and multiplying of the people and the effects of the forces that preserve their physical life, that is, . . . growth, prosperity, and success in all their forms" (*Blessing in the Bible and in the Life of the Church* [Philadelphia: Fortress Press, 1978], pp. 3-6).

[6]Those acquainted with Max Weber's typology of religion, as found in his *Sociology of Religion,* and anticipated in his *Protestant Ethic and the Spirit of Capitalism,* will be wondering how what I am proposing is related to his formulation, in which the fundamental distinction within salvation religions is that between what he calls "mystical religion" and "ascetic religion." Part of the answer lies in the fact that those religions that Weber would regard as dominantly mystical, I would regard as dominantly avertive; and those he would regard as dominantly ascetic, I would regard as dominantly formative. So our classifications are similar; nevertheless, we conceive the distinction differently: I think that it is a mistake to regard the degree of asceticism, of self-discipline, of what Weber calls "rationalization," as marking out any distinction here. As I have observed, the practitioners of avertive religion may be as self-disciplined as those of formative religion; it all depends on how strong are the impulses to turn to that higher reality, and how strong are those to continue luxuriating in this realm of inferiority. Furthermore, I think that "mystical" is a very misleading label to apply to the avertive religions, since an avertive religion need not be "mystical" in the usual sense of the word at all. There are more differences than these, but to point them out would require a detailed discussion of Weber's typology—a project which, though I cannot carry it out here, would in my judgment be eminently worthwhile.

[7]Fortescue, quoted by E. M. W. Tillyard, *The Elizabethan World Picture* (London: Chatto & Windus, 1948), pp. 24-25.

[8]Walzer, *Revolution of the Saints,* pp. 155-56. Cf. William J. Bouwsma: "The crucial difference between the two positions, between the medieval vision and that of the Renaissance, was an utterly different conception of the general nature of order; every other difference between them can be related to this. To put the matter in its simplest terms: in the medieval vision of reality, every dimension of the universe and every aspect of human existence were seen as part of an objective and cosmic system of order. But the Renaissance mind perceived nothing of the sort. Unable and frequently little caring to find coherence in the universe as a whole, it discerned only such limited and transient patterns of order as could be devised by man himself. Furthermore, the medieval vision identified a definite pattern in the universal order. All things appeared to be arranged in a hierarchy of complexity and value, an arrangement whose basis was ideal and therefore utterly static. In this conception some things were unalterably higher and therefore better, others were lower and thus inferior. But in the Renaissance vision there was no such hierarchy, and instead of stasis it saw merely, though often reluctantly, the incessant flux of things" (*Venice and the Defense of Republican Liberty: Renaissance Values in the Age of the Counter Reformation* [Berkeley and Los Angeles: University of California Press, 1968], p. 4).

[9]The connection between the avertive character of medieval religion and this hierarchical view of reality is indicated in these words of Bouwsma: "the medieval position tended to identify man with his intellect, and his ability to apprehend the pattern of universal order was closely related to the ultimate purpose of human existence. By contemplating its perfect structure and ascending its stages, man could, with his mind, rise from what was good to what was better, and finally approach and seek to unite himself intellectually with what was best. Contemplation was thus the noblest of pursuits, the highest path of existence; activity in the world of men and particular things was not only inferior but could chiefly be justified only by its contribution to something superior to itself" (*Venice and the Defense of Republican Liberty,* p. 5). The classic treatise expounding this view of contemplation as conducted by ascending the cosmic hierarchy of excellence is the early writing of Augustine, *De vere religione.*

[10]For a discussion of the development of this distinction with respect to

the state, see Quentin Skinner, *The Foundations of Modern Political Thought* (Cambridge: Cambridge University Press, 1978), vol. 2, *The Age of Reformation,* pp. 352-58.

[11]Troeltsch, *Social Teaching of the Christian Churches,* 1:303.

[12]Case, quoted by Walzer, *Revolution of the Saints,* pp. 10-11.

[13]Walzer, *Revolution of the Saints,* pp. 1-2. Cf. Bouwsma: "as subordinate members of a universal system men could be seen to have no right to govern themselves, and states no right to determine their separate courses of action. Self-determination, in this view, could only appear, in the deepest sense, as a violation of the very structure of reality, and political duty appeared to consist only in patient submission and obedience. Man, in this system, was always and necessarily a subject; he could not be a citizen" (*Venice and the Defense of Republican Liberty,* p. 6). Cf. Walzer: "Calvinist politics, indeed, radicalism in general, is an aspect of that broad historical process which contemporary writers call 'modernization.' Calvinism taught previously passive men the styles and methods of political activity and enabled them successfully to claim the right of participation in that ongoing system of political action that is the modern state. Not that modernity is in any sense the intentional creation of political radicals: few of the elements of the modern ('rational-legal') order detailed by Weber, for example, have much to do with radical aspiration. Calvinism is related . . . not with modernity but with modernization, that is, with the process far more significantly than with its outcome. The saint appeared at a certain moment in that process and is remembered afterwards for the dramatic part that he played and for the effects that he had rather than for his own motives and purposes" (*Revolution of the Saints,* p. 18). Add to this the following remark of Michael Oakeshott: "In considering the engagement to deliberate the conditions prescribed in *respublica* in terms, not of their authority but of their desirability, to imagine them different from what they are and to undertake or to resist their alteration, we are concerned with politics properly speaking. . . . Politics, then, is concerned with an imagined and wished-for condition of *respublica,* a condition in some respect different from its current condition and alleged to be more desirable" (*On Human Conduct* [Oxford: Oxford University Press, 1975], pp. 163, 168.

It will be evident that Walzer is following the Weber/Troeltsch line of interpretation of the significance of early Calvinism, and that my own interpretation likewise stands in that line. Let me here then take note of Quentin Skinner's scruples concerning this line (and particularly of Walzer's particular version of it). In his very important *Foundations of Modern Political Thought,* Skinner argues persuasively that in their theory of justified resistance, the Calvinists mainly took over arguments from the Lutherans, who themselves mined them from medieval law codes and legal theory; or, in the case of the French Calvinists, they took them over directly from a scholastic tradition of radical constitutionalism. Thus, concerning Walzer's thesis, Skinner suggests that "there seems to be a vitiating confusion underlying this approach to analyzing the role of Calvinism as a revolutionary ideology in early modern Europe. It is of course true that the men who argued in favour of revolution during this period tended to be Calvinists. But it is not true that in general they made use of specifically Calvinist arguments" (*Foundations,* p. 323). Several points should be made in response to this. For one thing, Walzer's central contention is that the Calvinists were the first modern *revolutionaries,* not that they were the first to have a *theory* of revolution. But secondly, even on the matter of a theory of revolution, a theory of justified resistance is not yet a theory of revolution; and I fail to see that in the whole medieval theory of resistance there is anything that even approaches a theory of revolution. Nevertheless, it must be granted that Skinner does make a very significant addition and correction to Walzer in his tracing of the Calvinist *theory* of justified *resistance* to medieval roots. On the other hand, Skinner himself shows that the Calvinists were the first to place the right to resistance in the hands of ordinary people, and this is one of Walzer's central claims.

All of this, though, is somewhat tangential to my own central thesis: Skinner focusses narrowly on the emergence of a theory of justified resistance, whereas what I argue is that in the Calvinists we find, full-blown, a religious vision different from that characteristic of the medievals—world-formative Christianity—a vision that includes a new "revolutionary" attitude toward society generally. The theory of justified resistance on which Skinner focusses is only *part* of this—though indeed a very important part.

Concerning the role of the laity in the Swiss reform, consider these words of Bernd Moeller: "What are the identifying marks of a 'Reformed' city? Among their external features they have in common the austerity of their divine service, the opposition to images, but above all the opposition of their pastors to the Lutheran doctrine of communion. In addition, the citizens of these cities worked with particular energy to perfect and consolidate the spiritual and moral life of the ecclesiastical and urban communities, to renovate public charity, public instruction, and civil discipline. Anticipating Calvin, they often set as their ideal a *civitas christiana,* or holy city, and in several places they came quite close to realizing this goal. But for our purpose it is most important to note the extremely significant role which the *lay element* played in all these activities. Of course, the late medieval tradition of strict civil control of morals in these cities probably accounts for the active participation of council members in the direction of church affairs and for the great importance of lay offices in the church. But, in addition, the Reformation in the cities of Upper Germany was especially characterized by the participation of the people, 'the common man,' who played an active role in ecclesiastical innovation as never before. Indeed, this participation was not limited to the introduction of the Reformation but involved its maintenance as well" (*Imperial Cities and the Reformation: Three Essays* [Philadelphia: Fortress Press, 1972], pp. 92-93).

[14]Bouwsma, *Venice and the Defense of Republican Liberty,* p. 29. For Bouwsma's general discussion of the breakdown of the hierarchical vision of politics, see pp. 11-17.

[15]Oberman, "The Shape of Late Medieval Thought: The Birthpangs of the Modern Era," in *Studies in Medieval and Reformation Thought,* ed. Heiko A. Oberman et al. (Leiden: E. J. Brill, 1974), vol. 10, *The Pursuit of Holiness in Late Medieval and Renaissance Religion,* p. 11. The same point has been made by Charles Trinkaus in these words: "what was going on was a tendency to secularize the sacred while simultaneously sacralizing the secular" ("Humanism, Religion, Society: Concepts and Motivation of Some Recent Studies," *Renaissance Quarterly,* 29 [1976], 688).

[16]Oberman, "The Shape of Late Medieval Thought," p. 25.

[17]Bouwsma, *Venice and the Defense of Republican Liberty,* p. 30.

[18]In the matter of the relationship between Augustinianism and Stoicism, these remarks of Bouwsma should be added: "neither Stoicism nor Augustinianism was, in the Renaissance, primarily a function of the availability and transmission of literary sources. They were rather responses to the deep and changing needs of Renaissance society and culture. These needs had been created by the growing complexity of European life in the later Middle Ages, and above all by the development of towns and the new vision of human existence towns increasingly evoked. For towns produced a set of conditions that made parts of Europe more and more like the hellenistic world in which both the Stoics and Augustine had been reared: the constant menace of famine and pestilence, urban disorders and endemic warfare in the countryside, incessant conflict among individuals, families, and social groups, a growing social mobility that left a substantial proportion of the urban population rootless and insecure, above all the terrible anxieties of a life in which the familiar conventions of a close and traditional human community had given way to a relentless struggle for survival in a totally unpredictable and threatening world.

"It was this situation to which scholastic culture seemed irrelevant, and which conversely Stoicism and Augustinianism sought, in their different ways, to interpret and remedy; and the needs of this grim predicament primarily explain why men sought and read Stoic and Augustinian writings" ("The Two Faces of Humanism: Stoicism and Augustinianism in Renaissance Thought," in *Studies in Medieval and Renaissance Thought,* ed. Heiko A. Oberman et al. [Leiden: E. J. Brill, 1975], vol. 14, *Itinerarium Italicum,* ed. Heiko A. Oberman with Thomas A. Brady, Jr., pp. 16-17).

[19]Bouwsma, "The Two Faces of Humanism," p. 52.

[20]Zwingli, "Of the Education of Youth," in *Zwingli and Bullinger: Selected Translations*, trans. Geoffrey W. Bromiley (Philadelphia: Westminster Press, 1953), p. 113.

[21]The ideas and practices of the early Calvinists and their relation to "modernization" have of course been much discussed, but for an especially judicious treatment, see David Little's *Religion, Order, and Law: A Study in Pre-Revolutionary England* (New York: Harper & Row, 1969).

[22]Troeltsch, *Social Teaching of the Christian Churches*, 2:610.

[23]Once again Troeltsch's insights are germane: Calvinism, he says, "co-ordinated the activity of the individual and of the community into a conscious and systematic form. And since the Church as a whole could not be fully constituted without the help of the political and economic service of the secular community, it was urged that all callings ought to be ordered, purified, and enkindled as means for attaining the ends of the Holy Community. Thus the ideal was now no longer one of surrender to a static vocational system, directed by Providence, but the free use of vocational work as the method of realizing the purpose of the Holy Community. The varied secular callings do not simply constitute the existing framework within which brotherly love is exercised and faith is preserved, but they are means to be handled with freedom, through whose thoughtful and wise use love alone becomes possible and faith a real thing. From this there results a freer conception of the system of callings, a far-reaching consideration for that which is practically possible and suitable, a deliberate increasing of the intensity of labour" (*Social Teaching of the Christian Churches*, 2:610-11).

[24]Calvin, *Calvin's Commentaries: The First Epistle of Paul the Apostle to the Corinthians*, trans. John W. Fraser, ed. David W. Torrance and Thomas F. Torrance (Grand Rapids, Mich.: Eerdmans, 1960), p. 153 (1 Cor. 7:20).

[25]Paraphrase of a point made by Calvin in his sermon on 1 Cor. 10:31-11:1, by Ronald S. Wallace, *Calvin's Doctrine of the Christian Life* (London: Oliver and Boyd, 1959), p. 155.

[26]Consider Calvin's caustic comments on the elitism of the monks in the *Institutes*, IV, xiii, 11. In this connection we should also be reminded of Calvin's break with the elitism characteristic of the humanists, in which the liberal arts were praised more highly than the manual arts (*Institutes*, II, ii, 14).

[27]Cf. Troeltsch, *Social Teaching of the Christian Churches*, 2:591.

[28]Marshall, quoted by Walzer, *Revolution of the Saints*, frontispiece.

[29]Cf. Walzer, *Revolution of the Saints*, pp. 100 ff.

[30]Troeltsch gives a fine summary: "In Calvin's view the individual is not satisfied with mere repose in his own happiness, or perhaps with giving himself to others in loving personal service; further, he is not satisfied with an attitude of mere passive endurance and toleration of the world in which he lives, without entering fully into its life. He feels that, on the contrary, the whole meaning of life consists precisely in entering into these circumstances, and, while inwardly rising above them, in shaping them into an expression of the Divine Will. In conflict and in labour the individual takes up the task of the sanctification of the world, always with the certainty, however, that he will not lose himself in the life of the world; for indeed in everything the individual is only working out the meaning of election, which indeed consists in being strengthened to perform actions of this kind. . . . The individual was drawn irresistibly into a whole-hearted absorption in the tasks of service to the world and to society, to a life of unceasing, penetrating, and formative labour" (*Social Teaching of the Christian Churches*, 2:588-89).

Chapter II

[1]See Talcott Parsons, *Societies: Evolutionary and Comparative Perspectives* (Englewood Cliffs, N.J.: Prentice-Hall, 1966), pp. 10-16.

[2]Talcott Parsons, *The System of Modern Societies* (Englewood Cliffs, N.J.: Prentice-Hall, 1971), pp. 27-28.

[3]For discussion of such criticisms, see, for example, Charles Taylor's *Hegel and Modern Society* (Cambridge: Cambridge University Press, 1979) and Peter Berger's *Facing up to Modernity* (New York: Basic Books, 1977).

[4]Wallerstein, *The Capitalist World-Economy* (Cambridge: Cambridge University Press, 1979), p. 5.

[5]Wallerstein, *Capitalist World-Economy*, pp. 5-6.

[6]Wallerstein, *Modern World-System*, p. 348.

[7]Robert L. Heilbroner, *The Worldly Philosophers: The Lives, Times, and Ideas of the Great Economic Thinkers*, 3d ed. rev. (New York: Simon and Schuster, 1967), p. 24. For a thorough discussion of the rise of a market economy, see Karl Polanyi, *The Great Transformation: The Political and Economic Origins of Our Time* (1944; reprint ed., Boston: Beacon Press, 1957), in which the author suggests that "no society could, naturally, live for any length of time unless it possessed an economy of some sort; but previously to our time no economy has ever existed that, even in principle, was controlled by markets. In spite of the chorus of academic incantations so persistent in the nineteenth century, gain and profit made on exchange never before played an important part in human economy. Though the institution of the market was fairly common since the later Stone Age, its role was no more than incidental to economic life. . . . While history and ethnography know of various kinds of economies, most of them comprising the institution of markets, they know of no economy prior to our own, even approximately controlled and regulated by markets" (pp. 43-44).

[8]In fact, remarks Wallerstein, "the multiplicity of states within the single economy has two advantages for sellers seeking profit. First, the absence of a single political authority makes it impossible for anyone to legislate the general will of the world-system and hence to curtail the capitalist mode of production. Second, the existence of state machineries makes it possible for the capitalist sellers to organize the frequently necessary artificial restraints on the operation of the market" (*Capitalist World-Economy*, pp. 69-70); in the same text he also notes that "the functioning then of a capitalist world-economy requires that groups pursue their economic interests within a single market while seeking to distort this market for their benefit by organizing to exert influence on states, some of which are far more powerful than others but none of which controls the world market in its entirety" (p. 25).

[9]See Andre Gunder Frank, *Crisis: In the World Economy* (London: Heinemann, 1980), pp. 172-262.

[10]Wallerstein, *Capitalist World-Economy*, pp. 68-69.

[11]Heilbroner, "The Demand for the Supply Side," *The New York Review of Books*, 11 June 1981, p. 37. Although there is indeed the analogy noted between wage labor and slave labor, to dwell on this exclusively is to overlook the fact that the move to wage labor has meant a sizable increase in freedom by self-determination. It is not accidental that people consistently prefer wage labor to other forms when they are given the choice.

[12]This is closely similar to the definition of capital offered by Alvin Gouldner: "Capital—to define it succinctly but generally—is: any produced object used to make saleable utilities, thus providing its possessor with *incomes*, or claims to incomes defined as legitimate because of their imputed contribution to economic activity . . ." (*The Future of Intellectuals and the Rise of the New Class* [New York: Continuum, 1979], p. 21). I drop the requirement that the object be a *produced* object; it seems to me that land, for example, can function as capital. Gouldner goes on to argue that labor and skills function as capital in our system; as will be clear from what follows in the text, I do not believe that this is true.

[13]Gouldner, *Future of Intellectuals*, p. 23.

[14]Heilbroner, "Demand for the Supply Side," p. 37.

[15]On the function of the semiperiphery in the world-system, see especially Wallerstein's *Capitalist World-Economy*, pp. 95-118. As to the content of the semi-

periphery today, Wallerstein states that "it includes the economically stronger countries of Latin America: Brazil, Mexico, Argentina, Venezuela, possibly Chile and Cuba. It includes the whole outer rim of Europe: the southern tier of Portugal, Spain, Italy and Greece; most of Eastern Europe; parts of the northern tier such as Norway and Finland. It includes a series of Arab states: Algeria, Egypt, Saudi Arabia; and also Israel. It includes in Africa at least Nigeria and Zaire, and in Asia, Turkey, Iran, India, Indonesia, China, Korea, and Vietnam. And it includes the old white Commonwealth: Canada, Australia, South Africa, possibly New Zealand" (p. 100).

[16]Wallerstein, *Capitalist World-Economy,* p. 71. Cf. Heilbroner: "capitalism, as I see it, is a world system, but not merely because it is linked by market forces. The unifying process of the world system of capitalism is the extension of the wage-labor system from the developed center to the 'underdeveloped' periphery, for the purpose of gathering surplus on a global scale" ("Demand for the Supply Side," p. 38).

[17]Wallerstein, *Capitalist World-Economy,* p. 73.

[18]See, for example, Reimar Schefold, "Religious Involution," in *Tropical Man, Yearbook of the Anthropology Department of the Royal Tropical Institute,* vol. 5 (Amsterdam, 1973), pp. 46-81, in which it is shown that sometimes when physical conditions change in a taboo-laden society, the result is an increase in role specialization. (I owe this reference to Prof. Sander Griffioen.) See also Clifford Geertz's *Agricultural Involution* (Berkeley and Los Angeles: University of California Press, 1963).

[19]This point is similar to that developed by Anthony Giddens in the second chapter of his *New Rules of Sociological Method* (London: Hutchinson, 1977).

[20]Cf. Peter L. Berger: "*modern consciousness entails a movement from fate to choice. . . .* What previously was fate now becomes a set of choices. . . . Destiny is transformed into decision" (*The Heretical Imperative: Contemporary Possibilities of Religious Affirmation* [Garden City, N.Y.: Doubleday-Anchor, 1979], pp. 11, 16).

[21]Ibid., p. 13.

[22]Max Weber, *The Protestant Ethic and the Spirit of Capitalism,* trans. Talcott Parsons (New York: Scribner's, 1958), p. 153.

[23]An implication of this is that technologically rationalized actions could not become a prominent part of the life of humanity until a certain alteration occurred in the *context* of our social world: there had to be a new kind of science, different from that of the ancients and medievals, and a new view concerning the benefits of science. If those alterations had not occurred in the *cultural* context of our social world, the growth of technologically rationalized actions would not have come about.

[24]Cf. Heilbroner: "The separation of work from the right to claim the product of work establishes the rationale for the organization of the work process typical of capitalism. This is an organization in which the volume of output per hour takes precedence over most other considerations, such as fatigue, interest, creativity, etc. The hallmark of this mode of organization is the 'division' of labor not just by occupational variety but by fragmentation of physical and mental tasks into their simplest components. This division is not a 'natural' tendency of mankind, and is not found in other societies to anything like the degree we find it in capitalism. The division of labor endows capitalism with its immense superiority with respect to productivity, but also saddles it with the need to maintain the strictest supervision over, and discipline within, the labor process" ("Demand for the Supply Side," p. 37).

[25]Peter L. Berger, Brigitte Berger, and Hansfried Kellner, *The Homeless Mind: Modernization and Consciousness* (New York: Random House, 1973), pp. 88, 89, 90; italics in original. Qualifying these statements, the authors also note that "it would be a mistake to ascribe to modern consciousness alone the discovery of a fundamental dignity underlying all possible social disguises. . . . The understanding that there is a humanity behind or beneath the roles and the norms imposed by society, and that this humanity has profound dignity, is not a modern prerogative. What is peculiarly modern is the manner in which the reality of this intrinsic humanity is related to the realities of society" (pp. 88-89). For an interesting slant on the decline of ethical pluralism, see

Benjamin Nelson's *The Ideal of Usury: From Tribal Brotherhood to Universal Otherhood* (Princeton: Princeton University Press, 1949).

[26]This of course raises the question of the tenability of Max Weber's thesis that the "worldly asceticism" of the Calvinists contributed decisively to the origins and spread of capitalism. The literature on this is now vast, but for especially good treatments, see R. H. Tawney, *Religion and the Rise of Capitalism: A Historical Study (Holland Memorial Lectures, 1922)* (New York: Harcourt Brace, 1926); Kurt Samuelsson, *Religion and Economic Action,* trans. E. Geoffrey French and ed. D. C. Coleman (New York: Basic Books, 1961); Michael Walzer, *The Revolution of the Saints: A Study in the Origins of Radical Politics* (Cambridge: Harvard University Press, 1965), pp. 300-20; and Andre Gunder Frank, *Dependent Accumulation and Underdevelopment* (New York: Monthly Review Press, 1979).

[27]Ch'ien Lung, quoted by Frank, *Dependent Accumulation and Underdevelopment,* p. 18.

[28]"Europe's . . . ability to dominate the rest of the world depended not upon her cultural superiority or economic strength but upon two technological break-throughs: the construction of large ocean-going sailing vessels and the development of gunpowder and naval cannons" (Keith Griffin, "Underdevelopment in History," in *The Politcal Economy of Development and Underdevelopment,* ed. Charles K. Wilber [New York: Random House, 1973], p. 70).

[29]On the origins of the *ideal* of freedom of self-direction, see Michael Oakeshott's *On Human Conduct* (Oxford: Oxford University Press, 1975), pp. 236-42.

[30]A general attempt to explain why secularization is more prominent in certain parts of the world than others can be found in David Martin's *A General Theory of Secularization* (New York: Harper Colophon Books, 1979).

[31]Berger, *The Heretical Imperative,* p. 26.

[32]Berger, *The Sacred Canopy: Elements of a Sociological Theory of Religion* (Garden City, N.Y.: Doubleday, 1967), pp. 132-33.

Chapter III

[1]Gutiérrez, "Notes for a Theology of Liberation," *Theological Studies,* 31 (1970), 249-50.

[2]Gutiérrez, *A Theology of Liberation: History, Politics and Salvation,* trans. and ed. Sister Caridad Inda and John Eagleson (Maryknoll, N.Y.: Orbis Books, 1973), p. 15. Subsequent references to this book (hereafter abbreviated *TL*) will be made parenthetically in the text.

[3]Gutiérrez, *Liberation and Change* (Atlanta: John Knox Press, 1977), part one, *Freedom and Salvation: A Political Problem,* trans. Alvin Gutterriez, pp. 84-85.

[4]For illustrations of the spread of this new consciousness, see part five of Andre Gunder Frank's *Crisis: In the World Economy* (London: Heinemann, 1980).

[5]See also *TL,* p. 84, and Gutiérrez, *Liberation and Change,* pp. 76-77.

[6]Croatto, *Exodus: A Hermeneutics of Freedom,* trans. Salvator Attanasio (Maryknoll, N.Y.: Orbis Books, 1981), p. 5.

[7]See also *TL,* p. 35, and *Liberation and Change,* p. 84.

[8]Gutiérrez, "The Hope of Liberation," in *Mission Trends No. 3: Third World Theologies,* ed. Gerald H. Anderson and Thomas F. Stransky (New York: Paulist Press; Grand Rapids, Mich.: Eerdmans, 1976), p. 67. Elsewhere Gutiérrez similarly speaks of his project as "a reflection on the theological meaning of the process of the liberation of man throughout history" (*TL,* p. x); and he also speaks of "the function of theology as critical reflection on Christian praxis in the light of the Word" (*TL,* p. 13) and of "reflect[ing] critically on the praxis of liberation" (*TL,* p. 14), etc.

[9]I have described Gutiérrez's approach as if his social-theoretical *interpretation* of his situation and his *project* in that situation are givens so far as the Word of God and the task of the theologian are concerned, and that the business of the theo-

logian is simply to interpret these givens in the light of the Word of God. Though this is usually the picture Gutiérrez draws, I do not think that he entirely means it thus. In any case, I would insist that the following points must also be kept in mind: (1) the Word of God comes as critique of, and guide and dynamic for, our praxis (project); (2) the Word of God ought to inform our social-theoretical analysis of our situation (this point is further developed in Chapter VIII of this text and also in my *Reason within the Bounds of Religion* [Grand Rapids, Mich.: Eerdmans, 1976]); and (3) we should also reflect on the Word of God itself, and, in so doing, we should see that it speaks of more than just social praxis.

[10]Gutiérrez, *Liberation and Change*, pp. 85-86.

[11]Speaking of the "client states" of the United States, Noam Chomsky and Edward S. Herman say that "as in Europe in the 1930s, only the church has survived as a potential protector of the majority"; and, speaking of Latin America, they say that "the churches fight a lonely battle as the last institutional protection of the mass of the population" (*The Washington Connection and Third World Fascism* [Boston: South End Press, 1979], vol. 1, *The Political Economy of Human Rights*, pp. 11, 262).

[12]Croatto, *Exodus*, p. 5.

[13]I shall not at this point stop to consider Kant's strategy of dividing us up into a transcendent self which is self-determining and an empirical self which is not. For an extended treatment of the whole issue of human self-determination, see my *Educating for Responsible Action* (Grand Rapids, Mich.: Eerdmans, 1980).

[14]See Georg Lukács, *History and Class Consciousness: Studies in Marxist Dialectics* (Cambridge: MIT Press, 1971).

[15]See Isaiah Berlin, "Two Concepts of Liberty," in *Four Essays on Liberty* (New York: Oxford University Press, 1970).

[16]See D. Th. Kuiper, *De Voormannen: Een Sociaal-Wetenshappelijke Studie over Ideologie, Konflikt en Kerngroepvorming binnen de Gereformeerde Wereld in Nederland tussen 1820 en 1930* (Kampen: J. H. Kok, 1972). See also D. Th. Kuiper, "Historical and Sociological Development of ARP and CDA," in *Christian Political Options* (The Hague: AR-Partijstichting, 1979).

[17]Herman Dooyeweerd, *Roots of Western Culture: Pagan, Secular, and Christian Options*, trans. John Kraay and ed. Mark Vander Vennen and Bernard Zylstra (Toronto: Wedge Publishing Foundation, 1979), p. 64. Subsequent references to this book (hereafter abbreviated *RWC*) will be made parenthetically in the text. For a more detailed discussion of these matters, see Dooyeweerd's *Critique of Theoretical Thought* (Philadelphia: Presbyterian and Reformed Publishing Co., 1955), 2:181-330.

[18]Goudzwaard, *Capitalism and Progress*, p. 191. Subsequent references to this book (hereafter abbreviated *CP*) will be made parenthetically in the text.

[19]For more on this, see Abraham Kuyper, *Calvinism: Six Stone Lectures* (Grand Rapids, Mich.: Eerdmans, 1931).

Interlude I

[1]Cf. Ernst Käsemann, "The Eschatological Royal Reign of God," in *Your Kingdom Come: Report on the World Conference on Mission and Evangelism, Melbourne, Australia, 12-25 May 1980* (Geneva: World Council of Churches, 1980).

Chapter IV

[1]Barth, *Church Dogmatics*, trans. T. H. L. Parker et al. (Edinburgh: T. & T. Clark, 1955-), vol. 2, *The Doctrine of God*, 1:386.

[2]Abraham Kuyper, *Christianity and the Class Struggle*, trans. Dirk Jellema (Grand Rapids, Mich.: Piet Hein, 1950), pp. 27-28, 50.

³World Bank, *Development Report,* August 1981, p. 11. Cf. these words of Francis Blanchard, Director General of the U.N. International Labor Organization, in his report entitled *Employment, Growth and Basic Needs: A One-World Problem*: "Today, in spite of the immense efforts that have been made, both at the national and international levels, a significant proportion of mankind continues to eke out an existence in the most abject conditions of material deprivation. More than 700 million people live in acute poverty and are destitute. At least 460 million persons were estimated to suffer from a severe degree of protein-energy malnutrition even before the recent food crisis. Scores of millions live constantly under the threat of starvation. Countless millions suffer from debilitating diseases of various sorts and lack access to the most basic medical services" (Report to the Tripartite World Conference on Employment, Income Distribution and Social Progress and the International Division of Labour [Geneva: International Labour Office, 1976], p. 17).

⁴Gunnar Myrdal, *Against the Stream: Critical Essays on Economics* (New York: Vintage Books, 1975), p. 72.

⁵Julio de Santa Ana, *Towards a Church of the Poor: The Work of an Ecumenical Group of the Church and the Poor* (Maryknoll, N.Y.: Orbis Books, 1981), p. 3.

⁶For a history of the church's attitude toward poverty, see Julio de Santa Ana's *Good News to the Poor: The Challenge of the Poor in the History of the Church* (Maryknoll, N.Y.: Orbis Books, 1979). See also Gustavo Gutiérrez's *A Theology of Liberation: History, Politics and Salvation,* trans. and ed. Sister Caridad Inda and John Eagleson (Maryknoll, N.Y.: Orbis Books, 1973), pp. 287-306.

⁷Calvin, *Institutes of the Christian Religion,* ed. John T. McNeill and trans. Ford Lewis Battles (Philadelphia: Westminster Press, 1960), 1:696 (III, vii, 6).

⁸Paraphrase of a point made by Calvin in his sermon on Deut. 4:39-43, by Ronald S. Wallace, *Calvin's Doctrine of the Christian Life* (London: Oliver and Boyd, 1959), p. 149.

⁹Calvin, *Commentary on a Harmony of the Evangelists, Matthew, Mark, and Luke,* trans. Williams Pringle (Grand Rapids, Mich.: Eerdmans, 1956), 1:304 (Matt. 5:43).

¹⁰Ibid., 3:61 (Luke 10:30).

¹¹Formulation of Calvin's thought by Wallace, *Calvin's Doctrine,* p. 151.

¹²Calvin, *Sermons of M. Iohn Caluine vpon the Epistle of Saincte Paule to the Galathians,* trans. Arthur Golding (London: Lucas Harison and George Bishop, 1574), p. 331 (sermon on Gal. 6:9-11); orthography modernized by the author.

¹³Calvin, *Sermons on the Epistle to the Ephesians,* rev. trans. (Edinburgh: Banner of Truth Trust, 1973), p. 457 (sermon on Eph. 4:26-28).

¹⁴Calvin, *Commentaries on the First Twenty Chapters of the Book of the Prophet Ezekiel,* trans. Thomas Myers (Grand Rapids, Mich.: Eerdmans, 1948), 2:224 (Ezek. 18:7).

¹⁵Calvin, *Calvin's Commentaries: The Second Epistle of Paul the Apostle to the Corinthians and the Epistles to Timothy, Titus and Philemon,* trans. T. A. Smail and ed. David W. Torrance and Thomas F. Torrance (Grand Rapids, Mich.: Eerdmans, 1964), p. 112 (2 Cor. 8:14).

¹⁶Calvin, Sermon XLIV on the Harmony of the Gospels (Matt. 3:9-10), quoted with reference by W. Fred Graham, *The Constructive Revolutionary* (Atlanta: John Knox Press, 1978), p. 71.

¹⁷Calvin, *The Sermons of M. Iohn Calvin vpon the Fifth Booke of Moses Called Deuteronomie,* trans. Arthur Golding (London: H. Middleton for George Bishop, 1583), p. 770 (Sermon on Deut. 22:1-4); orthography modernized by the author. Cf. this passage from Calvin's sermon on Deut. 24:14-18: "After that manner do the rich behave themselves often times . . . they espy some occasion or other to the intent they may cut off the one half of the poor man's wages when he knows not what to set himself about. The poor folk offer themselves to labor; they desire but to get their living if they could tell where. Whereupon you shall have a rich man say, 'This fellow is out of money and out of work; I may hire him now for a morsel of bread, for he

must yield unto me. . . . I will give him but half wages, and he shall be glad and fain of that' " (p. 860).

[18]*Calvin's Commentaries: The Second Epistle to the Corinthians,* p. 114 (2 Cor. 8:15).

[19]Kuyper, *Christianity and the Class Struggle,* pp. 48-49.

[20]Ibid., pp. 35-36.

[21]Ibid., p. 40.

[22]In this discussion on rights generally, and sustenance rights in particular, I am very much indebted to Henry Shue's *Basic Rights: Subsistence, Affluence, and U.S. Foreign Policy* (Princeton: Princeton University Press, 1980).

[23]Cf. Calvin: "If we see our neighbor stand in need of our succor before our eyes and fail him, if we perceive he is likely to sustain loss and we remedy not the matter, having the means to do it, we be condemned of felony before God. It is a hard case; men may well dispute of it . . . but all replying must be laid down, for as much as God has spoken it, his saying is an irrevocable sentence" (sermon on Deut. 22:1-4).

[24]Joel Feinberg, *Social Philosophy* (Englewood Cliffs, N.J.: Prentice-Hall, 1973), pp. 58-59.

[25]Bernard H. M. Vlekke, *The Story of the Dutch East Indies* (Cambridge: Harvard University Press, 1945), p. 178.

[26]The details here and in the ensuing discussion are taken from an unpublished paper, "The Drama of Bangladesh," by my colleague Eugene R. Dykema.

[27]Rene Dumont, *Lands Alive* (London: Merlin Press, 1965), p. 139.

[28]Nehru, *The Discovery of India* (New York: John Day, 1946), pp. 305-06, 295.

[29]"By the end of the sixteenth century . . . the agricultural economies of the Spice Islands, the domestic industries of large parts of India, the Arab trading-economy of the Indian Ocean and of the Western Pacific, the native societies of West Africa and the way of life in the Caribbean islands and in the vast areas of the two viceroyalties of Spanish America [were] all deeply affected by the impact of Europeans. . . . The results [of European expansion] on non-European societies were . . . sometimes immedate and overwhelming . . ." (E. E. Rich, *The Cambridge Economic History of Europe,* ed. E. E. Rich and C. H. Wilson [Cambridge: Cambridge University Press, 1967], vol. 4, *The Economy of Expanding Europe in the Sixteenth and Seventeenth Centuries,* p. xiii). For analysis of the European impact on other societies, see also Andre Gunder Frank's *Dependent Accumulation and Underdevelopment* (New York: Monthly Review Press, 1979) and Immanuel Wallerstein's *The Modern World-System II: Consolidation of the European World-Economy, 1600-1750* (New York: Academic Press, 1980).

[30]See Gunnar Myrdal, *The Challenge of World Poverty: A World Anti-Poverty Program in Outline* (New York: Random House-Vintage, 1970), p. 212.

[31]Keith Griffin, "Underdevelopment in History," in *The Political Economy of Development and Underdevelopment,* ed. Charles K. Wilber (New York: Random House, 1973), pp. 72, 74-75. In the same text, cf. Paul A. Baran's "On the Political Economy of Backwardness": "But if Western capitalism failed to improve materially the lot of the peoples inhabiting most backward areas, it accomplished something that profoundly affected the social and political conditions in underdeveloped countries. It introduced there, with amazing rapidity, all the economic and social tensions inherent in the capitalist order. It effectively disrupted whatever was left of the 'feudal' coherence of the backward societies. It substituted market contracts for such paternalistic relationships as still survived from century to century. It reoriented the partly or wholly self-sufficient economies of agricultural countries toward the production of marketable commodities. It linked their economic fate with the vagaries of the world market and connected it with the fever curve of international price movements.

"A complete substitution of capitalist market rationality for the rigidities of feudal or semi-feudal servitude would have represented, in spite of all the pains of transition, an important step in the direction of progress. Yet all that happened was that the age-old exploitation of the population of underdeveloped countries by their domestic overlords, was freed of the mitigating constraints inherited from the feudal tradition. This superimposition of business *mores* over ancient oppression by landed gentries resulted in compounded exploitation, more outrageous corruption, and more glaring injustice" (p. 83).

Cf. also Frank: "An examination of the location of the most ultra-under-developed 'depressed' regions in the New World today, regions characterised not only by exceptional poverty, but oppressive social institutions, extreme catholic clericalism or protestant fundamentalism, illiberal political organization, etc., reveals that they are all regions in which an earlier period of primary products production for export from the region has given way to decadence after their mines, soil, timber, or market were exhausted in the course of world capitalist development. . . . Though their present poverty is in part due to the exhaustion of their natural resources and/or to the dense settlement and erosion of inadequate agricultural lands in mountainous mining regions, the principal source of their present ultra-undevelopment is not so much physical as it is the social structure they have inherited from their 'golden years' of export boom. . . . Historical and comparative analysis thus leads to a revealing apparently paradoxical observation that was foreshadowed by Smith and systematised by Marx: the rich became poor and the poor became rich" (*Dependent Accumulation,* p. 23).

[32]Barnet and Müller, *Global Reach: The Power of the Multinational Corporations* (New York: Simon and Schuster, 1974), pp. 133-34.

[33]Myrdal, *Challenge of World Poverty,* p. 101.

[34]Ibid., p. 57; italics in original text.

[35]Ibid., p. 114; italics in original text.

[36]Andre Gunder Frank, *Reflections on the World Economic Crisis* (London: Hutchinson, 1981), p. 131. Earlier in the same text, Frank notes that in Germany "the average number of hours worked per year is between 1,700 and 1,800; in South Korea it is 2,800; in Malaysia it is 2,500. I want to stress, however, that 2,800 hours per year is an average for a country like South Korea; it is common to find people who work sixty, seventy, and even eighty-four hours a week (twelve hours a day, seven days a week) until they die or lose the ability to work. . . . Super-exploitation can be seen in the decline of real wages. This is happening in Brazil, where the real wage has fallen 40 percent since the military coup. In Argentina, the reduction in real wages since 1975 has been between 60 and 70 percent; in less than a year since the coup, there has been a 40 percent drop. In Chile real wages have fallen more than 50 percent since the military coup, to between 28 and 30 percent of their 1972 value" (pp. 61-62). According to Noam Chomsky and Edward S. Herman, "it is little wonder that the income share of the top 5% of income receiving units in Brazil rose from 44% in 1960 to 50% in 1970, that the share of the poorest 80% fell from 35% to 27.5%, and that only the top 10% of the population increased its relative income share. . . . According to *Business Week,* the *real* wages of the lowest 80% of the Brazilian population 'have been steadily dropping since 1964—the year the generals took over—despite a tripling of the gross national product to $80 billion' " (*The Washington Connection and Third World Fascism* [Boston: South End Press, 1979], vol. 1, *The Political Economy of Human Rights,* p. 58). For more on this issue, see also Peter Evans's *Dependent Development: The Alliance of Multinational, State, and Local Capital in Brazil* (Princeton: Princeton University Press, 1979).

[37]For an assessment of the overall benefits of multinational corporations within the Third World, see Ronald Müller's "The Multinational Corporation and the Underdevelopment of the Third World," in *Political Economy of Development and Underdevelopment,* pp. 124-51.

[38]"In order to provide these low wages, and indeed to reduce the wages from one country to another in the competitive bid to offer more favorable conditions to international capital, these governments need to destroy the labor unions, and to prohibit strikes and other union activity. Systematic imprisonment, torture, and as-

sassination of labor and political leaders, the imposition of emergency rule, martial law, and military government are used in one Third World country after another. Indeed, the whole state apparatus has to be adapted to this Third World role in the new international division of labor" (Frank, *Reflections on the World Economic Crisis*, p. 130).

[39]This alliance of business and government from the core with oligarchies in the periphery is nothing new. As Myrdal notes, "In the worldwide colonial power system as it functioned until the Second World War, *there was a built-in mechanism that almost automatically led the colonial power to ally itself with the privileged groups.* Those groups could be relied upon to share its interest in 'law and order,' which mostly implied economic and social *status quo.*

"To support its reign, the colonial power would thus generally feel an interest in upholding or even strengthening the inegalitarian social and economic structure in a colony. This was a major element in the laissez-faire tendency of colonial rule. . . . Often it even happened that new privileges and new privileged groups were created by the colonial power in order to stabilize its rule over a colony.

"There is no doubt that a similar mechanism has been operating after the liquidation of colonialism and that, now as before, it also has its counterpart in relation to those underdeveloped countries that were politically independent, primarily in Latin America. *This is the main justification for the use of the term 'neo-colonialism.'*

"When the political stability provided by colonialism had disappeared, it was only natural that the rich Western countries should feel a special sympathy for such a newly independent country where the rule was tightly kept by a conservative regime that preserved the social, economic, and political power situation inherited from colonial times.

"That business interests in the West would be more willing to invest in such a country was equally natural. It was also natural that they preferred to deal with the rich and mighty there. That this, in turn, strengthened those groups at home is equally self-evident" (*Challenge of World Poverty*, pp. 72–73; italics in original text).

In a later passage, Myrdal adds that "it is, moreover, easily observable that Western businessmen, however liberal they might be on their home ground, when operating in an underdeveloped country tend to become social and political reactionaries. To many of them a dictatorial upper-class regime, suppressing all opposition, is favored, even if it is extremely exploitative. To have to deal with such a regime facilitates business, which is difficult enough even if in the long run it becomes disastrous, not least for their own interests.

"Many enterprises also carry a historical load of reckless exploitation, corruption, and even plain fraud from earlier times when the enterprises were first started and property concessions acquired. . . . There are many . . . such potential scandals that must be prevented from exploding by keeping close to the oligarchy and often by bribing them" (pp. 264–65).

[40]Evidence for this claim can be found in Chomsky and Herman's *Third World Fascism*, especially pp. 44–46 and 53–60, as well as in chapter six of Frank's *Crisis: In the Third World* (New York: Holmes & Meier, 1980).

[41]For evidence, see chapter four of Frank's *Crisis: In the World Economy*.

[42]For samples of proposals and plans, see Denis Goulet's "Goals in Conflict: Corporate Success and Global Justice" (unpublished paper, University of Notre Dame, 1980); *Growth with Equity: Strategies for Meeting Human Needs*, ed. Mary Evelyn Jegen and Charles K. Wilber (New York: Paulist Press, 1979); George N. Monsma's "Biblical Principles and Economic Theory" (unpublished paper, Calvin College, 1980); *RIO: Reshaping the International Order*, ed. Jan Tinbergen (New York: New American Library, 1976); and Pierre Uri's *Development without Dependence* (New York: Praeger, 1976).

[43]The entire text of the letter can be found in *Fellowship* (Journal of the Fellowship of Reconciliation), Sept. 1977, pp. 14–15.

Chapter V

[1]Martin Buber, *Israel and the World* (New York: Schocken, 1973), p. 217.

[2]"The Epistle to Diognetus" (v:2-5), in *The Apostolic Fathers*, trans. Kirsopp Lake (Cambridge: Harvard University Press, 1913), 2:359-61.

[3]Isaiah Berlin, *Against the Current: Essays in the History of Ideas*, ed. Henry Hardy (London: Hogarth Press, 1979), pp. 351-52.

[4]Ibid., p. 346.

[5]Buber, *Israel*, p. 218.

[6]For a confirmation of this claim in the case of the Jews and Palestine, see Edward Said's *The Question of Palestine* (New York: Vintage Books, 1980).

[7]Berlin, "Two Concepts of Liberty," in *Four Essays on Liberty* (New York: Oxford University Press, 1970), p. 157.

[8]On this, see Karl Deutsch's *Tides among Nations* (New York: Free Press, 1979), p. 29.

[9]Buber, *Israel*, p. 219.

[10]Ibid., pp. 220-24.

[11]Kant, "Eternal Peace," in *The Philosophy of Kant: Immanuel Kant's Moral and Political Writings* trans. and ed. Carl J. Friedrich (New York: Modern Library, 1949), p. 454.

[12]Schleiermacher, quoted by Kedouri, *Nationalism*, p. 58.

[13]Harper, *Religion and the Higher Life: Talks to Students* (Chicago: University of Chicago Press, 1904), pp. 174-80.

[14]Meyer, quoted by Ivor Wilkins and Hans Strydom, *The Broederbond* (New York: Paddington Press, 1979), p. 203.

[15]Ibid., p. 209.

[16]Schocken, "Revisiting Zionism," *New York Review of Books*, 28 May 1981, p. 42. For an excellent survey of the relation of Zionism to nationalism, see Kohn, "Zion and the Jewish National Idea," in *Zionism Reconsidered: The Rejection of Jewish Normalcy*, ed. Michael Selzer (New York: Macmillan, 1970), pp. 175-212.

[17]Quoted by Elie Kedouri, *Nationalism*, 2d ed. rev. (New York: Praeger, 1961), p. 76.

[18]Meir, quoted by Frank H. Epp, *Whose Land Is Palestine?: The Middle East Problem in Historical Perspective* (Grand Rapids, Mich.: Eerdmans, 1970), p. 253.

[19]Goldmann, *Memories: The Autobiography of Nahum Goldmann* (London: Weidenfeld and Nicholson, 1970), p. 284.

[20]Ben-Gurion, quoted by Simha Flapan, *Zionism and the Palestinians* (New York: Barnes & Noble, 1979), p. 131.

[21]See Flapan, *Zionism and the Palestinians*, p. 135.

[22]Hannah Arendt had this to say concerning the event: "The end result of fifty years of Zionist politics was embodied in the recent resolution of the largest and most influential section of the World Zionist Organization. American Zionists from left to right adopted unanimously, at their last annual convention held in Atlantic City in October, 1944, the demand for a 'free and democratic Jewish commonwealth . . . [which] shall embrace the whole of Palestine, undivided and undiminished.' This is a turning-point in Zionist history; for it means that the Revisionist program, so long bitterly repudiated, has proved finally victorious. The Atlantic City Resolution goes even a step further than the Biltmore Program (1942), in which the Jewish minority had granted minority rights to the Arab majority. This time the Arabs were simply not mentioned in the resolution, which obviously leaves them the choice between voluntary emigration or second-class citizenship" ("Zionism Reconsidered," in *Zionism Reconsidered*, p. 213).

[23]Smilansky, quoted by Kohn, "Zion and the Jewish National Idea," in *Zionism Reconsidered*, p. 206.

[24]Regarding this issue, consider these words of Ahad Ha-am, writing in sorrow to his people late in life that the historical right of the Jews in Palestine "does

not affect the right of the other inhabitants who are entitled to invoke the right of actual dwelling and their work in the country for many generations. For them, too, the country is a national home, and they have a right to develop national forces to the extent of their ability. This situation makes Palestine the common land of several peoples, each of whom wishes to build its national home there. In such circumstances it is no longer possible that the national home of one of them could be total. . . . If you build your house not in an empty space, but in a place where there are also other houses and inhabitants, you are unrestricted master only inside your own house. Outside the door all the inhabitants are partners, and the management of the whole has to be directed in agreement with the interests of them all" (from *At the Crossroads* [1920], quoted by Kohn, "Zion and the Jewish National Idea," in *Zionism Reconsidered,* p. 202).

[25]Orwell, "Notes on Nationalism," in *The Collected Essays, Journalism and Letters of George Orwell* (New York: Harcourt, Brace & World, 1968), vol. 3, *As I Please: 1943-1945,* p. 370.

[26]Pinochet Ugarte, quoted by Andre Gunder Frank, *Crisis: In the Third World* (London: Heinemann, 1980), pp. 266-67. It seems to have been left to the rulers of Brazil to give "philosophical depth" to this new vision of the state, by a creative borrowing from the nineteenth-century German Romantics. Consider, for example, this description of Brazilian ideas from the Agencia Boliviana de Noticias in the *Estado de São Paulo,* 6 Aug. 1976: "The Brazilian military regime has served as a model for the new geopolitical concept of the state, which has already been adopted in various Latin American countries. It is principally based on the ideas of General Costa e Silva, chief of the President's civilian cabinet. This new model begins with the militarization of the powers which characterized the traditional state in the West, meaning the legislature, which is decorative, and the judiciary, which is not important. . . . The people is a myth; there are only nations, and the nation is the state. . . . War is part of the human condition and all nations live in the state of war. All economic, cultural, and other activities are acts of war for or against the nation. As a consequence, we must strengthen military power as a guarantee of national security. The citizen must understand that security is more important than welfare, and that it is also necessary to sacrifice individual liberty. The armed forces would be the national elite responsible for leading the state, and this is justifiable in Latin America by the volatility of the demagogic and corrupt civilians and by the requirements of war." Cf. also the following words of Pinochet Ugarte: "National security is the responsibility of each and every Chilean; therefore, this concept must be inculcated at all socioeconomic levels through knowledge of general civic duties. Specifically, in relation to the domestic arena, we must encourage patriotic values by disseminating our own cultural achievements in the variegated gamut of native art, and by teaching and constantly commenting on historical traditions and the respect for the past which the fatherland represents for us" (Costa e Silva and Pinochet Ugarte quoted by Frank, *Reflections on the World Economic Crisis* [London: Hutchinson, 1981], pp. 63-64).

On occasion one finds in the writings of the advocates of the national security state an utterly forthright assertion of national absolutism—as in this statement of General Costa e Silva: "The nation is absolute or it is nothing. A nation can accept no limitation of its absolute power" (quoted in *IDOC Monthly Bulletin* (Jan.-Feb. 1977), p. 3. Sometimes one even finds an absolutism of the military coming to expression—as in this secret memorandum of the elected civilian President Juan Boardaberry of Uruguay, dated 9 Dec. 1975: "It is becoming indispensable to change the Constitution. Power should be definitely vested in the hands of the Armed Forces, and their functions should be clearly defined. . . . The actions of the Armed Forces cannot be judged, since they act on the basis of norms that cannot be called into question . . ." (quoted by Frank, *Crisis: In the Third World,* p. 261).

Chapter VI

[1]Aquinas, *Summa Theologica,* 2a. 3, 3; 2b. 23, 8; 2a. 3, 4; 2a. 3, 5; 2a. 5, 3; *Summa Contra Gentiles,* 1, 2.

[2]Aquinas, *Summa Theologica,* 2a. 4, 8; 2a. 4, 3; 2a. 4, 7.

[3]Cf. Immanuel Wallerstein: "The trend towards structural consolidation of the [world-economy] over the past four centuries has included three basic developments. The first has been the capitalization of world agriculture, meaning the ever more efficient use of the world's land and sea resources in large productive units with larger and larger components of fixed capital. Over time, this has encompassed more and more of the earth's surface, and at the present we are probably about to witness the last major physical expansion, the elimination of all remaining plots restricted to small-scale, so-called 'subsistence' production. The counterpart of this process has been the steady concentration of the world's population as salaried workers in small, dense pockets—that is, proletarianization and urbanization. The initial impact of this entire process has been to render large populations more exploitable and controllable" (*The Capitalist World-Economy* [Cambridge: Cambridge University Press, 1979], p. 62).

[4]Aristotle, *Politics,* 1. 1. 1251^{b}12.

[5]For a theoretical account of this phenomenon of *fittingness,* see my *Art in Action* (Grand Rapids, Mich.: Eerdmans, 1980), pp. 96-121.

[6]Aquinas, *Summa Theologica,* 1. 5, 4. For a more detailed account of aesthetic excellence, see my *Art in Action.*

[7]For a vivid presentation of this conflict, see Chaim Potok's novel *My Name Is Asher Lev;* for an analysis of the dynamics involved, see my "Art, Religion, and the Elite," in *Art, Creativity and the Sacred: An Anthology in Religion and Art,* ed. Diane Apostolos-Cappadona (New York: Crossroad-Continuum, 1983).

[8]Calvin, *Institutes of the Christian Religion,* ed. John T. McNeill and trans. Ford Lewis Battles (Philadelphia: Westminster Press, 1960), 1:726-27 (III, x, 2-3). Cf. this passage from Calvin's commentary on Gen. 1:30: "God certainly did not intend that man should be slenderly and sparingly sustained; but rather . . . he promises a liberal abundance, which should leave nothing wanting to a sweet and pleasant life" (*Commentaries on the First Book of Moses, Called Genesis,* trans. John King [Grand Rapids, Mich.: Eerdmans, 1948], 1:100).

[9]Max Weber, *The Protestant Ethic and the Spirit of Capitalism,* trans. Talcott Parsons (New York: Scribner's, 1958), p. 53. Subsequent references to this book (hereafter abbreviated *PE*) will be made parenthetically in the text.

[10]Davie, *A Gathered Church: The Literature of the English Dissenting Interest, 1700-1930* (New York: Oxford University Press, 1978), pp. 25-26.

[11]For an insightful analysis of some of the "mechanisms" of our capitalist society that work to destroy our cities as humane places in which to live, see Charles Jencks's *The Language of Post-Modern Architecture,* 3d ed., rev. and enl. (London: Academy Editions, 1978), pp. 12-15.

[12]Mumford, *The City in History: Its Origins, Its Transformation, and Its Prospects* (New York: Harcourt, Brace & World, 1961), pp. 296-99.

[13]For a more thorough discussion of the nature, scope, and role of the aesthetic, see my *Art in Action* and "Art, Religion and the Elite," in *Art, Creativity and the Sacred.*

[14]Jacques Ellul, *The Meaning of the City,* trans. Dennis Pardee (Grand Rapids, Mich.: Eerdmans, 1970), pp. 160-62.

[15]Ibid., p. 163.

[16]It is easy to misinterpret Ellul's book and to misconstrue his views on these matters. At one point, for example, he suggests that "the Christian, like everyone else, is looking for a solution in laws. What should the Christian position be regarding these problems . . . ? Arrange things somehow, make city life possible; moralize the city, its leisure time, its work, its dreams. This is how Christians plan. What to do? God has revealed to us very clearly that there is absolutely nothing to be done. . . .

The city is a phenomenon absolutely removed from man's power, a phenomenon which he is fundamentally incapable of affecting. For man is not responsible for making the city something other than it is, as we have already seen. There is nothing to be done. And the problem does not change. . . . For God has cursed, has condemned, the city instead of giving us a law for it" (*The Meaning of the City,* p. 47).

What Ellul means is this: there is an "authority," an *exousia,* of the city— one of those quasi-personal powers of which the New Testament speaks in various places. Our human city is in the grip of this power, and there is nothing we can do to conquer it. "The city is an almost indistinguishable mixture of spiritual power and man's work. It has a very definite spiritual character, an orientation toward evil and away from good which in no way depends on man. And man is clearly not the one to change that inner spirit as he wishes—we see every day that he cannot change even the outer face" (p. 169). Of course we don't like to acknowledge this fact. So we give ourselves excuses. " 'We drew up beautiful plans for your cities,' the architects wail, 'and you did not build them.' This time it is because the money is missing that the demons are not exorcised. Next time it will be because a war has to be waged or a purge carried out. Poor, well-intentioned reason, always fluttering about, always running into irrational needs that can never be completely eliminated. It all adds up to man's dance of will and powerlessness as he faces the truth" (p. 168).

Accordingly, says Ellul, "we must not count on the urban specialists to give the city its simple character as one of man's works." But immediately he adds, "We must salute these idealists. They are right in doing what they are doing," though indeed, "they are wrong in believing they will ever get anywhere" (p. 168). Their endeavors are right; but they do not realize that "the struggle is too serious, too profound; it is taking place in a realm never reached by man" (p. 168). All in all, then, the work of the urbanists is "an uncertain attempt, groping toward a more balanced body, a healthier one, one with no soul other than that of its dwellers" (p. 167). They are oblivious to the dimension of the issues at stake. Yet we can see "a certain agreement between what they have done and what God has done, and which he continues mysteriously to foster until the time has come for the last great change" (p. 167).

In summary, it is the "power" which lies behind the city that has been cursed by God. With it God is engaged, through Jesus Christ, in eventually victorious battle. But God has not cursed the human beings who dwell in the city; for them he has love. And we are not to stay away from the city; we are to work so that it becomes more humane: "man's work as such is not condemned or cursed. What God judges and condemns is the power which from the beginning has been in the spirit of revolt, and, throughout the history of the city, in her spirit of seduction. The city as a power, as a spiritual reality, is what God rejects from his plan, and not the mere accumulation of stones and houses. . . . And God's will is to separate this power from man's work, in fact a part of man himself and his destiny" (p. 164); "the Scriptures teach that by Jesus Christ, God is snatching man's work from Satan's grasp and, as it were, giving it back to man, preparing it for other purposes. Man's work is no less valid; it is not itself engulfed in the fall and condemnation of the *exousiai.* This condemnation is not dragging man and his work down with it as though he were physically bound to it" (p. 167).

Interlude II

[1]In connection with this, see my *Educating for Responsible Action* (Grand Rapids, Mich.: Eerdmans, 1980).

[2]Quentin Skinner, *The Foundations of Modern Political Thought* (Cambridge: Cambridge University Press, 1978), vol. 2, *The Age of Reformation,* p. 202.

Chapter VII

[1]Alexander Schmemann, *For the Life of the World: Sacraments and Orthodoxy* (Crestwood, N.Y.: St. Vladimir's Seminary Press, 1973), p. 118. Subsequent references to this book (hereafter abbreviated *LW*) will be made parenthetically in the text.

[2]"The term 'sacramental' means that for the world to be means of worship and means of grace is not accidental, but the revelation of its meaning, the restoration of its essence, the fulfillment of its destiny. It is the 'natural sacramentality' of the world that finds its expression in worship and makes the latter the essential ἔργον [*ergon* = work] of man, the foundation and spring of his life and activities as a man" (*LW*, p. 121).

[3]For a sustained argument for the conclusion that God is not outside of time, see my essay "God Everlasting," in *God and the Good: Essays in Honor of Henry Stob*, ed. Clifton Orlebeke and Lewis Smedes (Grand Rapids, Mich.: Eerdmans, 1975), pp. 181-203.

[4]Johan van der Hoeven, "History and Truth in Nietzsche and Heidegger," in *Life is Religion: Essays in Honor of H. Evan Runner*, ed. Henry Vander Goot (St. Catharines, Ont.: Paideia Press, 1981), pp. 74, 75.

[5]Max Thurian, *The Eucharistic Memorial*, trans. J. G. Davies (Richmond: John Knox Press, 1960), part 1, *The Old Testament*, p. 22. In the discussion on "doing as memorial" that follows, I am much indebted to Thurian's insights.

[6]Cf. J. Severino Croatto: "I can celebrate the Passover only because the Exodus event occurred, but in this 'memory' I also recall the other moments of the people's liberation. Even the 'Passover' of Christ is a continuation of the Exodus. But any 'memory' has meaning for me only if I am in some way involved in a *present-day* process of liberation. Oppressors cannot celebrate the Passover; it would be a falsehood. At most, they might be able to re-adapt some pharaonic festivity. The Passover is of no use to them; it is a 'subversive memory' " (*Exodus: A Hermeneutics of Freedom*, trans. Salvator Attanasio (Maryknoll, N.Y.: Orbis Books, 1981), p. 23. Cf. also Gustavo Gutiérrez: "Without a real commitment against exploitation and alienation and for a society of solidarity and justice, the Eucharistic celebration is an empty action, lacking any genuine endorsement by those who participate in it" (*A Theology of Liberation: History, Politics and Salvation*, trans. and ed. Sister Caridad Inda and John Eagleson [Maryknoll, N.Y.: Orbis Books, 1973], p. 265).

[7]Calvin, *Institutes of the Christian Religion*, ed. John T. McNeill and trans. Ford Lewis Battles (Philadelphia: Westminster Press, 1960), 2:1421, 1424 (IV, xvii, 43; IV, xvii, 46).

Chapter VIII

[1]The epistemology that follows is more fully developed in my "Can Belief in God Be Rational if It Has No Foundations?", in *Faith and Rationality* (Notre Dame, Ind.: University of Notre Dame Press, 1983).

[2]In Pavlov's famous experiments in conditioned reflexes, you will recall, dogs were subjected to a "constant conjoining" of the sound of an electric bell with the presentation of food; after a time, the dogs' natural salivation at the sight of the food would come to be stimulated by the sound of the bell alone.

[3]See especially my *Reason within the Bounds of Religion* (Grand Rapids, Mich.: Eerdmans, 1976).

[4]See especially Jürgen Habermas's *Knowledge and Human Interests*, trans. Jeremy J. Shapiro (Boston: Beacon Press, 1971).

[5]Abraham Kuyper, *Principles of Sacred Theology*, trans. J. Hendrik de Vries (Grand Rapids, Mich.: Eerdmans, 1965), pp. 109, 110, 111.

[6]Ibid., pp. 112-13.

Postscript

[1]Goldmann, *The Philosophy of the Enlightenment: The Christian Burgess and the Enlightenment,* trans. Henry Mass (Cambridge: MIT Press, 1973), p. 82.
[2]Ibid.

CPSIA information can be obtained at www.ICGtesting.com
Printed in the USA
LVOW07s1541290115

424893LV00003B/491/P

3 4711 00224 2636

9 780802 819802